David J. Hesselg...av...
fessor of mission i... the S...
of World Mission a...d Eva...g...ls...
Trinity Evangelical Divinity
School.

Dynamic Religious Movements

Dynamic Religious Movements

CASE STUDIES OF RAPIDLY GROWING RELIGIOUS MOVEMENTS AROUND THE WORLD

EDITED BY DAVID J. HESSELGRAVE

BAKER BOOK HOUSE
Grand Rapids, Michigan

ISBN: 0-8010-4130-9

FOREWORD

At the end of Ecclesiastes the writer seems somewhat weary, and, taking a deep breath he says, "Of making many books there is no end" (Eccles. 12:12). Permit me to change this slightly and, with a sigh, say, "Of making many religions there is no end." We seemingly live in the days of which Christ spoke when He said, "Take heed lest any man deceive you: for many shall come in my name, saying, I am Christ; and shall deceive many" (Mark 13:5,6).

The pages of this book are a vivid reminder that we are living in an intensely religious world and also in an utterly religiously confused world. Man is on a search and is reaching out for something that he cannot define but that his soul demands.

This search and yearning is being strengthened by the anticipations that are being offered by numerous promises and movements. In his blindness man gropes about and is ready to follow and pledge his allegiance to almost any man or movement that appeals to his undefined soul-cry.

This book takes us around the globe and verifies the above generalizations. Man as an incurably religious being must have some kind of religion.

It is my hope that this book will find a large circulation. It is not exhaustive in its studies. It does, however, vividly portray samples of what is happening in the world. It is brief enough in each study not to weary the reader, yet it is definitive enough to give sound information. Much of the material in this book will be new to the reader; however, some topics he will find more exhaustively presented in separate volumes.

May this book bring us information needed for a more effective dissemination of Christian truth and the building of the Church of Christ. Surely there is much for us to learn in the manner in which other movements in various cultures are expanding. May it also impress upon us a sense of urgency for the proclamation of the gospel. And, may it loosen a volume of intercession for those who seek to present the Christ who saves men, sets them free and makes them whole.

George W. Peters
Professor Emeritus of World Missions
Dallas Theological Seminary

CONTENTS

PART FIVE
North America

PART SIX
South America

PART SEVEN
Southeast Asia

CONCLUSION

1 | INTRODUCTION

WHAT THIS BOOK IS ALL ABOUT

David J. Hesselgrave

"It won't be too long," a skeptic acquaintance said to me some years ago, "before religion will be a phenomenon of history and nothing more."

He was not alone in that opinion. He had some illustrious company. In fact, about that same time both he and I were becoming well acquainted—directly or indirectly—with outstanding educators who concurred. There were, for example, the logical positivists (including our own professor Dr. Herbert Feigl) who insisted that man is progressing to increasingly logical explanations of his world and experience. Metaphysical explanations will supersede religious ones, and metaphysics in turn will yield more and more ground to science.

Again, both of us were required to gain a rather thorough acquaintance with psychologists such as Sigmund Freud. The psychologists had their differences, of course, but many seemed to agree that religion is based upon illusion and that as mankind reaches maturity religion will be rendered unnecessary.[1]

---

1. Sigmund Freud, *The Future of An Illusion* (New York: Liverright Publishing Corporation, 1953).

Anthony F. C. Wallace had not yet written his *Religion: An Anthropological View*[2] (to which we will refer again in the concluding chapter) but we were well schooled in approaches to anthropology which looked forward to the extinction of religion. As a matter of fact, though we were not aware of it at the time, there were those Christian theorists who believed, not that all religions would die out, but that tribal religions and even the higher non-Christian religions were in for trying times and would gradually diminish if not disappear.

Yes, a quarter century ago, my skeptic friend boasted some illustrious company. But I am more convinced now than I was then that he—and they—were wrong. And it is more than my Christian faith that tells me so. In these twenty-five years I have witnessed the vitality of the various religions—often in the form of new, dynamic movements—in Asia, Africa, and even Europe and the Americas. I am now inclined to believe my Japanese professor friend who, shortly after the war, said, "If I wanted to become rich, I would not start a new factory but a new religion." Far from dying out, religious movements have a great attraction in the present century.

This book is about some religious movements that have experienced unusual growth. The writing of it was not undertaken in order to prove that religions are still "alive and well on planet earth" (though this book certainly supports that conclusion). To me—and to most of my colleagues who are involved in one way or another in the Christian mission—it hardly seems necessary to devote one's energy to that task. Rather, missionaries and missiologists will be interested in these case studies *as histories of the growth of varied religions in a variety of cultures during this century. And they will be concerned that all true Christians who· want to see the church of which Christ is the Head grow rapidly be informed and challenged by these records of growth.*

All of the contributors to this volume have done previous research on the religious movements concerning which they have written here. From my own experience and my interaction with some of the contributors I can attest that there is one

2. Anthony F. C. Wallace, *Religion: An Anthropological View* (New York: Random House, 1966).

question concerning these movements which has been asked more than any other. It is this: "What are the reasons for such phenomenal growth?" Yet, interestingly enough, this aspect of religion receives less attention in the literature than perhaps any other. Scholar after scholar—historian, anthropologist, sociologist, apologist—writes about religion and religions with scarcely a mention of growth factors. Numerous analyses of the features of religion do not even include methods of propagation as one of those features.

The reasons for this hiatus in the study and analysis of religious movements are undoubtedly varied and complex. But probably the most significant reason is that it is much easier to simply describe the history, doctrine, ritual, organization, and statistical growth of a religion than it is to explain the attraction that religion has for its members and the suasions that result in new converts. It is comparatively safe and simple to demonstrate *that* a religion is growing, but it is admittedly risky and difficult to explain *why* it is growing.

Ironically enough, for this and perhaps other reasons, the question that is asked most often about growing religions is answered least frequently. Therefore, that is the question to which we have directed these studies. History, doctrine and other aspects of religion are, of course, necessary to our discussions. Confusion would result from lack of that kind of information. But in this book history becomes primarily the story of growth; doctrine is related to growth; and so on. The focus, then, is on the growth of these movements. How have they grown? Why have they grown? And what can we learn from them?

Before we proceed to the case studies, however, some preliminary concerns merit attention.

A Matter of Definition

"Religion" and "religions" are terms that are common enough, but like many common terms they have an uncommonly large number of meanings. And it makes a great deal of difference which meaning we have in view. Edmund Perry's definition of religion reveals a definite Christian and theological commitment. He says that religion is "a generic term comprehending the universal phenomenon of men individually and collectively being led away from God in manifold ways by divers claims and systems."[3] The various particular religions, then, constitute instances of this phenomenon.

When a Christian views religion in this way he must either say that Christianity is not a religion or that gospel faith is to be distinguished from Christianity as such. In any case, to adopt Perry's definition involves a judgment that is outside the purview of this book. Let it be clear at the outset that in this book we have not set ourselves to the task of analyzing these religious systems so as to determine their truth or falsity, or the degree to which they qualify as being true forms of Christianity, Buddhism, Islam, or whatever. The authors undoubtedly do have their opinions on these questions, and by reading the lines they have written the reader will become aware of those opinions to some degree. But it must be clear that if the contributors' assigned task had been to evaluate the truth claims of these movements, they would have proceeded very differently. The truth question is important, but it is not all that is important. And it is not the question at hand.

A definition that fits what we have in view in this book is that of Edward Norbeck. He defines religion as "ideas, creeds, and acts of supernaturalism."[4] Because of its emphases on beliefs, acts, and the supernatural, this definition suits our present inquiry well. Since the authors are profoundly committed to the mission of the Christian church, they are keenly interested in the dynamics of growing religious movements that, like Christianity, are grounded in supernaturalism.

Like Perry, Norbeck is defining the generic term *religion*, however. In the present study we are more concerned with particular movements or systems that can be termed "religious" by this definition. Whether they are best classified as religions, churches, denominations, or sects will be a moot question here. That is not to say that the question is not worthy of consideration. As a matter of fact, there is an intriguing diversity apparent in the various religious movements which are the subjects

---

3. Edmund Perry, *Gospel in Dispute: The Relation of Christian Faith to Other Missionary Religions* (Garden City, NY: Doubleday and Company, Inc., 1956), p. 88.

4. Edward Norbeck, *Religion in Primitive Society* (New York: Harper & Row, 1961), p. 11.

of case studies in this book. Were one to attempt a categorization according to the types developed by J. Milton Yinger
among others,[5] most of the movements in this study would
probably be called "sects" because they are in conflict with
their respective cultures. The United Pentecostal Church in
Columbia, the New Apostolic Church in Germany, and the
Iglesia ni Cristo in the Philippines are clear examples of this.
Also within the "sect" category, Jehovah's Witnesses in the
United States and Ahmadiya in Pakistan (among others) might
be denominated "adventist sects" in that they seek to prepare
for the "new dispensation"; the Soka Gakkai in Japan might
be thought of as a "conversionist sect" because it seeks to
alter *men* and therefore the *world;* and it might be said that
groups such as Tong-il and Ahmadiya began as "charismatic
sects" but later developed into "sect movements" with complex
structures.

From still another perspective, it will be noted that movements such as the Zionists in Africa and the Umbanda in Brazil
encompass numerous smaller groupings which exhibit a certain
heterogeneity within the larger homogeneity. For the most
part, the others exhibit a significant degree of cohesiveness and
homogeneity in structure as well as in ritual and teaching.

In the context of this book we have avoided making these
distinctions and have used the phrase *religious movement* to
apply to all the groups under study. By using the phrase we
imply the following: (1) they are religious in the sense indicated by Norbeck; (2) they are recognizable, distinctive groupings; and (3) they exhibit more or less homogeneity and cohesiveness.

A Matter of Choice

We have said that the particular concern and approach
of this book are somewhat unique. That statement must now
be qualified. Numerous studies of the growth of Christian
churches have been undertaken by Dr. Donald McGavran and
his associates and students. Those studies are extremely valuable,
but in the nature of the case they are circumscribed. The question comes, "Is it not possible that we can gain additional

5. J. Milton Yinger, *The Scientific Study of Religion* (New York: The
Macmillan Company, 1970), pp. 251-82.

insights by focusing our attention on growing movements of *various* religious traditions as well as those of the Christian religion?" Just as the self-righteous compare themselves with one another (II Cor. 10:12) and thereby miss some important instruction, by comparing Christian churches only with other Christian churches we also miss significant data. Perhaps by comparing our Christian churches with spiritist or Buddhist or Muslim or syncretistic movements we will be instructed (and even somewhat shamed) and therefore better prepared to serve Christ more wholeheartedly and effectively. If so, this exercise will be worthwhile.

A study like the monumental inquiry of David Barrett into some six thousand nativistic movements in Africa represents an important step in the direction we have indicated.[6] That study merits careful attention whether or not one agrees with all of Barrett's conclusions. It also, however, is circumscribed in that it is limited to one continent and to movements which are related to Christianity. Those limitations represent the real strength of the work. But they also leave important questions unanswered.

The present work represents an attempt to determine growth factors in rapidly growing religions from different religious traditions *and* diverse cultures. The case study approach to inquiries of this kind is widely utilized. But it is recognized that we have selected twelve movements out of hundreds of growing ones that could have been chosen. No claim is made for representativeness other than that which stems from the religious, cultural and geographical diversity that is immediately apparent. These twelve movements should be looked upon as samples which are more or less representative. Our conclusions are therefore tentative and need the corroboration of further studies.

The Contributors

Scholars contributing to this book include twelve North Americans and one Swiss. Several scholars of other nationalities were originally included but personal and political fortunes were such that it became impossible for them to continue. The scholars

---

6. David Barrett, *Schism and Renewal in Africa* (Nairobi: Oxford University Press, 1968).

have all lived and carried out their research *in the countries in which the religious movements they examine have flourished.* In most cases they have lived in those countries for extended periods of time. (In the case of the Mormons and Jehovah's Witnesses, the authors are, of course, native to the same culture.) All of them have done extensive research on the movement concerning which they write. They are all Christians and are interested in the propagation of the religious faith they deem to be true and worthy of the allegiance of all men—that of Jesus Christ. This, however, has not deterred them from making objective analyses.

Finally, the author-scholars of these case studies have been encouraged by the editor to be true to their own style and to emphasize that which they deem important for our study. They have been furnished with a rather formidable list of questions on the growth of these movements for which we would like answers. But within the guidelines inherent in those questions they have emphasized the factors which they believe to be important; they have given brief attention to that which they believe to be of lesser importance; and they have omitted that which they believe to be of no importance whatever. It also must be recognized that in some cases certain important information is all but impossible to obtain.

Forthrightly and at the outset, therefore, the contributors and editor admit the limitations of the studies which we have undertaken. But for readers who are profoundly concerned for the future of the Christian church and mission—and these, we believe, will constitute the majority of our readers—we trust that the study of this book will prove to be an instructive experience. And for all readers irrespective of their motivation in availing themselves of this study, we sincerely believe that these are factual accounts of the growth of these movements. And facts have their own way of promoting causes which are righteous and true.

PART ONE

Africa

Phillip M. Steyne

Phillip M. Steyne was born to missionary parents in northern Natal in 1930. His early years were spent in close contact with the major ethnic groups of the area. He is married to Jeanne McDonald, who is likewise a child of missionary parents. They have four children. After serving a pastorate in Natal, the family came to the United States in 1954 where the author completed undergraduate work in philosophy at Roosevelt University, Chicago. He has received the M.Div. degree from Northern Baptist Theological Seminary. The Steynes have served two five-year terms with The Evangelical Alliance Mission (TEAM) in Swaziland and Natal, Southern Africa. Their ministry has been primarily educational in nature. In 1974, the author received the D.Miss. degree from Fuller Theological Seminary School of World Mission. Currently he serves as Chairman of the Department of Missions at Philadelphia College of Bible.

2 | THE AFRICAN ZIONIST MOVEMENT

Phillip M. Steyne

Contemporary black South Africa provides a home for an "underworld of sectarian Christianity." In these groups there has been an attempt to re-establish African values and beliefs while infusing them with Christian meanings. That the attempt has been successful from an African point of view is apparent when one realizes that their adherents number in the millions. Their vitality and influence demand the attention of observers of the religious scene in South Africa. Among these movements, none is more important than the African Zionist movement—the subject of this study.

Historical Overview

The beginnings of the African Church Independency movement can be traced back to the early nineteenth century. Very early in the history of culture contact there were those enterprising Africans who sought to ameliorate the impact of Western culture on tribal structures. In 1818 a Xhosa sought to integrate Western culture into a syncretistic messianism to compensate for the cultural voids and disintegration his people were experiencing with the coming of the white man and his Christian faith.[1] The breakdown of tribalism brought about by the efforts of European missionaries and the attendant secularism made it very difficult for the African animist to maintain self-hood and cultural integrity and identity.

By the twentieth century thousands of Christian converts in South Africa had already become part of the growing African Church Independency movements.[2] Some of them were a result of deliberate schism while others were spontaneous developments. At times the course of independency had nationalistic implications. Rather than resorting to revolution the African sought to air his grievances through religious structures. This he did by asserting his nationalism and traditions in meaning-ful religious ways of life. These have developed into indigenous expressions of African Christianity, though it may truly be said that theology seems incidental to these structures.

It is generally conceded that the term *Zion*, appended to many of these African church groups, was introduced by mis-sionaries coming from the apocalyptic church in Zion, Illinois. Their main teachings underscored divine healing, triune im-mersion and the second coming. It was one Daniel Bryant who baptized, in 1904, the first group of twenty-seven Zionist African believers in South Africa. In 1908, P. L. le Roux, a prominent European worker in the group, received the "bap-tism in the Holy Spirit." Africans in the group were not slow to follow.[3] The African Zionist churches, with their strong pentecostal leanings and practices, had been launched. It was not long before they incorporated within their structures tradi-tional religious forms that characterized their faith, at times, as being more nativistic than Christian.

Their growth has been phenomenal. They have swept thou-sands into groups which approach the Christian faith from an African perspective, with African initiative and leadership. No less than three thousand of these groups, claiming more than three million members, are presently registered with the South

1. Thomas Pringle, *Narrative of a Residence in South Africa* (Cape Town: C. Struik, 1966), p. 279. This work was originally published in 1834.
2. For a special bibliography on African Church Independency, see Bengt G. M. Sundkler, *Bantu Prophets in South Africa*, second edition (London: Oxford University Press, 1961).
3. Ibid., p. 48.

African government. Many more are seeking such registration and their growth carries on unabated. They constitute more than half of all black Christians in South Africa and many who hold membership in the mainline churches also adhere to some of these groups. Most have emerged spontaneously, taking root within the African culture and soil, and without the aid of Western church and mission agencies.

The nomenclature *African Church Independency* covers a variety of forms of religious expression. It ranges from ortho-dox Christian sects to neo-pagan cults. These variances make it difficult to group them accurately.[4] The demarcation line between blatant syncretism[5] and Christian independency is notoriously difficult to draw, for in the process of change from animism to Christianity it is well-nigh impossible to de-termine when a person has crossed, within his inner conscious-ness, the boundary line between the two.

In general these movements may be listed under three main classifications:[6]

(1) Ethiopians: those who seceded from white-controlled orthodox mission churches but who incorporated a few more traditional forms into their expression of the Christian faith.

(2) Zionists: those who seek to effect an indigenous expression of Christianity but do claim to acknowledge Jesus Christ as Savior and Lord.

(3) Messianic Movements: those who, under charismatic leadership, claim a special relationship to God. These may be Christian or in the process of becoming Christian.

Our study will focus primarily on the Zionist movements for in significant ways they are in the vanguard of establishing an indigenous expression of African Christianity.

---

4. B. A. Pauw, *Religion in a Tswana Chiefdom* (London: Oxford University Press, 1960), p. 8. Pauw describes the mixed multitude in the following way: ". . . a simple and clear-cut grouping into Christians or church people on the one hand and pagans on the other, is not possible because of the existence of a considerable but undefined middle 'group' consisting of people who claim to be church adherents but have no official church connections."

5. J. Spencer Trimingham, *The Christian Church and Islam in West Africa* (London: SCM Press Ltd., 1955), pp. 14-20. Here the author suggests a model whereby syncretism may possibly be scaled.

6. Bengt G. M. Sundkler, "The Concept of Christianity in the African Independent Churches," *African Studies* 4 (1961), 204-11.

In *Schism and Renewal in Africa,* David Barrett presents pertinent data on religious independency in 227 sub-Saharan African tribes.[7] Of these, the Zulus, numbering close to five million, have spawned the largest number of religious independency groups. It would appear that the military genius of the Zulu, dating back to the eighteenth and nineteenth centuries, has been carried over into the formulation of these new religious movements. In their tribal homelands, Kwazula (Zululand) and much of Natal, the names of mountains, valleys, rivers and streams often parallel those of the Holy Land. A mount Zion, a river Jordan, or whatever the ritual occasion calls for, can readily be found. But their search for parallel holy places is not limited to their homeland. Wherever the Zulu have wandered they have been able to make do with the environment in order to carry on their religious rituals.

African Zionism is not the possession of only the Zulu. It has reached into almost every tribe in South Africa, and its claim to numerical superiority over and above the messianic and Ethiopian movements can hardly be denied. It is a movement of major consequence and in many ways may hold the key to the future of Christendom in southern Africa.

The Church—Its Teaching and Life

Old Testament orientation. These groups approach the Old Testament with reverence and a sense of relief. To them it speaks of a faith unlike that practiced by Western Christians. To the African Zionist, the Old Testament is a source book of remembrance. Its atmosphere reminds them of their own traditional nomadic and pastoral life, their longing for offspring, their experiences of seedtime and harvest, and their sense of the presence and activity of divine power here and now.[8] The Old Testament reflects for them a continuous and direct revelation which is reinforced by sensible infusions of mystical powers. It also appears to condone polygamy as an economic and social structure; it depicts a sacrificial system; it refers to sacred rites and ritual prohibitions; it lists ritual objects like prophets' staffs,

---

7. David B. Barrett, *Schism and Renewal in Africa* (Nairobi: Oxford University Press, 1968).

8. G. E. Phillips, *The Old Testament in the World Church* (London: Lutterworth Press, 1948), p. 6.

cymbals, drums, and trumpets; it describes feasts and rites of passage like circumcision. All of these have their parallel in the traditional African religious system and for former animists they actualize, within the community, man's "beingness."

The Old Testament thus forms the foundation of the beliefs of these groups. They have tended to develop a church concept related to Old Testament forms and functions since they identify freely with its forms and find in it sanction for many of their traditional customs and rites. Conflicts between Old Testament and New Testament standards are usually decided in favor of the former. To them truth is to be found in Leviticus or Deuteronomy, with their detailed prescriptions and taboos.[9] With their aspirations for nationalistic identity in a white-dominated country, Zionist South Africans make Moses the central figure of the Bible. He exemplifies the African concept of leadership—that of liberator and also of lawgiver.

The African concept of solidarity, expressed in the emphasis on community, also finds its parallel in the life of Israel. The African proverb, "man is other men," is basic to tribal social structures and is thus carried over into their expression of Christianity. Even their conceptualization of sin is built on communal solidarity. Sin is that which disturbs the equilibrium in the community, that which produces unrest and disharmony, that which by harsh words and unbecoming acts causes violence and suffering.[10] Salvation is understood as a communal event, for man is not merely a solitary unit, but a "family." Their understanding of salvation is expressed in the African proverb: "I am because I participate."[11] Interdependence and mutual responsibility are touchstones of their expression of the Christian faith. Christianity is judged by its practical results, for as members of a "family" Christians are obligated to each other on every level—social, economic and spiritual.[12]

---

9. Sundkler, *Bantu Prophets*, p. 277.
10. A. I. Berglund, "The Rituals of the Independent Church Movement as Missionary Challenge," in Missiological Institute, *Our Approach to the Independent Church Movement in South Africa* (Mapumulo: Lutheran Theological College, 1965), p. 168.
11. J. V. Taylor, *The Primal Vision* (London: SCM Press Ltd., 1963), p. 93. This work was reprinted in 1972.
12. J. V. Taylor and D. Lehmann, *Christians of the Copperbelt* (London: SCM Press Ltd., 1963), p. 152.

This obligation is practiced in visible forms. Zionists freely engage in ritualistic participatory rites, for these rites serve to cement their relationships to God and to each other while also affirming the individual's "beingness."[13] To them beliefs without outward rites are meaningless. They think synthetically, communicate symbolically and believe that they must worship ritualistically. All of these characteristics are well illustrated in the life of the Israelites. The Old Testament, therefore, is a reflection of traditional African rites. And since integration into the African family depends on a series of rites of passage, by which the child is made a member of society,[14] Zionists do not frown upon the traditional African rites of passage. In fact, they have added their own confessions, absolutions, exorcisms, reparations, baptisms, prayers and purgations. In the case of Zionists, these ceremonies are not "once for all," but may be repeated as often as the individual senses his need. In a real sense they are mystically creative acts through which the individual is made a Christian and a member of the group.[15]

The spirit and the spirit world. Basic to African thinking and fully integrated into their approach to Christian faith is a central conceptualization alien to Western thinking. To them, every physical event has a metaphysical coordinate. Spiritual substance and significance, therefore, accrue to the most ordinary events of life. This phenomenon has led some observers to conclude that the African Christian holds his Christian faith in one hand and in his other hand the mysterious world of his traditional culture.[16]

The African understanding of spiritual reality takes special cognizance of "life force," ancestors and spirits. These all play a fundamental part in African socio-cultural structures and pervade the total life pattern of the individual. For example, the African closely relates physical life to the realm of the departed dead. Life is not limited to the time span of biological life nor is it terminated by biological death. Life is defined to

---

13. For a discussion on ritual see Pauw, *Religion,* pp. 146-211.
14. These are rites of separation, of transition and of incorporation. See Arnold Van Gennep, *The Rites of Passage* (Chicago: University of Chicago Press, 1960).
15. Taylor, *Primal Vision,* p. 130.
16. William D. Reyburn, "The Spiritual, the Material, and the Western Reaction in Africa," *Practical Anthropology* 6 (1959), 82.

include ancestorhood and symbiotic union is maintained in which the biologically dead depend upon the biologically living. The converse is also true.

African society is, therefore, based on a type of covenant relationship embracing the living, the dead and the unborn— a fact reaffirmed by the independent churches. "Life force"— implicit in this relationship—commences with the realization of personhood and extends into the future.[17] To speak of the "immediate dead" or the "distant dead" is still to include all of them in "life" and therefore in vital participation with the biologically alive. The psychological make-up of the African anticipates this and realizes the influence of the ancestors on the events of life.[18] Their "force" remains with the family to effect either benevolent returns or, if they should be disregarded, malevolent correctives. They are accorded powers to effect harmony, peace and blessing.

In the Zionist view, to disregard the ancestors is to ignore the fifth commandment. In the Western Christian view, to respect them *in this way* is to run afoul of the first commandment. Recognizing this tension, Zionist leaders assert with conviction and integrity that they simply respect their ancestors and do not worship them as outside observers maintain.[19]

Furthermore, these indigenous church groups recognize the presence and influence of other forces in the spirit world. They know that the African encounters existentially—not just theoretically—what the Bible identifies as devils, elemental spirits, cosmic powers and spiritual authorities.[20] They therefore seek to deal positively with the spirit world, making distinctions between God, ancestors and the powers of darkness. To their credit they do recognize the biblical prohibitions against sorcery, witches and witchcraft, while recognizing with

---

17. The *summum bonum* of life is possession of the greatest amount of this vital force. For a discussion see Fr. Placide Tempels, *Bantu Philosophy*, trans. A. Rubbens (Paris: Presence Africaine, 1959).
18. D. L. Makhatini, "Ancestors, Umoya, Angels," in Missiological Institute, *Independent Church Movement*, pp. 154—56.
19. Ibid., p. 155.
20. The Greek terms are: *diamonia, stoicheia, archai, exousia*—Eph. 6:12; cf. Lev. 17:7; Num. 21:6; Deut. 8:15; Isa. 13:21; 30:6; 34:14; Acts 16:16-18.

equal necessity exorcists, healers, ancestors and ministering spirits.

Holding to a powerful and immanent spirit world, Zionists regard the ministry of the Holy Spirit as of prime importance. They think of him as the one who has come, but also as the one who keeps coming and will come. His ministry is evidenced in the giving of guidance by means of dreams, visions, prophecies. He heals afflicted bodies. He drives away evil spirits. His power is visible—not merely believed, but also felt. Sometimes it seems that in their understanding the Holy Spirit is an influence rather than a person. Yet in their concept of spiritual reality all influences are personal, and this, of course, includes the Holy Spirit.

The church as a community. Being relationally oriented the Zionist concept of the church focuses on its community aspect. Mankind being a family, the church becomes an expression of that family.[21] In effect, it becomes the new tribal association. Within this "family" or "tribe" the member may unashamedly be himself, fully expressing his humanity, spiritually and physically. He may freely confess his sins without fear of rejection. Problems which disturb the harmony of the participant's environment are shared and committed to the family for this too is their responsibility. Within the communality[22] of the group the participant has every reason to believe that what concerns him concerns every member of the group. Nothing is too shocking for the family's hearing. Here he experiences compassion and some ritual demonstration of acceptance. Disharmonious situations are resolved and yield to genuine rejoicing.[23] In this intimate context the believer senses his worth to the group and the group's worth to his "beingness."

This sense of belonging carries over into the daily lives of Zionists as they seek to relate to each other.[24] They demonstrate very practically that there is an interrelatedness of

21. Taylor, *Primal Vision*, pp. 93-116.
22. Communalism is the traditional way of African life and is based upon relationships of interdependency, obligation and responsibility.
23. Sin, in African thinking, is related to broken relationships. See Berglund, "Rituals," p. 168.
24. It is quite common for members of these groups to assist each other in practical ways like obtaining employment and providing material assistance.

the physical, material, social and spiritual aspects of life. Thus their whole life-style, starting with their distinctive dress, demonstrates that they sense that they are "a chosen generation, a royal priesthood, an holy nation, a peculiar people" (I Peter 2:9).

When the group becomes too large this sense of fellowship, and therefore of community, is lost. The frequent secessions within African Zionism arise out of the need for intimate fellowship. Secessions lead to the creation of numerous new churches and groups.

Zionist worship. The most significant fact stressed in worship is the interrelatedness of church members. The distinctive dress mentioned previously is festooned with religious symbols which are intended to demonstrate the unity of members with Christ and with each other. Corporate worship is not confined to a staid liturgy. Oneness is expressed in rituals which demand the total participation of each worshiper. Rhythmic singing, dancing, group praying, testifying, slapping and massaging all serve to cement relationships into "true *koinonia.*" Baptism by immersion, repeated washings and other rites of purgation and purification, and frequent confessions also create a communality with each other and God. More is involved here than the belief that worship must be expressed symbolically and that symbolism must be ritualized in order to be effective. The ritual acts of the Zionists are strongly motivated by the urgent need to establish harmony with their personal environment, including the supernatural. These acts essentially become a search for reconciliation even though the dimensions of that reconciliation may be circumscribed so as to include but a small group.

Healing plays a very important part in Zionist faith and worship. Zionists believe that there are greater possibilities for healing in their churches than there are in Western medical hospitals. The laying on of hands, the exorcism of spirits, the vigorous shaking and even the slapping which accompanies such healing rites, are seen as more efficacious than are the impersonal administrations of Western medicine, because the individual actually participates in such rituals.[25] The rituals themselves demonstrate that harmony has been restored to

25. J. W. C. Dougall, "African Separatist Churches," *International Review of Missions* 45 (1956), 261.

the body and that the metaphysical cause of sickness has been dealt with effectively.

Special festivals form an essential part of worship. Not only do they provide substitutes for traditional pagan festivals, they also meet definite social needs in an atmosphere which reflects communal thanksgiving and well-being. Because of the exteriorized expressions of well-being at such festivals, healing rituals are considered to be more effective than at other times.

To demonstrate what the African Zionists consider to be important in their expression of Christianity we will attempt to give an eyewitness account of a typical worship service. On any given Saturday or Sunday the following scene repeats itself in most urban and rural areas.

Followed by a retinue of adherents festooned with green and blue crosses sewn onto long white garments, an African Zionist prophet leads his congregation to some open space or to the shade of some giant tree. Adherents carry wooden staffs, somewhat like a shepherd's crook.

At the site of gathering a few hymns are sung with zeal and apparent meaning. Hand-clapping accompanies the repetitious singing. Body movements add to the expression of meaningful participation. Then, without any visible sign the singing dies down as responsive "amens" and "hallelujahs" echo through the group. The prophet proceeds to relate some recently encountered meaningful experiences that stimulate the congregation to participate in a time of sharing. Some make confessions which are unadorned and straightforward. Others relate problems they have encountered. Whenever a note of mutuality is struck the amens and hallelujahs resound throughout the congregation. Sooner or later one or more of the members experience unusual physical reactions which elicit from others the acknowledgment of the presence of the Spirit (Umoya). Some appear to have convulsive fits which supposedly indicate a deliverance from evil spirits. The whole atmosphere is alive with the amens and hallelujahs of the congregation. This experience apparently not only confirms the testimonies, but also has a therapeutic effect on participants.

Singing is again taken up spontaneously. If a drum is available, its beat adds to the rhythm of the music and the tone of the meeting. As the singing dies down to the accompaniment of amens and hallelujahs, the congregation takes to praying. Everybody prays—some weep, some shout, some speak in tongues, some may again experience physical convulsions. There seems to be a bond which binds all together and yet they appear to be unaware of each other. There is no set time limit on this part of the service. It may require some fifteen to twenty minutes. Gradually a calm settles over the congregation again as the praying comes to an end. Amens and hallelujahs sound forth but they now appear to be indicative of an anticipation of what is to follow.

The time for the sermon has come. With no apparent preparation the Bible is opened and, if the prophet is literate, some passage may be read. Regardless of the context the exposition invariably focuses on the immediate needs of the congregation. The stress is on the human condition and what should or should not be done to realize well-being. Amens and hallelujahs are freely interjected. It is difficult for a Westerner to find continuity in the message, but the delivery is free and easy and involves the whole being of the preacher. There is no lack of words, explanations or exhortations. Upon the completion of the sermon—which may last an hour or more—the amens and hallelujahs sound even more boisterous than previously. They are followed by spontaneous singing.

While the singing is in process the participants group themselves. Those needing healing join the prophet in the center of a circle formed by the rest of the adherents. With staffs in hand, the circle begins to move as the participants start trotting and dancing—clockwise for the singing of one stanza and counterclockwise for the next, and so on. The drum beating and the singing provide an atmosphere which is charged with excitement and expectation.

Within the circle the prophet commences with the most important part of the meeting—a healing service which appears to be akin to exorcism. In this ceremony the candidate for healing is grabbed by the neck, or lifted by the arms, and vigorously and sometimes violently shaken, as the prophet shouts at the top of his voice for the demon to come out. This is done several times. Then the candidate is repeatedly slapped and the disease is "divined." The area of distress is located and specially treated, either with vigorous slapping or massaging. The candidate is then handed over to one of the assistants who helps the prophet in this ritual by continuing to massage and pray for the individual. Each candidate is thus exorcized, the distress divined and the ritual healing ceremony performed. Ashes may be used in the ritual, in which case they are mixed with the prophet's spittle and placed on the area of distress. Further instructions are given concerning the maintenance of physical well-being. The necessity of regular attendance at the meetings is stressed for this plays a vital part in continued healing. Having been convinced of some special need, some may drop out of the circle. They too go through the same procedure of healing.

If the occasion calls for new converts to be incorporated, this becomes an additional part of the service. This ceremony involves the exorcism of demons followed by repeated water immersion until the candidate is thoroughly exhausted.

At the conclusion of the healing service the members of the congregation contribute to the financial needs of the prophet. The entire service lasts from two-and-a-half to three hours. As the group disperses a lightheartedness and obvious satisfaction are evident, occasioned by the knowledge that each one has been ministered to and, in turn, has ministered to others.

Factors Contributing to Zionist Growth

The struggle for identity and authority. Historically, the separatism which is characteristic of African Zionists has been an important response to the rise of various kinds of dissatisfaction within the tribes.[26] Whether politically, socially or religiously motivated, the tendency toward schism has been expressive of the African's desire to find "a place to feel at home."[27] The security and comfort of belonging to a group are basic to the well-being of any individual. Religious independency, as expressed in the African Zionist movement, is an important contemporary expression of the search for such security in the maelstrom of modern culture change in South Africa. There rapid cultural disintegration is driving the tribal

---

26. Hilda Kuper, "The Swazi Reaction to Missions," *African Studies* 5 (1946), 177-88.
27. F. B. Welbourn and B. A. Ogot, *A Place to Feel at Home* (London: Oxford University Press, 1966), p. 135.

man, and even the marginal African city-dweller,[28] to attempt every means to hold together the fabric of his socio-cultural structures. One such attempt is the revitalization of the traditional religious system. The African tribesman is not a materialist and he cannot live without an ultimate concern to which he can give his whole self. Religion permeates his thinking and the Christian faith poured into traditional religious forms offers a functional alternative which appeals to a very large percentage of the Africans in their search for spiritual realization.

In his competition with the economic structure and its attendant dehumanization processes, so common to industrial societies, the African has sensed that he has been robbed of his selfhood and those values which give meaning to life. In order, therefore, to escape complete disorientation, socially and culturally, African independent church movements, like the African Zionists, have sought to guarantee a truly African tribal communal heritage akin to that of the old traditional structures. Thus, in their flight from complete Western encroachment, they have rediscovered and reasserted their African selfhood in these African forms of Christianity which anchor them in a rich past and offer a hope for a more promising future.

In times past the animist has been approached as a *tabula rasa* who would readily assimilate a new religious system without the necessity of integrating the new system of beliefs into the old traditions. The overlay of unintegrated Christian forms has not removed the tangible realities of the animist belief and value system. Culture contact only added to the problem of implanting Christianity, especially where the Africans have equated secular Western society with Christianity.[29] Therefore where culture contact has led to culture clash, religious independency appears to be strongest. When the secular European culture of the colonials, the "Christian" European

---

28. The vast urban complexes are in some respects melting pots of cultures. The people take from Western culture what may add to creature comfort and perhaps the philosophy that supports materialism, but the fundamental metaphysical philosophies are much slower in being assimilated into their patterns of thinking. See *Church and Culture Change in Africa*, ed. David Bosch (Pretoria: N. G. Kerk Boekhandel, 1971), pp. 66-68.
29. Welbourn and Ogot, *Place*, p. 135.

culture of missionaries, and the African culture of the tribesmen started to impinge upon each other, chain reactions were
set off that stimulated the African's proclivity to find "a place
to feel at home."

While most white churches and Western-oriented mission
societies and their related churches are either proclaiming a
generalized message of universal ultimate salvation, or are
focused entirely on social issues, there is a voice offering genuine alternatives to the stress arising out of the fragmented,
disrupted and disintegrating socio-cultural structures. This voice
—that of African Zionists—speaks and sounds like an African
voice and seeks to struggle with the spiritual needs of the
black people by relating to them a relevant message. This
message comes in African forms with a reinterpreted Christian
meaning. It elicits genuine fears in Western theological circles,
for it raises the problem of syncretism,[30] but it has a wide
appeal to animists and former animists for it provides "a place
to feel at home."

At a symposium on syncretism at Milligan College, Tennessee
(April 1974), Peter Beyerhaus confronted Western missions
with some of the obstructive factors that have encouraged the
rapid development of these groups and have thus added to
the problem of syncretism. These are: the failure of missionaries
to "convince many Africans that in Jesus Christ the Immanuel,
the 'God with us' has really appeared"; the failure of missionaries to appreciate New Testament eschatology; the failure
to develop a relevant pneumatology for Africa; and the failure
to achieve *koinonia* in a disrupted society.[31] These factors have
all had a profound bearing on the rise and rapid growth of
a syncretistic African expression of Christianity.

Leadership, organization and strategy. From a typical Western perspective it is exceedingly difficult to discern, describe
or define the organizational patterns and structures of the

---

30. When "Biblical ideas are detached from the person of God and Jesus
Christ and taken over into an essentially non-Christian structure and as-
similated into it," a system may be considered syncretistic. See M. L.
Martin, "Syncretism in Biblical Perspective," in Missiological Institute,
Independent Church Movement, p. 14.
31. Peter Beyerhaus, "The Christian Encounter with Afro-Messianic
Movements, The Possessio-Syncretism Axis Illustrated from South Africa,"
Symposium on "Syncretism," Milligan College, Tennessee, 1974, pp. 9-12.

African Zionist groups for, as sociologists Gerlach and Hine observe: "In the minds of many the only possible alternative to bureaucracy or leader-centered organization is no organization at all."[32] Likewise it is well-nigh impossible to discern a particular strategy for the propagation of their ideology. Both the infrastructure organization and an operational strategy for evangelism are closely related to normal practices inherent in indigenous socio-cultural traits which have been a basic part of communal tribal structures for many millennia.

Their rapid growth can be traced to their utilization of basic sociological and cultural factors. They have chosen to engage in church planting without foreign aid, both in personnel and financial assistance. They do not necessarily subscribe to a paid ministry or to a centralized church building. Their indigenous stamp makes them better able to communicate the "gospel" they preach. Their bold-faced rejection of Western forms has enabled them to adapt their own socio-cultural structures to meet the needs of their people. Their patterns of ministry, types of "ministers" and utilization of the laity conform more to known cultural patterns and make them more acceptable to their own people.

Five key sociological factors characterize their type of structures. These produce cohesion within the group and create forms of organizational structures while at the same time providing a dynamic operational strategy for recruitment. Social scientists Gerlach and Hine identify the same sociological factors in their study of the black power and pentecostal movements in the United States.[33] They are:

(1) A segmented, usually polycephalous, cellular organization composed of units reticulated by various personal, structural and ideological ties.

(2) Face-to-face recruitment by committed individuals using their own pre-existing significant social relationships.

(3) Personal commitment generated by an act or an experience which separates a convert in some significant way from the established order (or his previous place in it). This identifies

---

32. Luther P. Gerlach and Virginia H. Hine, *People, Power, Change: Movements of Social Transformation* (Indianapolis: The Bobbs-Merrill Company, Inc., 1970), p. 33.
33. Ibid., p. xvii.

him with a new set of values and results in changed patterns of behavior.

(4) An ideology which codifies values and goals, provides a conceptual framework by which all experiences or events relative to these goals may be interpreted, motivates and provides rationale for envisioned changes, defines the opposition, and forms the basis for conceptual unification of a segmented network of groups.

(5) Real or imagined opposition from society at large or from that segment of the established order within which the movement has risen.

Each of these factors—a close-knit cell group structure, face-to-face recruitment, a definite act of conversion, a distinctive all-encompassing ideology, and real or imagined opposition—is at the heart of the growth, appeal and momentum of the African Zionist movement. These factors must be taken into consideration, for they account for the "organization" within the groups.

The stereotypes associated with these indigenous groups do not lessen their integrity and ability to wrestle with the issues of organization and propagation. Because they are so unlike regular Western-type concepts of church organizations their structures are suspect. They are not socially disorganized nor do they build on deprived and deviant personalities. However, little is known or understood of their infrastructure. One of the baffling aspects of these movements is their lack of bureaucratic organization.

These groups fall into a type of organization characterized by *decentralization, segmentation* and *reticulation.*

By *decentralization* it is understood that no one person alone is in authority. Consensus is reached through group interaction. Egalitarianism is maintained as individual initiative and leadership are utilized. Power and authority are distributed among the group and yet one is recognized to be more than the others—a *primus inter pares* relationship. Leadership is therefore of a charismatic nature and yet the leader's regulatory power depends upon the group who accords him that responsibility. Reciprocally he must give priority to the welfare of the group. This is true whether he be called prophet, priest or bishop. His position is one of a benevolent chief or patriarchal headman. He symbolizes the well-being of the whole group. With this in mind we can understand the importance of the Zionist prophet. His popularity and prestige are a sign of success and blessing belonging to all.[34] Contributions are therefore gladly made to the cause and the leader. Unlike the Western value system, in the African system possessions are not considered to be ends in themselves. Rather, they prove to the African "that the presence of spiritual forces is at his service and that he stands in good with these."[35] The fact that spiritual forces are at his service places a special seal of blessing upon the effectiveness of his ministry and his church.[36]

By *segmentation* it is understood that there are groups or cells which are independent but which can combine to form even smaller units. Each cell or group may have its own peculiar distinctives. These may be socio-economic, ideologic, or geographic. Each interprets its own ideology in its own way. Each is grouped under its own leader or may split to form new cells. The fissiparousness of these groups is not a liability but rather the dynamic of the movement. Competition is excited by re-establishing goals and means. The group, the cause and the self are blended into this competition. It stimulates growth and encourages a greater sense of homogeneity.

Despite the search for identity and selfhood, attempts at cooperation are numerous. Someone whom Western observers would view as schismatic might become a champion for church union.[37] One such effort concerning itself with intergroup fellowship, theological studies and cooperative programs is the African Independent Churches Association (A.I.C.A.).

By *reticulation* it is understood that there is a weblike intersecting set of group linkages or relationships which are not tied together through a central point, but result from ties of various types and at different levels among the groups. This weblike communications system gives these structures inter-linkages which are most effective. These interlinkages provide

---

34. G. C. Oosthuizen, *Post Christianity in Africa* (Grand Rapids: Eerdmans, 1968), p. 208.
35. Reyburn, "Western Reaction," p. 81.
36. Ibid., pp. 80-81. The African thinks of possessions as "the manifestation of material witnessing to the abiding presence of one's Force . . . possessions witness to the quantity of his personal Force, his quantity of life, (and this) attracts others. . . ."
37. Sundkler, *Bantu Prophets*, p. 50.

not only an organizational infrastructure, but also channels for the propagation of ideology. Personal ties between members and their kinfolk; personal ties between leaders, traveling or itinerant "preachers"; ritual activities, ideological linkages and extra-movement connections which come from the broad range of social, economic, political and religious backgrounds and through networks of friends, associates and contacts outside the group—all serve as normal channels of communication and so provide the scaffold of "organization."

While there are these factors and other symbols, characteristics and tendencies which may classify the Zionists as a monolithic movement, each group claims its own peculiar distinctives. The names adopted by the respective groups may appear to Westerners as fanciful, if not downright ludicrous. Each group claims to have received its name by special revelation. The name accords status. The name also secures a mystical bond with a place in the Holy Land. The more distinctive the name the greater the claim to the supernatural enablement necessary to carry out the program relating to, and descriptive of, the place name. Thus the name *Apostolic Jerusalem Church in Zion* guarantees and secures the charter of the apostles; assures the miraculous events which attended the early church in Jerusalem, as described in the Acts of the Apostles; and promises the authorized religious program supposedly given by John the Baptist and sounded forth from Mount Zion in the Holy Land. All this is extremely serious and most significant, for it constitutes a claim to an effective faith and religious practice.

No one place may therefore qualify as headquarters of the African Zionist movement. Although some groups may be larger than others, no one group can speak for African Zionism in general. Here and there, especially in Natal and Kwazulu (Zululand), some places may be more important than others, but, generally speaking, wherever the group meets, that is the place of significance—an open field, a river bank, a mountain top, a tree or any building.

Future Prospects

In these groups there is a striving after reformation (not

unlike that which resulted in the German Reformation[38]), in which vernacular forms and indigenous control are central issues. The Africanization of Western forms, though important, becomes a steppingstone to the real aim—making Christianity completely indigenous within the African soil.

These indigenous Christian groups are "in process" in a way similar to that of the New Testament churches whose stories are recorded in Acts and the epistles. They are not fully formed as yet. Perhaps their plea to us is well expressed in the words of a current lapel button worn by many American teen-agers: "Please be patient with me; God is not finished with me yet."

The increase in literacy along with the availability and widespread distribution of the vernacular Scriptures, in both the Old and the New Testaments, holds out exciting prospects for the development of a truly African Christian church. Adaptation of traditional cultural forms which, though apparently instilled with new meanings, still perform those functions which in the traditional system assured psychological balance, may be a positive attempt to minister to the whole man.[39] The African Zionists' practice of community, the participation of the laity, their sense of belonging, their mutuality in worship and the use of ritual rites are all basic elements in the expression of a dynamic Christianity and are not foreign to Scripture.

The teaching and application of the Scriptures, endued with the ministry of the Holy Spirit, will undoubtedly increase Zionist understanding of scriptural emphases and will be the corrective for syncretistic tendencies. In some respects they have a long way to go in developing a Christocentric church, but in other respects they are near to the ideal. Whatever our evaluation, we must admit that they are dynamic, manifestly alive, and seeking further realization. Meanwhile, they remind black Christendom that Christianity offers more than what was found in the churches introduced by Western Christians.

---

38. The German Reformation was more than a revolt against the teachings of the Roman Catholic Church for national aspirations were also involved. See R. H. Murray, *The Political Consequences of the Reformation* (New York: Russell and Russell, 1960), pp. xvi-xvii.

39. Western Christianity acknowledges the need for a ministry to the "whole man," thereby objecting to the unscriptural dichotomy introduced by Greek philosophy.

Orthodox Christianity may again fail if it alienates the Zionists by judging them too harshly, in which case history may repeat itself in Africa.[40] Orthodoxy should choose a different course and approach them with compassion, concern and interest, sharing with them well-informed Christian instruction. Some are already doing this. Of their own accord there are those African Zionists who, though they were considered Christopagan just a few short years ago, are now both seeking and receiving Bible instruction at conventional Bible institutes. Donald McGavran advocates that many such schools be established and that we should not bewail the growth of these movements, nor seek to win them back into the fold of the mainline churches and missions. He further recommends that we accept them as part of the Christian scene and that we aid their leaders in getting a thorough knowledge of the Bible.[41]

When the Scriptures and the ministry of the Holy Spirit are brought to bear upon these groups we have every reason to believe that they will bring the masses of African animists to a living faith in Jesus Christ. The church in black South Africa is long overdue for a truly African expression of dynamic Christianity. Perhaps African Zionists are pointing in the right direction but they do need the content of Scripture to get them to their destination.

---

40. The north African church during the early centuries of Christianity produced some outstanding church fathers but did little to safeguard the future of Christianity. Christianity was never localized; it remained essentially an alien institution. The Muslim cause found it prepared soil for their ideology.
41. Donald McGavran, Introduction in Fred Burke, "Racialism and Denominationalism Completely Forgotten," *Church Growth Bulletin* IX (1973), 287-89.

Marie-Louise Martin

Marie-Louise Martin is a native of Switzerland. She studied theology in Berne, Basel (under Karl Barth) and Edinburgh, and received the D.D. degree from the University of South Africa where she did her dissertation, "The Concept of Messianism in the Bible and Messianism in Southern Africa." Subsequent to her ordination in 1938 she served in Switzerland as a pastor and then as a traveling secretary on behalf of missions. Proceeding to Africa she served in various places in southern Africa under the auspices of the Swiss Mission. She has held faculty positions at the Lemana Training Institution in northern Transvaal, the Theological School of Morija and the University of Lesotho, Botswana and Swaziland. In 1970 she founded the Kimbanguist Theological Seminary in Kinshasa, Zaire at the request of Tata Diangienda Kuntima, the son of Simon Kimbangu and the head of the Kimbanguist Church. Currently she is director and professor at that institution. She has published numerous monographs and has authored a book entitled Kimbangu *(Oxford: Basil Blackwell, 1975).*

3 | KIMBANGUISM:

A Prophet and His Church

Marie-Louise Martin

It started with a call to a humble African of the bush country of the Belgian Congo in 1918. It has developed into one of the most powerful religious movements in modern Zaire. It began as an oppressed community on the fringe of the organized church. It has emerged as a full member of the World Council of Churches. It is the "Church of Jesus Christ on Earth Through the Prophet Simon Kimbangu." Its history is a story of growth. In fact, its current membership exceeds four million souls!

The Historical Background

The ancient Kingdom of the Kongo was evangelized by the Portuguese even before the Reformation. Diego Cao arrived in 1482 at the mouth of the River Nzadi (which the Portuguese pronounced Zaire, since 1972 the official name for both the Congo River and the country).

It is in this part of Africa where we first find what we might term an independent African church. It broke away from the Roman Catholic Church during a period of great spiritual

and material crisis. The ancient kingdom had split into three
kingdoms. Christianity had touched but the surface. Christian
symbols were abused; crosses became fetishes to protect against
the assaults of wandering spirits.[1] In 1665 the Kingdom of the
Kongo suffered a total defeat at Ambouila by the Portuguese
allied with the Yak (Yaga? Bayaka?) warriors. After that defeat
three Kongo kings strove for supremacy. Prophets and prophetesses appeared.

Finally, the foundress of a national Christian Kongo religion
arose—a young Mukongo girl of royal blood, called Kimpa Vita
or Dona Beatrice. Her divine call was not unlike that of other
prophets and prophetesses in Africa. A Capuchin monk appeared to her and told her he was Saint Anthony—a saint greatly
revered in ancient Kongo. He conveyed a mission to her: preach
to the people and hasten the restoration of the ancient Kingdom of the Kongo. It was simultaneously a religious and a
political mission, because in Africa life cannot easily be de-
partmentalized in watertight sections.

Kimpa Vita is said to have died and risen. In that experience Saint Anthony took possession of her soul. The Catholic
saint thus replaced the ancient "possessor-spirit," or, if we
prefer Christian terms, Saint Anthony became for Kimpa Vita
that which for the majority of Christians is the indwelling
Holy Spirit. According to Balandier (who bases his report on
ancient Portuguese and Italian writers) Saint Anthony became
for her a "second god" that held the key to heaven. This same
motif is found in several independent African churches. It is
not a faint Western abstraction foreign to African philosophy.
Anthony assured Kimpa Vita of access to Nzambi a Mpungu,
the supreme God.

From this central figure, Saint Anthony, the movement
received its name: the Sect or Movement of the Antonians.
Dona Beatrice preached a black Christ, born in Sao Salvador
in northern Angola. Every Friday she died and went to God
to plead the cause of Negroes (as early as 1704!). She claimed
that she like the virgin Mary would have a child conceived by

---

1. Marie-Louise Martin, *Kimbangu, An African Prophet and His Church*
(Oxford: Basil Blackwell, 1975), p. 11.

the Holy Spirit. She gave birth to a male child, but the father was probably one of the apostles whom she had chosen.

In a very short time she had established a church and caused political revival by calling all the chiefs to the ancient capital of Sao Salvador. She substituted places in the Kongo for holy places in Palestine, as so many independent churches do even today. Why? Because Christ belongs to his people here and now—he cannot be a remote Savior, either in time or space. Thus, Sao Salvador was renamed Bethlehem.

The Capuchins had followed Beatrice's movements with great suspicion because the Roman Church seemed to collapse in the face of the advance of this heretical African church. On July 2, 1706, Dona Beatrice was burnt at the stake—another Joan of Arc!—with the name of Jesus on her lips.[2] In spite of her martyrdom and death the Antonians collected fragments of her bones to save as relics and continued as a movement.

Much of what was to happen later can be better understood in the light of the ideas which surfaced in the Antonian movement. It was a movement of reaction against European culture and religion, but also a first attempt to Africanize the preaching of the gospel and to express it in indigenous terms and forms. Christ became a black Messiah, that is, a Savior who identified with the unhappy Africans who had been exploited and sent away as slaves from the time the Portuguese arrived in their country.

At the end of the nineteenth century the Protestant missionary movement began its work in Zaire. At that time members of the Livingstone Inland Mission arrived. The first to tread the soil of Zaire was Henry Craven, who disembarked at Matadi in February, 1878. The Livingstone Inland Mission was followed immediately by the English Baptist Mission.[3] Other missions followed: the Swedish, the Presbyterians, the American Baptists, the Darbyist Brethren, and later, the Mennonites, the Disciples of Christ and others until there were about forty-six different Protestant denominations at work. They tried to penetrate this

---

2. Martin, *Kimbangu*, p. 17; A. Massamba-Debat, *De la Révolution Messianique à la Révolution Politique* [n.p. for political reasons. Massamba has been executed.] (Brazzaville, 1968).

3. J. R. Crawford, *Témoignage Protestant au Zaire* (Kinshasa: Protestant au Zaire 1972), p. 8.

immense country and bring the message of Christ, medical help and education to the most remote places.

After 1885 when the Berlin Conference of European powers assigned the territory of the Congo to King Leopold II of Belgium, Catholic missions tried once more to conquer the country. The king's ideal was a new Catholic "Belgium" in the heart of Africa. Relations between Catholics and Protestants were not always too happy, because the former enjoyed royal privileges unknown to the latter, who were rather regarded as disruptive foreigners.

In 1920 the Ethiopians, a religious (and political) Negro movement, made its appearance in the Congo. Its roots were in South Africa, Malawi (the Nyasaland) and also in the United States (Marcus Garvey). Its slogan was "Africa for the Africans." In the United States the Ethiopian movement had always been a separatist movement: away from the whites, back to Africa. In the Congo, the influence of the movement and its agent in Kinshasa (a certain Farnaya) seems to have been very insignificant, but its very existence frightened the colonial administration, as did any movement or utterance that did not conform to colonial mentality and aims.

Very briefly, this is the historical setting in which the prophet Kimbangu and his prophetic movement emerged.

The Prophet Kimbangu

His youth. Simon Kimbangu was born in 1889 in N'Kamba in the Lower Zaire, about seventy kilometers from Mbanza Ngungu (formerly Thysville) in hilly bush-country. His mother Lwezi and father Kuyela (both non-Christians) died while Kimbangu was still a small child. His name *Kimbangu* was given to him because it was the custom of the Bakongo people to shout "*kimbangu, kimbangu*" when a baby did not breathe properly after birth. Another deeper meaning is attached to the name, however. Kimbangu means "he who reveals what is hidden." There is also a related Kikongo word *kimbangi* that means "witness."

Kimbangu was brought up by his mother's younger sister, Kinzembo, as Congo custom demanded. She was a Baptist and a brave woman. She saved the life of a Baptist missionary, Rev. Cameron, by hiding him in her hut when enraged tribesmen attempted to shoot him. Before leaving her he blessed her and little Kimbangu—a meaningful gesture for Africans, because words of benediction as well as words of malediction are efficient words as in Hebrew tradition. The word itself effects what it signifies.

Kimbangu grew up at N'Kamba and attended the Baptist primary school. For a short while he was a teacher, then a catechist. He practiced agriculture and carpentry. In 1913 he married a young widow, Mwilu Marie, who after her young husband's death was given to Kimbangu as his wife in accordance with tribal tradition. She was the ideal wife for him. In 1914 their first child, Kisolokele Lukelo (Charles), was born. In July, 1915, Simon Kimbangu and Mwilu Marie were baptized according to the rite of the English Baptist Mission in the river Tonde near Ngombe-Lutete (Wathen Mission). The following year a second child was born named Dialungana Kiangani (Solomon), to be followed in 1918 by their third and last son, Diangienda Kuntima (Joseph).

Several stories of Kimbangu's early years still circulate: how he got ill and disappeared and was found through God's help by Kinzembo and cured; and how, simply by rubbing it in his hand, he "cured" a rotten coconut which had spoiled the garment of a friend. Such incidents have assumed a spiritual meaning in the Kimbanguist Church today: even a "rotten" heart can be cured and renewed by the love of Christ.

His call and ministry. It was in 1918 when the whole of Zaire, like the whole inhabited earth, was afflicted by a terrible epidemic of the Spanish flu. Lacking medical help, thousands died in Lower Zaire. The medical doctor promised by the Baptist Missionary Society did not arrive—he probably had more than enough to do in England! It was one night during this time of utmost distress and hopelessness that Kimbangu heard Christ's voice. It was a heavenly tongue that reached his ears; he understood it to mean, "My servants have become unfaithful. Take care of my flock. Lay hands on the sick and pray for them."

"I cannot," replied Kimbangu. "I am not educated. I am nobody. Send another one, a missionary or a priest."

But the voice spoke to him again and ordered him to go

to a certain place and meet the divine visitor. His wife wanted to accompany Kimbangu. He prayed about it.

"She may come," said the voice, "but she will not be able to understand." Tactfully, Mwilu Marie told her husband to go alone, because she realized that the meeting was meant for him.

The voice came to Kimbangu time and again. He refused to obey and instead packed his bundle and went to Kinshasa (then Leopoldville), about 220 kilometers to the north, under the pretext of earning some cash for his wife and children. But he had no success in his work because he had disobeyed the Lord. Finally he went back to N'Kamba, poorer than he was before. God's call reached him again; there was no escape.

On the morning of April 6, 1921, Kimbangu went to the market to sell some of his agricultural products, taking his seven-year-old son Kisolokele with him. On a hill opposite N'Kamba at Ngombe Kinsuka he had to pass a hut where a young woman with puerperal fever lay in agony on her mat. Believing Christ called him to enter the hut and pray for Nkiantondo (the sick young woman) Kimbangu entered, placed his hand on her head, and healed her in Christ's name. Instead of being grateful, Nkiantondo accused Kimbangu of having bewitched her previously.

"You have come now only to take your curse from me," she shouted at him.

Kimbangu tried to explain to her that he was not a sorcerer or a witch doctor, but a simple Christian who had obeyed his Lord's call.

This was Kimbangu's first healing, and on that very day the movement, which in 1956 became the "Church of Jesus Christ on Earth Through the Prophet Simon Kimbangu," had its beginning.

At first Kimbangu's fellows were afraid of him. But when more miracles occurred, they began to flock to him. Paralyzed people were healed, blind received their sight, the deaf were made to hear, all kinds of diseases were cured, a child was resurrected. Up to five hundred people at a time came to N'Kamba—some coming from as far as northern Angola and from Boko beyond the river Zaïre in what is today the People's Republic of the Congo (formerly the French Congo). To assist with the large crowds, Kimbangu found helpers on whom the same gift of God's Spirit was bestowed—one of them is still alive and active today (Mikala Mandombe).

There was joy on the hills of N'Kamba and in the surrounding countryside. Christ's salvation was proclaimed in songs which the people "seized" in visions even as they still do today. While Kimbangu healed and prayed, a choir sang the glory of the Savior Jesus who had come to save blacks and whites. At no time was there any animosity against whites, though the whole movement was a genuine African movement. Kimbangu not only healed, he also preached, forcefully, simply, convincingly: "You cannot serve Christ and put your trust in man-made fetishes. Either you trust Christ wholeheartedly and get rid of your fetishes or remain bound with the chains of Satan."

Hundreds of fetishes were thrown away. What had not been possible through the preaching of white missionaries happened when Kimbangu preached. Africans realized that one of their own people had been chosen as God's *Ntumwa* (envoy, apostle). Through Kimbangu, Christ revealed himself to the poorest and most forgotten blacks. Now Christ became a reality, and was no longer only a remote figure in an ancient tale of the white people. Christ lived in their midst through the Holy Spirit in N'Kamba. Kimbangu was doing Christ's work. Through Kimbangu they perceived Christ. Hence the joy. N'Kamba became the New Jerusalem. All these events were made possible through the working of the promised Holy Spirit who had come down in abundance on this simple black catechist Kimbangu.

This is the church's theology in a nutshell: Christ became real to the Africans through Kimbangu, there had been a new outpouring of the Holy Spirit, and there was the anticipation of the coming glory of the New Jerusalem—all right there in poor, simple N'Kamba on that remote hill so far from all the luxuries of Western civilization.

In his dealings Kimbangu attempted to follow the biblical pattern. Like Christ (and in accordance with Kikongo custom) he asked people who knelt down before him, "What do you want me to do for you?"

The story of the paralyzed woman who had been carried all the way from Angola to N'Kamba is most touching.

"What shall I do for you?" Kimbangu asked.

"*Tata* (father), that I may walk again."

He prayed and told her to stand on her feet. But it was in vain! She repeated her humble request. Kimbangu offered another prayer. Still there was no success. The woman began crying: "What a worry for those who have carried me here. They will have to carry me all that long way back to Angola. What sin have I committed that there is no healing for me?"

Moved by her tears Kimbangu once more prayed and asked the Lord to help this poor woman. Then he took her by her hand, and lifted her up. She tried to walk—very carefully at first—then her legs became normal again and there was tremendous joy when she walked like any healthy woman.

Kimbangu's mission was not only that of healing, but first and foremost, that of leading people to Christ. His hearers were urged to repent of their sins, believe in Christ, submit to his commandments, and obey biblical injunctions. Faith in Christ, repentance, forgiveness through Christ—this was the heart of Kimbangu's simple preaching. He warned those who wanted only health or a material blessing. The last judgment was a reality for him. There must be no watering down the biblical truth. The way to salvation is faith in Christ, personal surrender and obedience. All who received healing or spiritual advice were sent to the well just below N'Kamba to bathe three times "in the name of the Father, the Son and the Holy Spirit." To Simon Kimbangu, outward cleansing was the sign of spiritual cleansing from sin and evil desires. Spiritual and material realities are not two separate realities, but one reality—the one expressing the other. Greek dichotomies are foreign to African philosophy.

Hostility. Opposition came from different quarters: the existing churches were not satisfied with that "self-styled prophet"; Roman Catholics were angry because not a few of their converts had gone to Kimbangu to find healing, or to listen to his preaching and receive his blessing. As a consequence, chapels emptied. Catholics accused Protestants of encouraging such nonsense by putting the Bible into the hand of untutored people who would necessarily "misuse" it. Protestants, who were foreigners in the Belgian colony, could not take the accusation lightly. They kept a watchful eye on the movement. Belgian traders were especially angry because some of their employees had gone to N'Kamba to be healed or to accompany the sick. They also feared a revolution when so many blacks came together. They spoke of subversive activities and of Ethiopianism (of which Kimbangu had no knowledge).

Actually, Kimbangu taught nonviolence, obedience to the authorities, and punctual payment of taxes. Nevertheless, only five weeks after the beginning of the movement, authorities sent the administrator of Mbanza Ngungu, Mr. L. Morel, to go and investigate. Morel was received by the prophet and his helpers. When they saw him the Spirit of God seized them and they spoke in tongues. Then they took him to the place where Kimbangu healed the sick. Morel watched a while, then wanted to retire. Against the advice of the inhabitants of N'Kamba he had pitched his tent next to Kimbangu's place. Singing continued throughout the night. Morel was annoyed. To him Kimbangu and his followers were madmen, so he reported to his superiors that arrest was not advisable, but that Kimbangu should be discreetly taken away to a mental hospital. He also tried to enlist Protestant and Catholic help against the movement, being fearful—with some reason—that an epidemic of some sort could result from so many people with diseases going to N'Kamba.

But the most dangerous opposition arose from the ranks of Africans who wanted to be prophets and to join Kimbangu in common actions. Some sought simply ecstatic experience such as glossolalia and trembling. Others had political aims and prophecies: the imminent coming of a great Kingdom of the Kongo and the expulsion of all whites. Kimbangu sent them away as "sons of the devil." But when the colonial authority put Kimbangu into prison for good, the day for these aspirants had dawned. They crowned themselves with the name of the martyr Kimbangu, and carried on in a way that did much to discredit Kimbanguism.

Arrest and imprisonment. Traders continued to exert pressure on the colonial administration to do something against this prophetic movement in N'Kamba because other less harmless prophetic movements had sprung up. Morel was sent back with a detachment of twenty-five soldiers to arrest Kimbangu. When he arrived at N'Kamba, there was considerable confusion. Somebody threw a stone at the soldiers. A trigger-happy soldier shot a child. During the confusion Kimbangu escaped to Mbanza Nsanda with his helpers and his son Kisolokele. There he taught his disciples, evangelized, and healed. Though sought by the Belgian authorities, nobody betrayed him.

He remained near Mbanza Nsanda until September 12, 1921, when he returned to N'Kamba.

"My hour has come," he confessed. "Those who want to use violence must leave me."

He was arrested and chained by the commander, Snoek, and taken (together with Mikala Mandombe, then a girl of about sixteen to eighteen years) in chains to Mbanza Ngungu. His followers and sympathizers also were taken to prison; and one of his helpers, Therese Mbonga, died in prison of ill treatment. Among the prisoners were many Protestants who had sympathized with Kimbangu. As a matter of fact, there was hardly an African Baptist who was not in sympathy with Kimbangu. Protestant missionaries were not even permitted to visit the prisoners.

A few days after Kimbangu was taken prisoner his wife, Mwilu Marie, and his three sons were also apprehended. In prison, Kimbangu's wife was mistreated and whipped. Even though he was only seven years of age, Kisolokele had to appear in court to testify whether he had knowledge of any miracles wrought by his father. Though threatened with a beating, the young child testified that his father had cured many suffering people. The boy was later to be removed to a Roman Catholic boarding school at Boma, where he had to live separately from his family. Outwardly he became a Roman Catholic. Of course, in Boma he had the chance to receive an excellent education.

On October 3, 1921, Kimbangu was tried. He was accused of hostility toward whites, of sedition, and of having hindered a civil servant in the exercise of his functions (Kimbangu had escaped when arrested by Morel). Neither witnesses nor counsel for the accused were admitted. After the death sentence was pronounced, missionaries Ross Phillips of the English Baptists and Joseph Clark of the American Baptists went to see the governor general in Boma to deliver a petition for pardon. The British Baptist Mission in London sent a similar petition to King Albert of the Belgians. The death sentence was commuted by the king to life imprisonment in Lubumbashi (then Elisabethville) prison, thousands of miles away from N'Kamba.

Before being taken away from the prison in Mbanza Ngungu, Kimbangu asked to see his wife and children. His request was refused at first. But when the train that was to take him to Kinshasa was delayed, Kimbangu was allowed to say farewell to his family. He blessed Mwilu Marie (who was to lead the movement through a period of secrecy) and his sons—first the youngest, Diangienda (who would become his successor), then Dialungana (the guardian of the holy city N'Kamba—Jerusalem), and finally the eldest son Kisolokele (who would look after the family upon his release from exile).

Kimbangu's weeping followers asked him: "Tata Simon, what do you leave behind for our guidance?"

"You have the Bible; it is and always will be your guide," he replied.

This partially explains why so little material about Kimbangu and his teaching is available. He never had the ambition to create his own doctrine. He advised his followers to go to their own churches while remembering the hymns and all that N'Kamba had meant to them.

Kimbangu was first taken to Kinshasa where he was given 120 lashes. He survived and was then taken the long way by boat and train to prison in Lubumbashi. He was given a tiny cell where he spent much of the next thirty years. His conduct in prison was exemplary and in 1935 there were proposals to free him. However, since it was a time of numerous prophets and messianic movements, it was feared that Kimbangu's release might encourage rebellion.

He never saw his family again. On October 4, 1951, he became ill and was taken in chains to Lubumbashi hospital where he was kept under strict guard. He died on October 12. His family was not informed of his death, but it is said that in a mysterious way he appeared to his son Diangienda, who at that time was serving the Belgian administration in Kananga (then Luluabourg). Reluctantly, Diangienda's Belgian senior officer phoned to Lubumbashi prison only to discover that Kimbangu had died twelve days previously, and had been buried by friends.

All sorts of tales surrounded Kimbangu's death. For instance, it was reported that on his deathbed he had denied his faith and mission and had become a Roman Catholic. Diangienda insists that he examined the evidence and found no proof whatever to support the allegation.

In spite of the imprisonment and death of Kimbangu, the movement continued underground and experienced tremendous growth.

The Spread of the Kimbanguist Movement
1921-1959

N'Kamba was destroyed by the Belgians, though a single military post was retained there. People were prevented from assembling near the sacred well for prayer, hymns and healing. Mwilu Marie with her two smaller sons (the eldest had already been banned to Boma) was allowed to return to the neighboring village, Ngombe Kinsuka, but severe restrictions were placed upon her. No one was to see or help her in any way. Nevertheless, she survived, and, in spite of police surveillance, some believers managed to meet with her. Between 1921 and 1924 she was able to lead the movement because measures against the Kimbanguists were not strictly enforced.

After 1924 the government responded to certain incidents and pressures by moving to suppress and eventually exterminate Kimbanguism. The movement went completely underground and what was heard of Kimbanguism was mainly reports of pseudo-Kimbanguist groups which emphasized ecstasy and prophecies of the imminent return of Kimbangu "through the air" to reign over a kingdom of blacks in central Africa.

Large numbers of true Kimbanguists were placed in concentration camps—some in the most remote places in the forests. But wherever believers came together, they kept their religious observances as they plowed their fields and built their villages. Their way of life attracted many people and these communities became centers of evangelization.

In 1949 the leader designate, Kimbangu's youngest son Diangienda, began his ministry in secret, visiting groups here and there, praying for the sick and laying on hands for healing. He and a few helpers of the second generation reportedly "received the gift of the Spirit" when they were in prison or in concentration camps. When no such *bansadisi* (healers) were available, the community prayed for the sick—without laying on hands but applying some of the water from N'Kamba when it was available.

Great strength was derived from hymn-singing. Hymns were sung daily in the concentration camps and in the Kimbanguist communities. In fact, down through the years new hymns have been "seized" and added to the Kimbanguist repertoire until their number has become so large that it is impossible to incorporate all of them into one hymnbook.

When in 1954 a more liberal (socialist) government took over in Brussels, increased toleration was extended to Kimbanguists, and they were even allowed to hold open-air services. The reaction of other churches to this policy was negative. They disliked the prospect of the movement coming to the fore again. They were also disturbed because some of their members participated in the Kimbanguist meetings.

The Kimbanguist *movement* was forced to become a *church* with its own structures in 1956. And a *church* it became—but a church that was neither Catholic nor Protestant, but African. Its worship, organization and fellowship fairly breathed the cultural air of its African environment. The Kimbanguist Church had a tremendous advantage when compared to the mission churches. At the same time it should not be supposed that practices such as polygamy and sacrifices to ancestors were allowed in the new church, for such was not the case.

In 1957 there was another change of government in Brussels and the new men in power initiated another persecution of Kimbanguists. On June 11 of that year five Kimbanguist pastors of Kinshasa were arrested. Others were put on a government blacklist. Some young Kimbanguists working in government offices took the initiative: they wrote to the United Nations Organization and to the Belgian Parliament to protest this religious persecution. Kimbanguists also wrote a letter to Governor General Petillon, whose private secretary was none other than Tata Diangienda, the prophet's son. They wrote: "Tomorrow we shall be at the sports stadium, unarmed. Either arrest us all and execute us, if necessary, or else grant us religious freedom."

While Petillon considered the matter Kimbanguists in Kinshasa made ready to be arrested at the stadium. The governor general referred the matter to Brussels. Meanwhile he declared that Kimbanguists could meet for their services.

On December 24, 1959, the Kimbanguists received official recognition and permission to function normally. Since Mwilu Marie had passed away, Tata Diangienda left his well-paid job with the Belgian administration and took over the leadership of the church (later to be assisted by his two brothers). Encouraged, a million followers emerged from all parts of Zaire, the French Congo, and Angola. The movement began to spread into Tanzania, Burundi, the Central African Republic, Gabon and Zambia through spontaneous evangelization by lay people.

Developments Since 1960

In January, 1960, scores of parents came weeping to Tata Diangienda's home in the humble township of Ngiri-Ngiri in Kinshasa. Their children had been turned away from Catholic and Protestant schools, and there were but very few state schools at the time. Most of the schools—right up to university level—were in the hands of the churches. Parents wondered what to do with their children who had been turned away from the church schools. As a result, Kimbanguists joined together to teach their children in any available place—in plots between houses, in little houses placed at their disposal by faithful believers, and even under trees. In a short time the church was able to care for thousands of school children. They were taught by volunteers. High school boys built their own college at N'Kamba in 1962. The program was enhanced when the government stepped in and paid the qualified teachers in Kimbanguist schools.

On June 30, 1960, the Belgians left and the Congo became an independent state. The first years of independence were difficult. East and West had their material interests and the Congo became the playground of foreign powers—among them the United States, Russia and China. It was a sorry state of affairs. Millions died in various rebellions. In Europe and America people talked of the whites (including missionaries) who were victims. But the number of blacks who were victims of the manslaughter outnumbered the whites by far. During this troubled time the Kimbanguist Church stuck to its principle of nonviolence. Each believer was left to decide for himself whether he wanted to take part in politics and was free to choose the party which he found closest to his ideals. Tata Kisolokele became a minister of state in the Congolese government, but retired because of ill health.

In 1965 the revolution of General Mobutu put an end to intertribal fighting and restored order in the country, but misery and suffering were everywhere. The Kimbanguist Church never separated body and soul to care only for the salvation of the soul. It took social action: a colony for jobless people was created in 1964 at Lutendele near Kinshasa. Dispensaries were established to treat the sick. Youth movements multiplied: dramatic groups, choirs, and the *surveillants* (guardians of church property who also keep watch for thieves during open-air services). A women's movement was initiated in order to teach reading, writing, crafts and skills to women, and to care for abandoned and delinquent girls.

In 1962 a school for the training of ministers had been inaugurated in N'Kamba in order to unify church worship and administration. Men with little education but with love and zeal for the church were admitted.

Much later, in 1970, a theological school was created in Kinshasa for students with a high school education who desired to become the future leaders of the fast-growing church. With a church membership of four million it has become apparent to Kimbanguist leaders that there is need for a well-trained ministry, though finances are extremely limited. At the founding of the theological school Tata Diangienda asked white collaborators to train his future clergy, provided they were willing to accept the church and its way of life, and put themselves into the African way of thinking and expression. Students were challenged to work for their living during the five-year course of study. From the first group to receive their diplomas new theological tutors will be recruited. One is already at work.

Meanwhile, in September, 1975, the theological school had to move to the farm at Lutendele some thirty kilometers outside of Kinshasa. Jobless students have started an agricultural project and are proud of their Lutendele, as the campus also is called. Students still working in Kinshasa travel by school bus to Lutendele either in the early morning or in the late afternoon in order to attend lectures. At present (1976) some eighty students are thus being trained for the ministry of the church.

Perhaps the greatest event to occur in the years from 1960 to 1975 was the transfer of the mortal remains of Simon Kimbangu to his home village, N'Kamba. For years the desire of Kimbanguists had been to take the prophet home. Several early attempts had failed due to the opposition of the Belgian administration. Finally, in March, 1960, the sons of Kimbangu and some of the officials of the church went to Lubumbashi and took the coffin by rail and boat to Kinshasa. Since permission to enter Kinshasa with his coffin was not forthcoming, a place was prepared in Matadi-Mayo. There on April 2 of that year a great ceremony was held. The following day the "Return of the Prophet" was completed: the procession reached N'Kamba by car. The remains of Simon Kimbangu were placed in a mausoleum. Each year the mausoleum is opened on the occasions of the great pilgrimages to N'Kamba—at Christmas and on April 6 (to commemorate the beginning of the Kimbangu movement). Plans call for a large church building to be erected in N'Kamba for the many religious services held for pilgrims coming from far and near.

Organization

The organization of the Kimbanguist Church is simple and hierarchical. At its head is the youngest son of Simon Kimbangu, Diangienda Kuntima. An outstanding leader and orator, he attracts thousands to his meetings in Kinshasa and elsewhere throughout Zaire. At the base of the organizational structure are the minister-evangelists and their helpers and the believers of the local churches. The large majority of ministers are laymen with secular employment. The same is true of their catechist-helpers. Ministers have received education at gradually rising levels since 1962. Catechists receive three months of special training at N'Kamba. More stress is put on charismatic ministry than on education. And though ministers receive ordination, they are still thought of as laymen—and all laymen as the "people of God."

A simple diagram of church organization reveals the basic pattern of leadership.

The spiritual head (Diangienda)
Adjunct spiritual heads (Dialungana and Kisolokele—
the other sons of Simon Kimbangu)
Bansadisi (healers)
Legal representatives of churches in the various countries
Regional representatives and their staffs
Subregional representatives and their staffs
Main parish ministers, evangelists and helpers
Parish-section ministers, evangelists and helpers
"The faithful"

Evangelistic Outreach

There is no mission board or evangelization committee in the Kimbanguist Church. The structure of the church is new, and still adaptable to the various needs. Everyone has the duty to evangelize. There are, of course, ministers (many still without training). There are also catechists (or evangelists) and deacons, both male and female. Each parish, in fact, is subdivided into sections, each with its own ministers, catechists and deacons. But every Kimbanguist tries to win his brother. This is not always easy, especially in centers like Kinshasa. But even there Kimbanguist conduct (no alcoholic drink, no adultery and fornication, no smoking, willingness to help anyone in need, nonviolence) attracts attention. Some mock and jeer but others respond positively. It is amazing how many people join the church in Kinshasa every year. More than a thousand candidates were received into church membership at Kinshasa in one day on December 1, 1974. Some had been unbelievers; others had belonged to some church, but had not seen it from the inside for a long time!

Such services are not uncommon. Hundreds find Kimbanguist characteristics appealing. And upon joining the church, the new member becomes involved in one of its organizations: the dramatic society, choir, women's association, and so forth. There they find identity, belonging and activity.

Another factor in the outreach of the Kimbanguist Church is the emphasis on meeting the physical and spiritual needs of the people. For example, some women regularly work on the church farm at Lutendele to raise manioc for the needs of the church and to feed poor people. Pastors regularly pray for the sick, for blessing and for other special needs. The house of Tata Diangienda is open day and night to those who are in need. When he leaves Kinshasa on a trip to the interior of Zaire or to another country he takes his brass band and a team of co-workers. Thousands come to greet him and not a few see in him what the older generation had seen in his father: a concern for the simple and poor. They find that he has a word of comfort for them. The following Sunday they are likely to visit a Kimbanguist church.

Kimbanguist music and hymn-singing constitute an extremely important evangelistic appeal. Hours—not minutes—are devoted to singing at the services. Every visitor is greeted personally and has a song dedicated to him. When someone dies, the church members come and sing all night. The words and tunes of Kimbanguist songs are easily learned and not soon forgotten. Music of this sort appeals to the African.

Kimbanguists from a large district meet twice a month to collect money by means of a *nsinsani* (giving competition): as the music plays, groups form and compete against each other, the most generous one winning the victory. This is a way of financing many church projects without much help from outside. The Kimbanguist Church has never accepted money from any agency that might interfere in the determination of her projects. Most Kimbanguist ministers earn their livelihood in secular professions. This method of self-help and joyful competition at the *nsinsani* attracts many people. They first join one of the *nsinsani* groups, and later they may join a catechism class and become members of the church.

One of the most powerful means of evangelization is the numerous spiritual retreats which were inaugurated in December, 1972, by the women's movement. Since 1973 all members of the Kimbanguist Church—men and women, old and young, take part in a five-day retreat far from the noise and bustle of town or even village life. Special teams of men and women have been formed to conduct the retreats. We shall say more about them later. But this much should be said here: a large number of non-Kimbanguists seem to be desirous of participating in these retreats. They seem to be an effective tool for the "re-evangelization of the evangelized" and the evangelization of the unevangelized. They have given a new intensity to the spiritual life and mission of the church.

Worship and Spirituality
in the Kimbanguist Church

A knowledge of worship and spirituality in the Kimbanguist Church implies participation in its manifold expressions of faith. It also implies spiritual involvement and submission to church discipline. Solid information in this area of church life can only come from within. My observations are based on my own participation in the life of the Kimbanguist Church. It is an African church with African forms of expression. This has often puzzled people, especially those coming from other traditions and different cultural backgrounds.

A few examples are in order.

(1) When an outsider arrives at a service or at the humble residence of the spiritual head of the church, he sees people kneeling before the leader and he jumps to the conclusion that Kimbangu and his son are God and black Messiah to their converts. He ignores the fact that in many African societies kneeling is the polite way of approaching persons of authority.

(2) After the sermon visitors are greeted by name and with a piece of music played by the brass band or the flute orchestra, or sung by the choir. If the visitor comes from a foreign country he is greeted with a special hymn containing the prophecy of Kimbangu to the effect that in times to come men and women from east, west, south and north will come and worship together with his followers. The music is followed by clapping hands "in the name of the Father, the Son and the Holy Spirit." People who are used to silent and solemn worship are perplexed by the joyful noise of the people in the church. They question the spirituality of a church so different from the puritan or pietistic forms of spirituality evidenced in many Western churches.

(3) Some visitors attend a Kimbanguist service with the expectation of hearing what they call "real African music"— the rhythms and drums known in Zaire as *tam-tam*. They are disappointed at the character of the Kimbanguist hymns and songs. There are drums, but not necessarily of the type they expect. Some have termed the Kimbanguist music a blend of "revival songs" or "Salvation Army style music" and the rhythms

and harmonies of Africa. They are critical of so many "un-African musical elements" in a supposedly "authentic African church." They forget that the Kimbanguist Church wants to be representative of both the universal church and the church of Christ *on earth*.

(4) Some visitors are profoundly disappointed not to find dancing in Kimbanguist worship. They have been persuaded that "Africa dances her faith." However, since the time of Simon Kimbangu, dancing has not been permitted in the churches because in many tribal societies in Zaire, dancing has a lascivious, erotic character. During the *nsinsani*, however, groups do march around with rhythmic steps.

These few examples show that the cult of the Kimbanguist Church is lively, though orderly. Speaking in tongues and trembling occur from time to time, but they are not promoted. Rather, the emphasis lies on a life of prayer, love, faith and honesty which is a living testimony in a world of impiety, hatred, jealousy and dishonesty.

Spirituality and daily living. All activities are permeated by a spirit of worship. Grace is said even before drinking a bottle of Coca-Cola. No new car (or other object) is put in use before it has been blessed with holy water. Before taking a journey—even a short one in the snarled traffic of Kinshasa—a prayer is said, and *N'Kamba* water is used. Thus the material is surrounded and permeated by the spiritual.

Prayers are said in the morning, at noon and in the evening (by the family, the congregation or the individual). There is a hymn of prayer which helps Kimbanguists in their effort to remain in contact with God. Church workers interrupt their schedules for prayers before beginning their work, and again at noon and before leaving. At the theological school lectures begin and end with prayer. The Western dichotomy—here spiritual life, there material life—makes no sense in African Christianity.

Worship services. Services for worship are held on Sundays, Wednesdays (a special holy day) and Fridays. Attendance at Sunday services is compulsory for a Kimbanguist unless he is ill or is required to work.

The services often last for a whole day, especially the big *nsinsani*. Even an ordinary service starts at 8:00 A.M. and does not end until 1:00 or 2:00 P.M. so people usually bring their lunches in little plastic buckets. The services themselves are simple. The opening hymn is followed by prayer and the reading of a psalm. Then the text of the sermon is read and the sermon is delivered. The sermon itself is usually given in a very animated way and is often punctuated by questions from the congregation or the singing of a hymn which brings home the preacher's point. Children are not overlooked. As a regular part of the service they receive a blessing. The services usually close with prayers and a benediction.

The healing of the sick through Tata Diangienda or one of the *bansadisi* (the close associates of Simon Kimbangu during his lifetime) is important but usually takes place at Tata Diangienda's home during the week rather than on Sundays. Holy water—a visible symbol of cleansing from evil and disease—is used in conjunction with these prayers for healing.

Rites and symbols. Twice a year baptismal services take place. The child, having come of age, decides for himself whether he wants to become a Christian or not. He enrolls at the local parish and takes catechetical instruction. After that he is baptized—not by water, but by the Spirit—by being lifted up by a minister especially appointed for the work. Usually there are thirty ministers officiating at the big baptismal services. There is no second baptism for those who previously belonged to another church. Men and women who have failed to live up to the standard of the church are put under discipline. After an intensive talk with the minister and having rearranged their affairs, they present themselves to the church on the same Sunday as the baptism and are readmitted with joy.

Holy communion was introduced at the fiftieth anniversary of the church in 1971. Very deep reflection preceded the introduction of communion. What elements were to be used? Who was to partake of the communion? How many times a year? Elements available in Africa were chosen, since Christ is not incarnate in the Mediterranean countries alone. A cake made of potatoes, maize and bananas serves as the body of Christ, and honey dissolved in water as the blood of Christ. The elements are consecrated before use and then represent the real body and blood of Christ. All who are faithful Kimbanguists partake of the holy communion. It is always a great feast. The people of one parish after another come and kneel at the huge improvised communion table. About one hundred communicants can be served at a time. About thirty ministers and even more deacons and deaconesses assist. Those who give holy communion are all clad in white. Otherwise no clerical garb is used in the Kimbanguist Church. The *surveillants* wear their green and white uniforms as in all services. Both green and white are symbolic colors and represent hope and purity.

Symbolism in the church is not elaborate, but it does go beyond that inherent in baptism and holy communion. Stars which decorate church implements represent Christ at the right hand of God. Three doves stand for the fulness of the Spirit, for the Trinity, and also for the unity of the three sons of Simon Kimbangu who make all major decisions of the church in remarkable unity of spirit and mind. The symbol of the cross is used sparingly because from the time of the Portuguese evangelization in the ancient Kongo, it often has been represented as a powerful fetish.

Church retreats. We have briefly touched on the retreats of the church. Regular attendance at some of the five-day retreats is compulsory (for the time being at least). Theological students must attend a special retreat one day a month, in addition to other retreats. Retreats are under the leadership of specially chosen teams of men and women who have charismatic gifts. On the first evening (and, if there are many participants, right on through the night) open confessions take place "to vomit one's evil and get rid of the dirt." One by one, members come before one of the leaders for confession. Everyone is obliged to make a full confession of his sins "before the witnesses in heaven and on earth." One day of complete fasting without food or even a drop of water is also compulsory. Many fast for three full days. Sermons are preached, hymns are sung, regular prayer times are observed and during certain hours, Bible studies, interrupted by prayers, are held in small groups. Visions received by participants during these retreats are remarkable. Not a few are cured from diseases. Many reconversions and new conversions take place. Fetishes are thrown away; reconciliation in families and among neighbors takes place. Lukewarm Christians come back and get involved in the church. Retreats are indeed an important factor in the numerical and spiritual growth of the church.

Church discipline. The Kimbanguist Church has been accused of being legalistic. It must be admitted that certain features of Kimbanguist teaching and life would seem to support this accusation. The Ten Commandments are emphasized. Modesty is a virtue. Children learn respect for their elders. Members are not allowed to smoke or drink alcoholic beverages. Dancing is prohibited. (When the government revived the old lascivious tribal dances in the name of patriotism, many Kimbanguists were fined or imprisoned for not yielding on this point and those who did participate were disciplined by the church.)

Church leaders believe these emphases to be necessary. Premarital sex, wife-beating, drinking and dancing are common features of African life. Furthermore, as Africans move to towns and cities, individuals have to make more and more decisions on their own. In this context, the law is emphasized. Personal behavior is an important theme in Kimbanguist sermons, and that is especially true of the sermons of Tata Diangienda. But it is not forgotten that the law without the gospel is impotent and irrelevant.

Special teachings. Is there any special doctrine that distinguishes the Kimbanguist Church from other churches? Kimbanguist doctrine is biblical doctrine and this is the reason why she was accepted as the first independent African church in the World Council of Churches in 1969. But the place of Simon Kimbangu needs some explanation. He, as well as his wife, Mwilu Marie, are occasionally invoked in Kimbanguist worship. According to African tradition one cannot go directly to the highest authority. One must humbly submit his request to an inferior—in this case Simon Kimbangu. He will take the request to Christ. But nothing prevents the Kimbanguist from addressing his prayer directly to the Lord, and this is what most of them do. Also the term *god* can be used for Kimbangu or Diangienda though the latter makes it abundantly clear that he is not the Father of Jesus Christ, but only a simple and sinful human being. The term *god* in this context does not refer specifically to the God whom we know from the Bible, but merely designates a being who is superior. When as a professor I have to give a clear order to students (an order which may be linked to a promise), I am "god." We may think along the lines of Martin Luther, who regarded the preacher as a man who speaks God's word. The African would say that while the preacher speaks, he is "god." Different word usages in different cultures often cause misunderstandings, and Europeans and Americans must beware of premature judgment and of hunting for heresies. A serious look at Exodus 4:16 would be a great help in this situation.

As the envoy of God, Simon Kimbangu is not dead. He lives with God—as Jesus promised—because God is the God of the living and not of the dead. He can appear to his disciples in times of distress and need. He can say a word or a prayer. He intercedes before God for the church and thus protects it against the attacks of the evil one. Kimbangu had the gift of prophecy and some of his prophecies have come true: his country has become independent; his church has made immense progress; and there is brotherhood with whites who used to be the oppressors, but for whom Simon Kimbangu prayed daily while he was on earth.

In all spheres the church is making progress, and to what has been written today, much will have to be added in the future. Certainly, the Kimbangu Church has its backsliders. The discipline of the church is too strict for them. They have been caught in the quest for material goods and high positions, or they disdain the risk of being laughed at when they say that they are Kimbanguists. But there is a hard core of faithful people, not only among the old, but especially among the young. Many of them are in training. Thus Kimbanguists dare hope to achieve the aim of the Church sooner than expected— the aim to send messengers to many more countries, in Africa and abroad, who will testify in their own way to what they have received from God and thus encourage their brethren elsewhere, even in Europe and America.

PART TWO

Europe

Frederick O. Burklin

Frederick O. Burklin, the son of missionaries, was born and raised in China. He received his training at Grace College (B.A.), Grace Theological Seminary (M.Div.) and Westminster Theological Seminary. Since 1961 he has been on the faculty of the German Bible Institute in Seeheim, Germany, teaching in the areas of systematic theology and New Testament. He has served in that institution as dean of men and registrar and, since 1966, has been academic dean.

4 | THE NEW APOSTOLIC CHURCH

Frederick O. Burklin

The movement that culminated in the *Neuapostolische Gemeinde* (New Apostolic Church) had its origin in England in the first part of the nineteenth century. A group of earnest Christians united in prayer for an outpouring of the Holy Spirit, since they deemed him to be missing in the life of the church. One of the more influential circles within the larger group met at the Albury Park estate of a London banker, Henry Drummond (1786-1860). Their concern was that Christ's church might truly become a spotless bride, fully prepared to meet its returning Lord.

About 1830 in many parts of England and Scotland, but particularly in Glasgow, "strange events" took place such as prophesying, speaking in tongues, and healings. They caused a furor in the press but were considered by the Albury circle as confirmation of their expectations. One member of the circle, Edward Irving (1792-1834), was dismissed from his London pastorate and started his own congregation. He took a prominent role in the movement, preaching the imminent return of the Lord and the Babylonian apostasy of the Christian world.

Through the exercise of prophecy some members were informed of their high vocation, and a few were designated as apostles. Ultimately, twelve men were declared to be apostles and were solemnly ordained to that ministry on July 14, 1835, in London. The aim of these prophets and apostles was to unite the divided church according to the pattern established by Paul in the New Testament. The apostles established the teachings of the church and watched over it, while the prophets interpreted the spiritual secrets of the Scriptures. When the prophets called out certain members for spiritual ministries, they were examined and ordained by the apostles. A new movement had emerged.

For one year the twelve apostles lived at Albury Park in order to plan for the future and also to study the Scriptures. They concluded that the Holy Spirit and sound doctrine are imparted through the apostleship only. Scripture recognizes the apostles alone as the center of authority, of doctrine, and of unity. All Christendom was to be divided among these apostles as the "princes of the tribes of Israel." They were to travel in assigned areas in order to ascertain and evaluate spiritual conditions and religious practices.

They also decided to direct a respectful epistle to the ecclesiastical and secular heads of Christian nations, appealing for correction of the abuses of Christianity and for general reform. They made it clear that this reform would come from God through the divinely ordained offices of the apostolate.

Returning from their survey trips, the apostles set themselves to the task of unifying the church and preparing it for Christ's return on the basis of the faith revealed in the Bible, and in the Apostolic, Nicean and Athanasian Creeds. To accomplish this purpose they reinstituted the four offices of apostle, prophet, evangelist, and pastor for the whole church (Eph. 4:11). Functions within local congregations were to be administered by officers occupying three hierarchical positions: angels or bishops, elders or presbyters, and deacons. A liturgical order of services was issued with a view to uniting a divided Christendom. Such were the organization and mission of the Catholic Apostolic Church.

All was not to go smoothly for the movement, however. One of the leading exponents of change in the church, particularly in Germany, was Fritz Krebs (1832-1905). As he gained control over the movement in Germany, he propounded the teaching that the words of the living apostles had an authority that equaled those of the early apostles. He also stressed the unity of the apostles *(Aposteleinheit)* rather than their equality.

Not all were willing to accept Krebs's teachings. A break with the original Catholic Apostolic Church resulted and the New Apostolic Church was born. It should be noted in passing that the actual founding date of the new organization is later than the date maintained by the church itself. As Kurt Hutten writes, "It did not originate in 1863, as maintained by itself, but rather in 1897-98 when Krebs carried through his concept and broke with his antagonists."[1]

Actually the apostles of the older church had insured either a gradual demise of the movement or a radical change by failing to resolve the problem of succession. In 1901, Apostle Woodhouse—who had been assigned to the "tribe of Reuben" in southern Germany and Austria and who was the last surviving apostle—died. More recently, the last remaining deacon to be ordained by the "original" apostles also died. With no one left to perform the all-important liturgical services, the Catholic (or Old) Apostolic Church has been gradually dying out.

The New Apostolic Church, on the other hand, remedied the situation by appointing new apostles to fill the vacancies left by the death of the "original" apostles. Appointments were not limited to twelve and as a consequence the number of apostles has gradually increased until currently more than forty men serve in this capacity. More important than the actual number, however, is the fact that the new church has provided for continuing leadership and in so doing has made growth possible. In fact, Krebs's teaching and actions had cleared the way not only for apostolic succession, but for a consolidated authority in the apostolate. "To the apostles alone, barring all other offices, was assigned the *exclusive authority to transmit salvation (exklusive Vollmacht der Heilsvermittlung)*."[2]

---

1. Kurt Hutten, *Seher, Grübler, Enthusiasten*, tenth edition (Stuttgart: Evangelische Buchgemeinde, 1966), p. 635.
2. Ibid.

It was only a short step from joint authority of the office of the apostles to the primacy of the main apostle *(Stammapostel)*.[3] All power was said to derive from him. He administers the mysteries of the Holy Spirit. A strictly hierarchical church polity was the result.

Main apostles Hermann Niehaus (1848-1932) and Johann Gottfried Bischoff (1871-1960) ably, though ruthlessly, consolidated their leadership and control of the church. *Stammapostel* Bischoff claimed that he had received a revelation from God that the Lord would return for his own during Bischoff's lifetime. He made this declaration in a Christmas message in 1951 and it was accepted as dogma soon afterwards. It was preached in almost all services, and every "sealed" person was bound to it. This dogma, of course, guaranteed that New Apostolics were in a state of election and would be saved out of the world while others would be left behind. Anyone who dared to utter a doubt was condemned. Some did, and recriminations and strife resulted.

But another and perhaps greater challenge to the movement was yet to come. Bischoff unexpectedly died on July 6, 1960. Shock and consternation swept through the church. However, the college of apostles speedily elected a new main apostle, Walter Schmidt, who declared that the past *Stammapostel* could not have been mistaken. God had simply altered his plans. The churches accepted this excuse and were content that the mercy seat of God was occupied again and that the fount of salvation continued to flow. Their "Moses" was not allowed to enter the promised land but the new "Joshua" would lead his people in. Gradually the churches recovered and a greater soberness seemed to prevail.

As proof of their new-found equilibrium the transition of authority from Schmidt to *Stammapostel* Ernest Streckeisen was made without difficulty in January, 1975. Whereas death had terminated the reigns of the previous main apostles, the reasons given for Schmidt's retirement from office were old age and ill health.

---

3. The German designation *Stammapostel* expresses a twofold meaning. It refers to a tribe like one of the twelve tribes of Israel, but also to a trunk from which stem all the branches. The main apostle became the conductor, even an originator of all blessings to others.

Growth and Its Causes

By 1925 the German membership of the New Apostolic Church had reached 138,000. This number increased to over 343,000 by the end of 1953. By that time a significant number of adherents—just over 121,000—had been added to the church in other countries, making a grand total of almost 465,000 members. By the time another decade had passed, the membership in the apostolic districts of Germany had swelled to some 420,000 and the world total was over 600,000 members in some 5,000 churches administered by 47 apostles and 30,000 other officers. During the decade from 1964 to 1974 little or no growth was reported in the German districts, but considerable growth occurred in other countries. A report of membership statistics for 1973-74 reveals not only the relative numerical strength of apostolic districts, but also the unique pattern of New Apostolic organization.[4]

Europe:	Federal Republic of Germany	335,000	Evidently including Denmark, Sweden, Greece, Turkey and Lebanon.
	German Democratic Republic	85,000	
	Holland (with Belgium)	12,000	
	France	10,000	
	Switzerland (including western Italy, Spain, Czechoslovakia, Hungary, and Poland)	45,000	
Canada:	(Including England and Ireland, the United States, Jamaica, Columbia, Peru, Venezuela, the Philippines, Japan, Korea, India, Ceylon, and Rumania)	108,000	Includes in the United States 21,000

4. Cf. Oswald Eggenberger, *Die Neuapostolische Gemeinde* (Munich: Chr. Kaiser Verlage, 1953) and Hutten, *Seher, Grübler, Enthusiasten.* The 1973-74 statistics come from an authoritative source.

Africa:	186,000	Includes in republics of South Africa: 110,000
		Rhodesia: 6,000
		Zambia and Malawi: 70,000
South America:	66,000	Includes in Argentina and Brazil: 50,000
		Uruguay: 15,000
Australia:	2,000	
Indonesia:	7,000	
TOTAL	856,000	

Church leaders do not readily co-operate with outsiders who inquire into the affairs of the church. Repeated requests by the author for printed information concerning their history and teachings have been either ignored or politely but firmly turned down. Abuse by outsiders and protection against mis-representation have been given as reasons. Thus the writer has had to rely on secondary materials for much of his informa-tion, including that of a statistical nature. Moreover, though the church is not a secret organization which bars outsiders from its services, the writer was requested to refrain from taking notes during worship services because it was "against procedure."

In any case, the reasons for the growth of the New Apostolic Church would not seem to be exactly those which we might ordinarily expect.

In the first place, the New Apostolic Church maintains no seminaries or training institutes in which their clergy receive education and preparation for the ministry. They pride them-selves that their officers and ministers have grown out of the local churches and have become bearers of the Spirit of Christ while serving as unpaid workers.

In the second place, the church has not produced any sig-nificant literature for propagation purposes. Subscriptions to such periodicals as *Wächterstimme (Voice of the Watchman)* are available to believers only. Indeed, the church has pro-duced but a meager literature for its own members.[5]

In the third place, though the church has engaged in evangelism and missionary activity in the past, it no longer emphasizes this. No campaigns are conducted by its leaders. No door-to-door visitation is practiced by its members. Rather, the church relies mainly on person-to-person contact with family members, relatives and neighbors in its efforts to propagate the faith. This may be one of the reasons for a somewhat slowed growth rate in recent years, especially in Germany.

But the question remains. Why has the New Apostolic Church grown so significantly down through the years in comparison to other church groups, especially those within the same socio-cultural context of Germany? It is the author's contention that the reason is to be found in the sense of security, eliteness and belonging which has accrued to its authoritarian leadership structure, dogmatic teachings, and close-knit fellowship, and that these are closely related. To these factors, then, we will turn our attention.

Organization, Authority and the Apostolate

The hierarchy and church organization. The New Apostolic Church is a well organized and highly disciplined church. The administration follows a hierarchical pattern: the main apostle *(Stammapostel)* is the highest authority and heads the whole church; the regional apostle *(Bezirksapostel)* oversees several districts, each of which is headed up by either an apostle or a bishop; the "apostle" or "bishop districts" are made up of a few (usually four to seven) "elder districts" presided over by chairmen, elders or evangelists; these "elder districts" are com-

---

5. New Apostolic literature cited in Eggenberger and Hutten include the following books:

Die Amter und Sakramente der Neuapostolischen Kirche (Frankfurt am Main: College of Apostles, 1935).

Fragen und Antworten über den Neuapostolischen Glauben (Frankfurt am Main: J. G. Bischoff, 1938).

Lehrbuch über Fragen und Antworten zum Gebrauch für den Religionsunterricht der Kinder und Konfirmanden in der Neuapostolischen Gemeinde (Frankfurt am Main: College of Apostles, 1933).

Neuapostolisches Gesangbuch, fifth edition (Leipzig: Neuapostolischer Verlag, 1921).

Niehaus, Hermann, *Hilfsbüchlein* (1908).

———. *Allgemeine Interne Hausregeln Nebst Glaubensbekenntnis* (General Board, 1908).

prised of a number of congregations in given localities; and finally, each local congregation is under the direction of a church president *(Gemeindevorsteher)* functioning as pastor, church evangelist or priest. Also, in addition to the first or regular priests, there are numerous supporting ministries such as assistant priests, deacons and subdeacons.

In their own presentation of the offices of the church, the New Apostolics now start with the main apostle and proceed down the hierarchy to the subdeacon. This is just the reverse from listings given earlier in their history, and it emphasizes the authority of the apostles in contradistinction to the authority that finds its roots in the local churches. The prophetic office with which the earlier apostles were related has been superseded by the apostles and especially by the *Stammapostel.* The explanation is given that prophecy was needed only in the initial stages of the church. In the economy of God, the Holy Spirit now works through the apostles to teach his people, and prophets are no longer needed.

The apostles and their authority. The apostolate, then, is a unique characteristic of the New Apostolic Church. Due to the efforts of the apostles, when Jesus Christ returns he is to find a church that will be like the church founded by the apostles of the first century. Thus, the New Apostolic Church considers itself to be a continuation of the early apostolic church and an anticipation of the true future church of the end times. Other churches may possess a certain measure of divine life, but it is the *Neuapostolische Gemeinde* in which Jesus Christ has revived the apostolic office. "That we possess again today in the apostolic churches the original status is a great miracle; it is grace."[6]

The apostles are ambassadors and messengers who function as God's intended substitutes for Jesus Christ in his church. Along with such responsibilities as preaching, teaching, and judging, they dispense the Holy Spirit to believers through the sacrament of sealing (see below). They also appoint other officers to positions of leadership within the church. According to Oswald Eggenberger's summary the apostles are *am-*

6. *Brot des Lebens,* 1949, no. 22, pp. 173-74, as quoted by Eggenberger, *Die Neuapostolische Gemeinde,* p. 45.

bassadors of the Lord who have been sent and authorized by him to represent him on earth.[7] They are *custodians* of Christ's heritage, completing the redemption of mankind. Jesus Christ rules, heals and blesses through the apostles who are the ascended Lord's extended hands on earth. They are the *revealers of God's teachings.* The teaching of the apostles bears the mark of revelation. Through them God's Spirit speaks to his church. Upon their words the church can build—and build, as it were, upon bedrock.

This close relationship between Christ and the apostles finds its clearest expression in the New Apostolic phrase, *"Jesus in the apostle."* Jesus Christ came in the flesh and continues to live in the flesh today by working in and through the apostles. Recently, however, there has been a gradual modification in the way the church views this doctrine in that it stresses the spiritual presence of Christ in the apostles more than his physical presence.

Apostles are appointed by the *Stammapostel.* No formal training is necessary. University education is considered to be incongruous with the spiritual calling of the apostle. How could one learn about the kingdom of God in secular schools?

The marks of apostleship are love, patience, truthfulness, service, sacrifice and pastoral care. The office of the apostles is legitimized by their activities and work. A church will flourish where apostles function in power. In this connection, reference is made to I Corinthians 9:2 ("you are the seal of my apostleship," RSV) and II Corinthians 3:2 ("ye are our epistle") to show that a prospering church is a validation of the apostolic office.

In summary, it is apparent that the apostles are mediators between God and man. Without them no salvation, no true life in God would be possible. They have power to remit sins and to cleanse from iniquity. Their words carry as much authority as those of Scripture. The New Apostolic Church hymn sums it up well: "Blessed is he who found the shepherd through grace and the office of the apostle" *(O selig, wer den Hirten fand durchs Gnaden und Apostelamt).*[8]

---

7. Ibid., pp. 49-52.
8. *Neuapostolisches Gesangbuch* (Frankfurt am Main: Friedrich Bischoff, n.d.), no. 535, stanza 4.

Other officers and their functions. The following offices are listed in the 1952 edition of *Questions and Answers* (question 224): main apostle, assistant main apostle, district apostle, church apostle, bishop, district elder, district evangelist, pastor, church evangelist, priest, deacon, and subdeacon.[9]

The highest office after that of apostle is that of bishop. He is the mainstay of the apostle, supporting him and functioning as priest of the priestly offices.

The elder heads up a large congregation or several smaller congregations either as a church or district elder. He is to care for, lead, and govern the church(es) in his trust as a man mature in faith and dedicated to the apostle.

A pastor, evangelist, or priest also could be in charge of a local church. The pastor is the first priest among other priests in the church. He is to safeguard the apostolic teaching of Christ by instruction and admonition, and proclaim the forgiveness of sin in the power and name of the apostle. The evangelist is under the pastor (or as a district evangelist he is under the district elder), and has to declare the gospel of Christ. The priest cares for the church in a priestly manner, and comforts and prays for those in his care. All officers from the bishop down to the priest have authority to baptize, forgive sins, and administer communion.

The deacon helps to maintain order in public worship services and to bear witness to the teachings among those who lack faith and knowledge both inside and outside the church. He is to be an example of love, zeal, fidelity, faith and peace. One of his duties is to gain new members.

The subdeacon has to prove himself on a preliminary level before he may advance up the ladder to a higher office.

Priests and deacons alternately visit the families of the church on a regular basis, usually once a quarter.

No remuneration is given for services rendered by an officer of the church except in those cases where the office demands all the time and energy of its occupant so that he is forced to give up his secular vocation.

---

9. Quoted by Eggenberger, *Die Neuapostolische Gemeinde*, p. 64.

The Teachings of the Church

Inevitably the teachings of the New Apostolic Church have been touched on already. It is not the writer's purpose to present here an exhaustive analysis and evaluation of their doctrines but only to establish a basis for understanding the attraction the church holds for many. One explanation for the staying power of the New Apostolic Church is to be found in the nature of its teachings.

The creed of the church. The New Apostolic Church has a confession of faith expressed in ten articles. The first three articles embody the Apostles' Creed as used in the Christian church from the earliest times. Article four speaks of the living apostles sent by the Lord Jesus Christ to teach, forgive sins, and baptize with water and in the Holy Spirit. Article five refers to the officers within the church—they are appointed by the apostles from whom all gifts and powers flow. Articles six through eight deal with the sacraments of baptism, communion, and sealing. The ninth article formulates eschatological views referring to Christ's return, the resurrection and rapture of the prepared ones, the millennial reign, and final judgment. The last article treats of the authority of government.

Two kinds of revelation. In the New Apostolic view the Bible is considered to be a very important document because it contains teachings propounded by Jesus and his apostles. It is to be read publicly and privately and is to be preferred above all other books. But it does not stand alone. The catechism asks, "Thus the Bible is not the only foundation of true faith?" And the answer given is, "No, but it is an essential adjunct to it.[10] Since the Bible is a document of the past it takes a secondary place to the "living word" of the apostles of today. The *written word* and *living word* are complementary to each other. Though important and profitable, the Bible is no substitute for today's messengers who proclaim true teachings and administer the sacraments of grace.

---

10. *Lehrbuch* (1916), question 615, as quoted by Eggenberger, *Die Neuapostolische Gemeinde*, p. 55. *Fragen und Antworten, Lehrbuch für den Religionsunterricht* is their catechism, written by Niehaus originally, and revised repeatedly (new editions appeared in 1916, 1924, 1938, and 1952).

Two kinds of faith. It is illuminating to see how the New Apostolics look at faith. A distinction is made between two kinds of faith depending upon the source. There is the historic faith as recorded in the Bible. Then there is the living and hopeful faith centered in the preaching of the apostles active in the present world. Faith must go beyond mere belief in what happened in the past. In other words, it must go beyond belief in the written word to belief in the living word. What is important is not what *was* but what one *has*. To *possess* is more than to *believe*. "Faith focuses on Christ in the apostle; but the apostle is visible; thus faith becomes sight."[11]

The role of the *Stammapostel*. The longing for a manifestation of God's Spirit has been present from the inception of the church. To the New Apostolic believer the Holy Spirit seems to have become incarnate in the person of the *Stammapostel*. The main apostle becomes the visible guarantee of the individual's salvation. Through the sacraments the members are joined to the true church which alone is the continuation of the original church of the apostles of the first century. The greater the authority and power in the office of the apostolate, the greater the security of the individual members. The *Stammapostel*, therefore, takes the role of a mediator who is equipped with the Spirit's authority. He dispenses grace and blessing. He will give rest to the weary and heavy laden.

Kurt Hutten aptly observes that the power of salvation vested in the main apostle flows from him in two streams: one is of a pastoral nature *(seelsorgerlicher Art)*, the other of a sacramental kind.[12] As his representatives, the church officers counsel and shepherd the members extensively. And the three sacraments of baptism, sealing, and communion assure the individual of his salvation. "In the close relationship to the officebearers and the reception of the sacraments by faith the attainment of the goal promised by Jesus is guaranteed to everyone who seeks grace."[13]

The three sacraments. The first sacrament is baptism. Infant baptism is standard practice in the New Apostolic Church.

---

11. Eggenberger, *Die Neuapostolische Gemeinde*, p. 81.
12. Hutten, *Seher, Grübler, Enthusiasten*, pp. 650f.
13. *Lehrbuch* (1952), article 221, as cited by Hutten, *Seher, Grübler, Enthusiasten*, p. 651.

But for any covenant of baptism to be recognized it must be either performed or validated by an officer of that church.

The second sacrament is the sealing of the member, usually enacted within half a year of the baptism of the child. This rite is to be administered only by an apostle because he dispenses the Holy Spirit, thereby activating the regeneration of the individual. The sealed person will be born of the Spirit of Christ and renewed in his mind, thus becoming a child of God. On the day of his sealing he receives eternal life. A life of obedience to the apostles will make him a conqueror who will participate in the first resurrection and in Christ's millennial kingdom.

The third sacrament, communion, is celebrated every Sunday as part of the worship service. Its importance is indicated by the fact that it is customary to schedule an additional service on Sunday afternoon for those who cannot attend the Sunday morning service. The officiating priest (as we have noted that their ministers are sometimes called) pronounces absolution after which the members receive the wafer and cup as confirmation that their sins have been forgiven.

With these sacraments New Apostolics possess a guarantee of salvation. Though a believer may fall from grace, by returning to union with the apostles and receiving absolution through their authority, eternal bliss can be assured.

The life of piety. Though the believer's salvation is dependent upon the authority dispensed by the apostolate, he is called to a life of self-denial and conquest over sin by the power of the Holy Spirit. Jesus Christ has set the example. Like him, the believer has to do battle with the powers of evil in order to attain perfection. But as a recipient of the Holy Spirit through the sacrament of sealing the believer is redeemed and able to overcome.

Emphasis is placed on a life of piety. The New Apostolics have their taboos: sports, jazz, theaters. Regular attendance at church services is expected of all members. Inexcusable absence over a period of time can result in dismissal from membership.

Worship Services

The worship services in the New Apostolic churches are quite simple. A typical order of service would be as follows:

(1) An opening hymn.

(2) Prayer.

(3) Scripture reading.

(4) A sermon or talk by a church officer.

(5) Music by a mixed choir.

(6) A sermon or talk by a church officer (complementing the first one).

(7) The praying of the Lord's Prayer by the congregation.

(8) The proclamation of remission of sins.

(9) The celebration of communion.

(10) A closing prayer.

(11) A congregational hymn.

(12) The benediction.

In addition to the Sunday services, regular services for prayer are scheduled. At these services individual members are encouraged to pray such petitions as may be suggested by the district apostle.

There is a certain spontaneity in the simple services of the churches which must be attractive to those attending. Sermons are not prepared ahead of time because it is the spiritual condition of the speaker which makes it possible for him to declare the "present deeds of Jesus." Participants are encouraged to sing the hymns from dedicated hearts. The preface of the New Apostolic Hymnal states: "Sung in this spirit they [the songs] lift the hearts of God's children and prepare the way for the word of the Lord which in our days is being proclaimed purely and clearly by the apostles given again to his church tions of the apostles is the occasion of spontaneous expressions of thanksgiving. In the presence of the *Stammapostel,* Ernst Streickeisen, at a service in November 1975, the statement was made: "No one on earth is comparable to the *Stammapostel* by Jesus."[14] And the assurance that comes through the ministra- who alone has the key to save. To him the power, authority, and gifts have been granted from God to redeem."[15]

---

14. *Neuapostolisches Gesangbuch. Notenausgabe zum Gebrauch bei allen Gottesdiensten der Neuapostolischen Gemeinden. Auf Beschluss des Apostelkollegiums bearbeitet und herausgegeben.*

15. Personal notes taken surreptitiously at a church service in Darmstadt, Germany on November 2, 1975.

Conclusion

The New Apostolic Church has faced difficulties which could have occasioned its demise, and undoubtedly have had the effect of slowing its growth. In Germany, at least, its expansion has slowed somewhat. And it should not be overlooked that the church still comprises a small minority of less than 1 percent in West Germany. One negative factor has been the disappointment experienced by some members because of the accommodation of church leaders with National Socialism previously and with Communism today. Another obstacle to growth was the death of main apostle Bischoff—premature in view of the dogma that Christ would return during his lifetime. An apparent gradual de-emphasis on evangelistic activity may prove to be a most important deterrent to rapid growth in the future.

Nevertheless the New Apostolic Church has proved itself to be a resilient and dynamic movement. In the German context especially, curious outsiders are attracted by its vitality and, initially at least, they do not find its teachings to be very different from those of other churches. Once they have been lulled into the fold, they experience the sense of security that comes with membership in a church where apostles, by their word and ministration, dispense grace and salvation.

PART THREE

The Far East

A. Leonard Tuggy

A. Leonard Tuggy was born in 1929 in Port of Spain, Trinidad. His parents were missionaries to Venezuela. He came to the United States at an early age. He graduated from UCLA with a B.A. degree in astronomy in 1953. In 1956, he received a B.D. degree from Fuller Theological Seminary. From 1958 until 1973 he with his family served with the Conservative Baptist Foreign Mission Society in the Philippines. During the year 1967 to 1968, he studied at the School of World Mission, Fuller Theological Seminary, where he received his M.A. degree. The following year he spent with Church Growth Research in the Philippines, surveying churches there. This research resulted in the book, Seeing the Church in the Philippines, *which he co-authored with Ralph Toliver. He is also the author of* The Philippine Church: Growth in a Changing Society *(Grand Rapids: Eerdmans, 1971), and a volume on the* Philippine Iglesia ni Cristo, *which is being published in the Philippines. In 1973, he received the D.Miss. degree from the School of World Mission at Fuller Theological Seminary, and since that time has been serving as the Overseas Secretary for Asia of the Conservative Baptist Foreign Mission Society. Dr. Tuggy and his family now reside in Wheaton, Illinois.*

5 | IGLESIA NI CRISTO:

An Angel and His Church

A. Leonard Tuggy

When Pope Paul arrived in the Philippines (for his special visit) on November 27, 1970, representatives of four major religious bodies met him. One was from the Iglesia ni Cristo; the others represented the Roman Catholic Church, the National Council of Churches in the Philippines, and the Moslem community. In this way the virulently anti-Catholic Iglesia ni Cristo dramatized its position as a leading Philippine religious body.

The Iglesia ni Cristo is significant not only in the Philippines. As one of the largest, most powerful and dynamic independent, indigenous churches in the Third World, the Iglesia ni Cristo demands our careful study. Most Americans are surprised to find out that about three hundred members (nearly all Filipinos) are regularly attending its Los Angeles "local," and that it has bought and refurbished an older Methodist church building in Queens, New York, as part of its "foreign" mission.

What is the story of Iglesia ni Cristo? Can we discover the reasons for its remarkable growth? Why has it been so successful in propagating its teachings in areas where other churches have grown only with great difficulty? These questions will give direction for this investigation.

The Lengthened Shadow

A great institution is often but the lengthened shadow of its founder. The Iglesia ni Cristo was so powerfully molded by its founder, Felix Manalo, that it is often referred to by outsiders as the "Church of Manalo," or *Manalistas,* rather than as the "Church of Christ," which is the literal translation of its name. To tell Felix Manalo's story is to a large extent to tell the story of his church, so tightly are the two intertwined.

Felix Manalo Ysugan was born on May 10, 1886 in Taguig, Rizal province, about eight miles southeast of Manila along the shores of Laguna de Bay Lake.[1] His parents chose the name *Felix* ("Happy") from the roster of saints for that particular month. Later, when Felix was a young man, he dropped his father's surname and adopted that of his mother, Manalo ("Victor" in Tagalog); so he became known as the "Happy Victor."

Felix Manalo's formal schooling was very limited, probably extending to only two or three years. But while still a young boy, he showed strong leadership traits which were to stand him in good stead throughout his life. He apparently was a restless, active, even pugnacious young man.[2] His mother was a devout Roman Catholic who made sure that young Felix attended his catechism classes where he learned the common prayers and fundamental doctrines of the Roman Church.

While still a teen-ager, Felix Manalo began a spiritual quest which was to lead him through five denominations before he decided to start his own. His first religious exploration focused on a group of religions, called *colorum,* which were mysterious, secretive, and centered around pilgrimages to a sacred mountain. However, Felix became disillusioned by the deception practiced by a leader of one of these groups, left the religion, and moved to Manila to begin making his livelihood there.[3]

Soon after moving to Manila, Felix witnessed a debate between a Roman Catholic priest and a Protestant minister concerning the use of images. Impressed by the minister's ef-

1. Dolores G. Garcia, "Felix Manalo: The Man and His Mission," *Pasugo* (July 27, 1964), p. 179.
2. Julita Reyes Sta. Romana, "The Iglesia ni Cristo: A Study," *Journal of East Asiatic Studies* (July 1955), p. 331.
3. Garcia, "Felix Manalo," p. 180.

fective use of the Scriptures, Manalo joined the Methodist Church in 1904 and began studying at their Bible school. His studies were interrupted by the death of his mother, and when he returned to school he enrolled at the Presbyterian Ellinwood Bible Training School. But it was not long before he heard the preachers of the Christian Church and became convinced of their view of baptism.[4]

Manalo's quest was not yet over. As a young Christian Church evangelist, he attended a Seventh Day Adventist meeting to debate the missionary. The outcome of this encounter was that Manalo was converted to Seventh Day Adventism in 1912. He became one of their workers, but within a year he was charged with immorality and excommunicated from this church.[5]

While still a Seventh Day Adventist worker, Felix Manalo began to think of starting his own church. After his separation from the Adventists, the idea took root and bore fruit. Significantly, Manalo experienced a "call," such as other "prophets" have experienced down through history. In early November, 1913, Manalo closeted himself with his Bible for three days. When he emerged from this experience, he said to his wife, "Let's go!" Giving his shoe business to a friend, he left everything to begin his mission. Taken in by Christian Church sympathizers, he began to gather a group of believers around him, and then a new church was founded.

What was Manalo's message during those days? He seems to have majored in attacking the Roman Catholic Church. He preached against gambling and drinking, and dealt with topics such as "Body, Soul, and Spirit," "The New Heavens and New Earth," and "Where Are the Dead?" His message in the early days of his church may not have been noticeably different from the message being preached in many Christian churches, though it may have had some apocalyptic notes borrowed from the Adventists. Nevertheless, the young church was definitely Filipino, and Manalo was its unquestioned leader.

---

4. Arthur L. Tuggy, "The Philippine Iglesia ni Cristo: A Study in Independent Church Dynamics" (D.Miss. dissertation, School of World Mission, Fuller Theological Seminary, Pasadena, CA, 1974), pp. 42ff.
5. Ibid., pp. 45ff.

Contrary to some reports, the new church did not grow very rapidly during its first years. Felix Manalo quickly proceeded to register it with the Philippine government, however. The date of official registration was July 27, 1914, the day which witnessed the beginning of the First World War. About 1922, Felix Manalo came to see a tremendous prophetic significance in this date, and claimed that it closed the period of the sixth seal as described in the seventh chapter of Revelation.

In 1919, Manalo left his fledgling church in the hands of his assistant ministers and went to the United States to study religion for one year. After his return to the Philippines, the Iglesia ni Cristo continued to expand northward into central Luzon until 1922. At that time the groups suffered a serious schism led by Teogilo Ora, one of the pioneer ministers.[6] Very possibly Manalo developed his special "messenger" doctrine in an effort to re-establish his leadership in the church. In spite of the Ora schism, the Iglesia ni Cristo maintained at least twenty-nine local congregations in 1922, with a total membership of about three thousand.

Quickly recovering from the damage caused by the schism, the Iglesia ni Cristo entered a period of accelerated growth during which it multiplied congregations throughout the heavily populated provinces of central Luzon and began its movement southward. By the beginning of the Second World War it had entered both the Ilocano-speaking northern Luzon provinces as well as the port city of Cebu, gateway to the influential Visayan Islands in the central Philippines.

The unsettled and difficult conditions of the war years greatly hindered the aggressive propagation of the teachings of the Iglesia ni Cristo. However, since its members were scattered over the archipelago during that disruptive period, a base for future growth was provided. Manalo was able to keep his church administration intact, and was ready to move ahead again once the war was over. By 1945, after a development of thirty years, the Iglesia ni Cristo had grown from a struggling little group in Manila to a large, powerful church with a membership of possibly forty thousand. Among Protestant groups, only the Methodists were larger.

---

6. Ibid., pp. 71f.

After the war, the Iglesia ni Cristo exploded all over the Philippines. In the newly independent Philippines, this church, with its strongly indigenous character and emphasis on the national language (Tagalog), fit the emerging nationalistic mood. Moreover, its strong anti-Catholic posture attracted many among the disillusioned masses. Moving forward on several fronts simultaneously the Iglesia planted congregations in extreme northern Luzon and the Western Visayans (central Philippines), and entered southern Mindanao in force.

The story of how the Iglesia began its work in the western Visayan Islands is especially instructive. Two provinces, Iloilo and Negros Occidental, were opened through the efforts of teams of men employed by Atlantic Gulf and Pacific Company— the large construction firm in which Felix Manalo had found his first converts so many years before. This firm built several large sugar refineries in these provinces with construction teams made up of Iglesia members. Not only did these construction crews actively propagate their faith, they also were able to build chapels for the newly formed congregations.[7]

During the postwar period, the Iglesia ni Cristo not only has grown numerically and geographically, it also has become politically powerful and fabulously wealthy. All of these factors are interrelated. As the church membership grew, the giving grew proportionately. Because Manalo taught that the Bible required all church members to vote as a block ("think the same thing," Phil. 2:2), the Iglesia vote was increasingly sought by rich and powerful politicians. As it grew in power and finances, the Iglesia began to acquire prestige by constructing large ornate cathedral-chapels (it refuses to allow its church buildings to be called anything but "chapels"!). Its building program was climaxed in 1971 by the construction of a $3,000,000 headquarters building which was more expensive than the residence of the Philippine president—Malacanang Palace.

The Iglesia's founder, Felix Manalo, died in 1963. Many predicted that the church would splinter when Manalo was off the scene but careful preparation for an orderly transition of power to his handsome son, Erano, had been made some ten years previous to the founder's death. Erano Manalo took

---

7. Ibid., p. 95.

the reigns of leadership and continues to lead the Iglesia ni Cristo today. Among the new developments which he has been able to spearhead is the beginning of foreign missions (priority being given to the United States with its numerous Filipino immigrants).[8] Today the Iglesia is larger than any Protestant denomination in the Philippines. Latest census figures (1973) give 475,000 members. These members congregate in 2,584 locals which are served by 1,902 ministers. This represents a religious force that must be reckoned with in any serious consideration of religion and politics in the Philippines.

What the Iglesia ni Cristo Teaches

The Iglesia ni Cristo is unashamedly doctrinal in its approach. It claims to be more true to the Bible than any other church. For almost thirty years it has been forcefully propagating its teachings through its widely read monthly magazine, *Pasugo (God's Message)*.

What are the most important elements of its doctrinal structure according to its own literature? What are its distinctives which lead its members to believe that it is the only true church?

Teachings about God. In common with other Christian churches, the Iglesia ni Cristo strongly affirms the unity of God; it emphasizes the doctrine so strongly, in fact, that no room is left for the Trinity. It quotes John 17:3 ("that they might know thee, the *only* true God") and I Corinthians 8:6 ("But to us there is but one God, the Father") to undergird its contention that the one God spoken of in Scripture is the Father, not the Son, nor the Holy Spirit. Its arguments, however, are all against tritheism, not against trinitarianism. The Iglesia places itself within the Judeo-Christian tradition by teaching that God is a Spirit, One, Eternal and Almighty Creator of all things, and worthy to be worshiped by all men.[9] It stands against all image worship and saint veneration as practiced by the Roman Catholic Church.

---

8. Brandon V. Rosquites, "Barria Maligaya: A Sanctuary in the Wilderness," *Fifty-Fifth Anniversary of the Iglesia ni Cristo* (Manila: Iglesia ni Cristo, 1969), p. 11.

9. *Lsang Pagbubunyag sa Iglesia ni Cristo* (Manila: Iglesia ni Cristo, 1964), p. 1.

About the Bible. In their own words, "the Iglesia ni Cristo believes that the words of God are written in the Bible." It assumes biblical inerrancy and emphatically rejects church tradition and other sources of revelation. It holds to the *infallibility* of the Scriptures, but denies their perspicuity. According to the Iglesia, the ordinary Christian cannot correctly understand the Scripture unless it is interpreted for him by authorized ministers. Thus it is that the basis of authority for the Iglesia ni Cristo is not simply the Bible, but the *Bible as interpreted by God's messenger, Felix Manalo.*

About Jesus Christ. An Iglesia minister was once asked about the Iglesia's belief concerning Christ. He answered, "Yes, we believe in Jesus Christ, but we do not believe that he is true God. We believe in only one true God, the God of creation. Jesus Christ is a great Saviour and was commissioned by God to be the Saviour."[10] Though Manalo seems not to have attacked the doctrine of Christ's essential deity in the earlier days of the Iglesia, since the 1930s the Iglesia has pointedly denied the deity of Christ. It denies his pre-existence, stating that only "in purpose" was he with God in the beginning.

About the church. The Iglesia ni Cristo believes that Christ's great purpose on earth was to establish his church through which his people would be saved. It points to his words in Matthew 16:18: "I will build my church." Whose church? "My church"—the church of Christ, or, in Tagalog, the Iglesia ni Cristo. Following restorationist and Adventist precedents, it teaches that the true church disappeared after the time of the apostles, when it was led astray by "false prophets" (to be identified, it says, with Catholic priests). But Jesus taught that there are "other sheep." These, the Iglesia teaches, are those who will come from the Far East in fulfillment of the prophecy in Isaiah 43:5, 6 (Moffatt).

A special form of the doctrine of limited atonement is taught by the Iglesia ni Cristo. Since the church was purchased by the blood of Christ (Acts 20:28), only faithful members of the true church (the term, of course, refers only to the Iglesia ni Cristo) are redeemed by Christ.[11] This leads the Iglesia to its

10. Far East Broadcasting Company, "Research Center Bulletin," April 17, 1970 (mimeograph), p. 3.
11. *Lsang Pagbubunyag,* pp. 33ff.

doctrine of salvation through the church, which we will discuss below.

Teachings about Felix Manalo. The Iglesia ni Cristo undergirds its organization with its unique doctrine concerning its founder, Felix Manalo. According to his own teaching, he fulfills the prophecy in Revelation 7:2, 3 concerning the "angel ascending from the east, having the seal of the living God." Building on this passage, the Iglesia has developed its doctrine that Felix Manalo is God's last messenger, his special *Sugo* (commissioned messenger), the angel of the east. Felix Manalo's special mission, according to Iglesia doctrine, was to preach the "true" gospel and to snatch the true believers as a "ravenous bird" (Isa. 46:11) from the false religions in which they are trapped. As the *Sugo,* he was the authorized interpreter of the Bible and leader of the church.

Teachings about the way of salvation. The Iglesia ni Cristo agrees with Christians that man's basic problem is sin. And it also agrees that Christ's death offered the solution to this problem. But it differs as to how a person can appropriate the benefits of Christ's death. The Iglesia ni Cristo stands against the Reformation doctrine of salvation through repentance and faith. Salvation is obtained through faith in Christ, but this entails becoming part of Christ's body, which is the church, and the true church is the Iglesia ni Cristo (Rom. 16:16). In summary, a person is saved by being baptized and joining the Iglesia ni Cristo. To the Iglesia, propagandizing the Iglesia ni Cristo is equivalent to evangelizing; and they are not embarrassed to use the word *propagandize.*

Other teachings. The Iglesia also teaches "soul-sleep"—that is, when a person dies, his soul also dies and has no consciousness.

It stresses the second coming of Christ, but teaches no millennial rule of Christ on earth. Evil persons will be condemned to the lake of fire, there to be tormented forever.

The Iglesia ni Cristo raises to doctrinal importance a matter which most Filipino Christians take to be a matter of Christian liberty. That is the question of eating *dinuguan,* a Filipino delicacy made from cooked blood, and served with rice cakes. Tying together Acts 15:19, 20 (the apostolic decree forbidding the eating of blood because of the stumbling block it would be to the Jews) and Matthew 12:32 (concerning the sin of blasphemy against the Holy Spirit), the Iglesia ni Cristo concludes that anyone eating *dinuguan* in defiance of "what seemed good to the Holy Spirit" sins against the Holy Spirit.

Thus through a very literalistic and tendentious approach to biblical interpretation, the Iglesia has built up its own particular system of doctrine which is close enough to orthodox Christian teaching to attract many, but cannot be said to be orthodox.

A Special Kind of "Total Mobilization"

The Iglesia ni Cristo is organized like an army. (Before the introduction of martial law, some of its ministers were known to carry revolvers!) A member once told me, "If you touch an Iglesia member, the whole church can be mobilized against you in twenty-four hours!" That was quite likely an exaggeration but it did reflect one member's appreciation of his church's organization and power.

At the top of this powerful hierarchical structure is Erano Manalo, who has absolute power and is answerable to no one. He does have a cabinet of "generals" who advise him, and who direct the various departments of the church's work. The cabinet includes the Administrative Secretary, General Evangelist, Auditor General, General Treasurer, and the Manila Division Minister.[12] The two financial officers are particularly important because *all* Iglesia monies are channeled through headquarters. This involves many millions of pesos every year. But it is also significant that one of the offices is that of General Evangelist, presently filled by Teofilo Ramos, who not only directs the entire propagandizing work of the church, but is himself extremely effective as the Iglesia's chief debater and (Tagalog) polemicist. Cipriano Sandoval, the Administrative Secretary, is probably the most highly educated official in the Iglesia.

Under the cabinet in rank and directly responsible to Manalo are the sixty-four division or provincial ministers who oversee the church organization in the various Philippine provinces. They are very active in propaganda work and in training the ministers under them.

---

12. *Fifty-Fifth Anniversary of the Iglesia ni Cristo*, p. 64.

Approximately 2,000 ordained ministers serve the Iglesia ni Cristo in its 2,600 local congregations. In addition there are many evangelists and workers, some paid, but many not. From this pool of workers the ministers are chosen and trained. A man must prove himself in the field before he can be considered for ministerial training and ordination.

The Iglesia ni Cristo teaches that the church is the organization as a whole, and that the ministers are under it, not under the local congregations (which are not called churches, but simply "locals"). Each local, however, is carefully organized. A head deacon is appointed and is responsible to the local minister. Under this head deacon are the deacons and deaconesses. But the organization of the local does not stop there. The entire congregation, whether numbering fifty or a thousand, is organized into committees of about seven members each. Each committee has its own president, vice-president and secretary. These committees are extremely important, both for disciplinary purposes, and also for propagation. If a member becomes lazy, he will be reported by his president. If a new contact is made by a member, he notifies his committee which immediately mobilizes to follow up the new contact, and if possible bring the minister to the contact's home. Thus though every member is not an evangelist as such, every member is mobilized for propagation.

Propagation Principles and Methods

Many Filipino church leaders are naturally very critical of the Iglesia ni Cristo's system of doctrine, but feel that its propagation methodology has been notably successful and contains many lessons for other churches in the Philippines. Propagation methodology, being heavily conditioned by environment, is not always easily transferable from one culture to another. On the other hand, some methods undoubtedly have a more universal application. Before describing the Iglesia's successful methods, we will look at three important principles of propagation which have guided the Iglesia as it has expanded throughout the islands.

The first of these principles is that of *extensive propagation*. The objective of the Iglesia ni Cristo has been to grow throughout the whole of the Philippines. It has not waited for established congregations to become strong before beginning new ones in new areas. By adopting this nation-wide (and now world-wide!) strategy, the Iglesia has had no built-in limitation on its growth. A church which refuses comity agreements, believes it is the true church, and has a very distinctive message, finds it easy to adopt such a policy.

This principle of extensive propagation also applies to the local level. When the Iglesia begins a local congregation in a Philippine town, it is not satisfied with simply entering a new town. It seeks to propagate its message into every district and barrio. It also seeks to penetrate the various strata of society, including youth and the higher classes.

The second principle is that of *intensive propagation*. While workers from other churches tend to schedule home Bible studies or teaching sessions once a week, hard-working Iglesia ministers will go to an interested home *every* night (except Sunday and Thursday nights when regular worship services are scheduled at Iglesia chapels). Iglesia converts are literally inundated with personal attention. Their time is so completely monopolized by the Iglesia that competing options fade into the background. In its teaching methods the Iglesia has discovered the strategic value of constant repetition of key doctrines. "Overlearning" or saturation teaching imbeds Iglesia teaching in the minds of converts. Other churches may shy away from such an approach because it smacks of brainwashing and, treating the individual as an object, demeans the human personality. But the basic validity of the intensive principle remains. Spiritually effective disciple-making cannot be done in a haphazard, undisciplined way. To borrow a modern medical term, new converts need "intensive care."

In a previous section of this chapter, we have described the Iglesia's special version of *total mobilization*. This is the third important propagation principle which we can observe in the Iglesia methodology. What we have in the Iglesia ni Cristo is a particular type of mobilization for a definite purpose—the purpose of propagation. The Iglesia ni Cristo does not say, "Every member is an evangelist." But it does demand that every member be tied very closely into the church organization so that the church can move forward as a unit. Though the min-

ister is unquestionably the leader in the local, every member
bears a responsibility for the propagation of the faith.

In propagating its faith, the Iglesia ni Cristo has used many
methods—open forums, house meetings, mass media (including
radio and its well-known magazine *Pasugo*) and large religious
rallies. But it is probably best known for its religious debates.
In an age which stresses religious toleration, the Iglesia's aggressive, hard-hitting debating style seems anachronistic; yet
we must attribute much of its past growth to the skill of its
debaters. True, in recent years the number and frequency of
these debates have dropped off dramatically, but whether this
has been the result of a lack of challengers, or a change in
policy, is not clear.

In the days before martial law Iglesia ni Cristo debates
could be quite a production. To help catch the flavor of a
typical debate, I will reproduce a first-person account of an
actual debate which I witnessed. The "opposition debater" was
Rogelio Baldemor, a Filipino Baptist pastor and my co-worker.
He writes of the encounter in the following terms:

I got out of the jeep at the Sariaya town plaza. A crowd was
already milling around the basketball court, excitedly waiting for
the widely advertised debate to begin. I saw many jeeps and
buses parked near the plaza. These had been chartered by the
Iglesia ni Cristo to bring their members from surrounding towns
to bolster their "cheering section" during the debate. That evening I was to meet one of this sect's most able debaters to defend
the doctrine of the deity of Christ, a doctrine which they
vehemently reject.

Why did I accept this challenge to debate? I knew that
public debates were one of their chief means of gaining converts, and I also knew the scriptural injunction that the servant
of the Lord must not strive or quarrel. But did not the Apostle
Paul himself engage in public debate on occasion to present
the Gospel to the masses?

At the time this debate was held we were just beginning a
church in Sariaya, about a 15-minute drive from Lucena City
where I am pastor. We had been repeatedly challenged by the
Iglesia ni Cristo to defend our doctrines publicly. They charged
that we were actually afraid to do so. After much prayer I
decided that I must meet them publicly. The Lord assured me
that no matter what the provocation He would enable me to
remain cool and Christian in my spirit.

I would only agree to what we call an "Oxford-style" debate. Each side would have three stands of 20 minutes each, and after each stand the other side would have five minutes to interrogate the speaker. We agreed that each listener would be his own judge. A neutral moderator and timekeeper (a Roman Catholic and former vice-mayor of the town) also had been agreed upon.

Since this was to be "their show" the Iglesia ni Cristo provided the loud-speaking equipment. I soon noticed that the microphone which they had for me was noticeably weaker than the one their debater was using. Their team consisted of one chief debater and an assistant, both district ministers. The assistant was busy checking my Scripture references throughout the debate. Three or four other ministers were also on the platform. I, feeling a little like the prophet Elijah, was the only one on our side of the platform. I was confident of the truth of our position, but knew their reputation for unfair tricks.

I began by citing many Scripture verses which teach the deity of Christ. The Iglesia ni Cristo accepts the inspiration of the Scripture, so I bore down heavily on the biblical evidence. I cited Hebrews 1:8 where the Son, that is Christ, is clearly referred to as God. When the debater stood up to interrogate me he very neatly passed over all the clear verses I had mentioned and zeroed in on a verse with exegetical problems.

During his stands the Iglesia ni Cristo debater emphasized that the Bible refers to Jesus as a man, and that Jesus called Himself a man when He was here on earth. I emphasized in turn that I believed Christ was true man as well as true God, so those verses referring to Him as man were no problem to me. But I also pointed out that for every verse he could cite calling Christ a man, I could cite many more which referred to Him as God or God's Son.

The partisan nature of the crowd, especially that part of it close to the platform, soon became obvious. As the Iglesia ni Cristo debater made some of his very familiar points he gradually increased the volume of his voice until he reached a climax of intensity, and then his followers would burst into applause as if it had been rehearsed.

As the evening wore on he became more and more personal in his attacks on me. He tried desperately to make me angry, but I felt an extraordinary calmness and control. So, his tactic failed. I heard later that the local parish priest had remarked that the Iglesia ni Cristo won the debate in insults, but the Baptists won in truth.

During my last stand I did something that they had not expected. I brought out a large blackboard and gave a simple, illustrated exposition of Philippians 2:5-11 which I called "The Three Stages of the Life of Christ"—before His incarnation, when He took human form, and when He was glorified. I stated that we could explain any verse about Christ in the Bible by simply placing it in its proper place in the stages of Christ's existence. The Iglesia ni Cristo debater did not answer this presentation, but merely went back to the Scriptures which teach that God is one, and He gives His glory to no one else. I closed the debate by asking him if Christ made a mistake in accepting Thomas' worship in John 20:28, 29.

After the debate we sportingly shook hands and then went our separate ways. I have noticed since then that the ordinary ministers of the Iglesia ni Christo will not discuss doctrine with me, because I have faced the top man in this area.[13]

Debates such as we have just described have both their positive and negative aspects. Undeniably, Philippine audiences enjoy such sharp, hard-hitting public debates. Many older church leaders were converted by listening to Protestants debate Roman Catholics. Public debates have forced the Iglesia and its teaching on the consciousness of millions of Filipinos. They also have forced Iglesia leaders to study the Bible in great detail, and have helped them perfect the "question and Scripture answer" teaching method which they use in sermons, instruction classes and magazine articles. Negatively, Iglesia debates have become repetitive and predictable—therefore their impact has greatly weakened. The real issues are constantly skirted, and the skills of the debaters, rather than truth itself, have become the important issue. Iglesia ni Cristo debates have tended to become more like sporting events (complete with cheering section!) than religious meetings.

A very significant force in the propagation of the Iglesia ni Cristo has been the *Pasugo* magazine. The name refers to the message which a *sugo* or messenger brings, and is loosely translated by the Iglesia as "God's Message." This magazine has been the Iglesia's primary written instrument of propagation and indoctrination. It features articles in both Tagalog and

---

13. Rogelio Baldemor and Leonard Tuggy, "I Debated the Iglesia ni Cristo," *Conservative Baptist* (Summer 1972), pp. 6-7.

English written by Iglesia leaders, usually in question and Scripture (proof text) answer style. Most of the articles are obvious attacks on Roman Catholic doctrines and practices, and bear such titles as "Let Us Forsake the Habitation of Demons!" "Roman Catholics Do Worship Images," and "Priestly Celibacy and the Holy Scriptures."

More recently, the Iglesia ni Cristo has established a nation-wide network of radio stations which broadcast daily expositions of Iglesia doctrine. These stations were shut down when martial law was declared by President Marcos in September, 1972, but subsequently have been allowed to operate again.

A Philippine Rhetoric

In discussing methods of propagation we may become so engrossed with the external mechanics that we overlook the inner logic of persuasion that is actually operating in Iglesia methodology. By the time people decide to become Iglesia members, it is clear that they have been persuaded to adopt a new system of beliefs. But how has the Iglesia persuaded them? What is the rhetoric by which the Iglesia moves men? What are the positive and negative characteristics of that rhetoric?

From our study of the Iglesia ni Cristo, the following generalizations about the appeal of Iglesia persuasion seem justified.

(1) The Iglesia ni Cristo appeals to a widely accepted standard of authority. The Bible is recognized by most Filipinos as having divine authority.

(2) It has sought to construct an internally consistent, tightly logical system of doctrine. Iglesia doctrine may not be deep, nor wide-ranging, but it is carefully thought through, and is logical, if one grants the Iglesia's basic presuppositions.

(3) It does not try to fight battles on too many fronts at once. It has only a few basic themes which are repeated over and over again.

(4) Its arguments are well-honed, and are readjusted to meet new attacks.

(5) It always speaks from a position of strength. It is the "true church," so all other churches must (according to its logic) defend their right to exist.

From our perspective, Iglesia ni Cristo rhetoric reveals some *negative* characteristics which need to be noted.

(1) It is based upon faulty hermeneutical principles. It uses Scripture references out of context and without regard to the intent of the original authors.

(2) It depends on a superficial logic. Sharpness is valued over truth.

(3) *Argumentum ad hominem* is frequently resorted to. The opponent's person is attacked, not merely his position.

(4) Its use of sarcasm often verges on superciliousness, so it is often less than convincing.

(5) It never deals with the strengths of opposing viewpoints, only their weaknesses.

(6) It focuses attention on the organization, not on the teaching.

Among the various Philippine peoples, the Tagalogs have been known throughout their history as the orators of the nation. Felix Manalo was a Tagalog, and his oratory lies at the heart of Iglesia rhetoric, for rhetoric fundamentally involves the art of oratory. We conclude that according to some standards, Iglesia rhetoric leaves much to be desired. As is clear from the above paragraphs, Iglesia debaters do not strive for elegance or even appropriateness, though they give the appearance of aiming for clarity and correctness. But if the aim of oratory is to instruct, to move, and to delight or entertain, Iglesia orators do well. Evidently, many Filipinos are persuaded by the positive aspects of Iglesia rhetoric and are willing to overlook the weaknesses which might in fact be decisive factors to other audiences.

What can we learn from Iglesia ni Cristo propagation? Independent Third World churches—orthodox, mildly or seriously heretical as the case may be—are a fact of world-wide Christianity in the late twentieth century, and traditional churches in the West need to study them in depth. These churches have much to teach us about the different shapes the Christian church must take as it grows throughout the vastly different cultures of the world. The Iglesia ni Cristo is no exception.

Many Western missionaries have doubted the ability of nationals to organize and govern their own churches in an efficient and orderly manner. The Iglesia ni Cristo belies every assertion that nationals are incapable of operating their own church with their own personnel and depending on their own resources. Iglesia worship services contrast favorably with many services conducted by missionaries, and the attentive audiences must be the envy of every non-Iglesia preacher who has seen nodding heads in his congregation.

The Iglesia ni Cristo is nothing if it is not Filipino. It did not have to adapt to its culture, it grew out of it. All who doubt that an indigenous church can succeed must ponder the phenomenon of churches like the Iglesia ni Cristo. Having said this, we should also point out that, as someone has said, nationalism is the sin of which no one repents; and this sin probably lies at the heart of some of the Inglesia's doctrines as well as its appeal.

The basic principles of effective propagation which the Iglesia has put into practice as described in this chapter would seem to be universally valid. Strategy that incorporates the principles of extensive and intensive propagation, and of total mobilization, should prove effective. For those working in the Philippines, at least, certain other features of Iglesia propagation methodology can also be adopted. Methodists in the Philippines, for example, have held barrio (village) evangelistic meetings which have been preceded by a series of open forums, patterned very much after the open forums held by the Iglesia ni Cristo.

In other cultures, Iglesia methodology would not be suitable, though some aspects of it likely could be adapted to local situations. An example might be the Iglesia's "question and Scripture answer" indoctrination technique.

Possibly the greatest lesson which we can learn from the Iglesia ni Cristo is a lesson in motivation. The Iglesia grows because it aims to grow. All of its efforts are focused on expansion. Churches, like people, probably will not attain what they do not aim at. The Iglesia ni Cristo is an example of a church wholly dedicated to this aim, and it has grown as a result. To its own hurt, however, the Iglesia seems to have made growth its only aim. Therefore it seeks the destruction of other churches. For Christians, church growth should be a means to greater ends—the glory of God and the triumph of his truth in all the world.

Everett N. Hunt, Jr.

Everett N. Hunt, Jr., was born in 1933 in New Jersey, the son of a Methodist minister. After graduation from Asbury College in 1954, he attended Temple University School of Theology and later received the B.D. degree from Asbury Theological Seminary. In 1958 the author began missionary work in Korea where he conducted Laymen's Training Institutes in over four hundred churches. Returning to the United States he received the M.A. and Ph.D. degrees from the Divinity School of the University of Chicago. He is the author of a number of journal articles in both English and Korean. His interest in missions in Korea is indicated by a major article titled "Protestant Beginnings in Korea, 1885-1890, A Study in Accommodation" (also the subject of his Ph.D. dissertation). The article appeared in the Journal of Seoul Theological Seminary, 1973. *Dr. Hunt presently teaches at Seoul Theological Seminary in the areas of missions and religions.*

6 | MOON SUN MYUNG AND THE TONG-IL

(Unification Church)

Everett N. Hunt, Jr.

There are a possible two hundred-fifty newly emerging religions in Korea.[1] Twenty-seven of these are related to Buddhism, twenty-five to Christianity, three to Confucianism, five to other Chinese religions, and five to Japanese religions. The rest are either indigenous to Korea or relate to the general category called Eastern Learning.[2]

Few of these new religions are known outside of Korea, but there is one glaring exception—the Holy Spirit Association for the Unification of World Christianity, known most often as Tong-il (the Korean word for unification) or Unification Church. In Roman letters it is often abbreviated H.S.A. (Holy Spirit Association).[3]

---

1. The term used in Korea is *Shin heung Chong kyo* which literally translated is "new rising religions." A large number of these have emerged since the end of the Korean War in 1954—thus the word *new*.

2. The best introduction to new religions in Korea is Tak Myung Hwan, *Hangook Eh Shin Heung Chong Kyo* (*New Religions in Korea,* no publication data available). Tak is the family name.

3. Tong-il publishes a very complete information brochure entitled *Ahn Nae* (Seoul: Holy Spirit Association Press, 1974). It is hereafter referred to as *Information,* which is the translation of the title.

The Founder and the Founding of Tong-il

Moon Sun Myung[4] was born January 6, 1920. He grew up in the north Korean province of North Pyongyang in a small farming village near the sea. Moon's father was a farmer and the father of six girls and two boys—Moon being the younger son. The family being a traditional Confucian family, Moon's early training included the study of Chinese. When he was ten years old his family converted to Christianity and became most zealous in that faith.[5]

At the time of his family's conversion to Christianity, Moon gave up his Confucian studies and began a typical public school education with more emphasis on science and mathematics than on traditional Eastern literary studies.

Moon seems to have been a very sensitive child. At a tender age he began to ponder the meaning of life, the problem of human suffering, and the fallen state of man. He determined to dedicate his life to serving the needs of mankind.

On April 17, 1936, when Moon was sixteen, he claimed to receive a revelation from Jesus after which he decided to spend his life in the service of heaven.[6] Moon continued his studies, completing his elementary education in his home area, his middle school work in Seoul, and his high school education in Japan. Reports differ as to how much education Moon received after high school.[7]

Moon's followers claim that their teacher is specially endowed for his life's mission. They point to his strong body, clean appearance, and air of serenity and generosity. He is said to

4. Moon's name is given in the usual Korean order. Moon would be the last name in English but is listed first in Korean. Koreans refer to him as Teacher (Sunsaeng) and not Reverend as he is called in America.

5. Information gives the best description of Moon's early life but unlike many religions, not much is made of his birth and early life.

6. In traditional Confucian terms, heaven was the divine ruling power of the universe and not the eternal abode of God and the saints as in Christianity.

7. Information says he received his high school education in Japan. Tak says in New Religions in Korea that Moon attended Waseda University in Japan; Moon himself claims to have graduated, but Tak says there is no record of it. Choi Syn Duk in "Korea's Tong-il Movement" (The New Religions of Korea, Transactions of the Korean Branch of the Royal Asiatic Society, XLIII 1967) claims that Moon graduated from Waseda University with a major in electrical engineering.

be respectful toward heaven, to possess supernatural mental powers, and to have developed a character without deficiencies of any sort. They believe him to be a man of high ideals, with strong perseverance and will power. They say that contact with Moon gives the impression that he is well qualified to bring East and West together.

In Moon's personality, his accomplishments, and his unchanging ideals, Tong-il followers see evidence that God is especially near to Korean people. By believers, Moon is seen as a representative Korean man.

By the end of the Second World War, Moon had completed work on his basic principles and began to teach them within Christian churches. Before long he felt it necessary to come out of the traditional churches in order to carry on his work. It was not until 1954, however, that Moon officially organized the Holy Spirit Association for the Unification of World Christianity.[8]

Beginning in 1960, Moon began to expand his teaching internationally. In 1970 he made America the new center of his ministry and since that time he has carried out his activities while living there.

Sources of Authority

The basic source for Tong-il teaching is the book, *Lectures on Basic Doctrine (Wul lee Kang Non)*. The English edition is called *Divine Principle*.[9] This book is described as "encompassing the profound thought of the Orient and based upon Christian beliefs and ideology."[10]

The book is divided into two parts. The first part contains chapters with titles which would fit into any standard work of Christian systematic theology: "Principle of Creation," "Fall of Man," "Consummation of Human History," 'Advent of the Messiah," "Resurrection," "Predestination," and "Christology."

---

8. For a list of the more important dates in the history of Tong-il, see Appendix A.

9. The Korean version is *Wul lee Kang Non* (Seoul: Sungwha, 1966). This is a collection of lectures on basic doctrine which is published in English as *Divine Principle* (Washington, DC: Holy Spirit Association for the Unification of World Christianity, 1973).

10. *Divine Principle*, Foreword.

In the second part the chapter titles sound less familiar: "Providential Age for the Foundation of Restoration," "Providence of Restoration Centering on Moses and Jesus," and a lengthy one, "Providential Age of Restoration and Age of the Prolongation of Restoration from the Standpoint of Providential Time-Identity." Although Moon Sun Myung's picture is in the front of the book, authorship is not specifically attributed to him within the volume. Nevertheless, it can be safely assumed that it is a faithful presentation of his teachings.

The relation between the doctrines of Tong-il and the Bible is clearly spelled out. The *Divine Principle* emphasizes that truth is unique, eternal, unchangeable, and absolute. However, "the Bible is not the truth itself, but a textbook teaching the truth."[11] The conclusion is drawn that though truth is absolute the textbook is not. Though the New Testament was adequate for teaching the truth to people two thousand years ago—"people whose spiritual and intellectual standard was very low"—it is not sufficient to meet the needs of men today.[12] In the early days of Christianity truth could be expressed in parables and symbols. Today truth must be expressed "with a higher standard and with a scientific method of expression" in order to speak to modern man.[13]

As a sign of the inadequacy of the Bible, the *Divine Principle* points to the variety of interpretation which has resulted in the rise of numerous denominations. It prophesies that "since the source of denominational divisions is not in man but in the expressions used in the Bible, the divisions and quarrels cannot but increase."[14]

As a matter of fact, not only the Bible but also the scriptures of other religions have proven inadequate to speak to contemporary man's predicament. "Scripture can be likened to a lamp which illuminates the truth. When a brighter light appears, the mission of the old one fades."[15]

Interestingly enough, the *Divine Principle* cites *biblical* references in order to demonstrate that a new truth must appear

---

11. Ibid., p. 9.
12. Ibid., p. 131.
13. Ibid., p. 132.
14. Ibid., p. 131.
15. Ibid., p. 132.

in the last days. That new truth cannot come from "any man's synthetic research in the scriptures," or from the human mind.[16] It must come as a revelation from God himself. More, this new truth has *already appeared:* "With the fulness of time, God has sent his messenger to resolve the fundamental questions of life and the universe. His name is Sun Myung Moon."[17]

The *Divine Principle* proceeds to elucidate Moon's answers to the problems of man which have been given directly to him in repeated revelations from Jesus himself. However, the *Divine Principle* makes no claim to be the whole of the final truth. It is only part of it: "We believe with happy expectation that, as time goes on, deeper parts of the truth will be continually revealed."[18]

A quick overview of the *Divine Principle* reveals Moon's "new truth" to be a revisionist approach to certain basic Bible teachings coupled with his particular understanding of human history and the history of Christianity. Definitely influenced by oriental philosophical and religious concepts, Moon's teachings are mathematically inclined and present an impersonal, technical view of man's predicament and the ultimate solution. There are frequent passages which, while not explicitly naming Moon, quite obviously refer to his central role in the final restoration of mankind.

Basic Teachings[19]

In the general introduction to *Divine Principle,* Moon sets forth his view of man's problem.[20] In the "original mind of man," which refers to man's inmost self, man delighted in the law of God. However, after the fall a new principle was introduced. Ever since that time man has struggled between this original mind and the fallen mind. This is the basic conflict of life.

Moon sees man as having two aspects: the internal or spiritual and the external or physical. Likewise, there are

---

16. Ibid., p. 15.
17. Ibid., p. 16.
18. Ibid.
19. For a succinct statement of basic teachings see Appendix B.
20. Though Moon is not listed as the author, the *Divine Principle* does claim to be his teaching. Hereafter we will consider Moon as the source of these basic teachings.

two aspects of knowledge (internal and external) and two of ignorance. Man's internal ignorance—that is, his spiritual ignorance—leaves him unable to answer such questions as: What is man's origin? What is the purpose of life? Do God and the next world exist? What are good and evil?[21]

Throughout human history, Moon asserts, men have been seeking truth both internally and externally. Man's search for internal truth he calls religion while his search for external truth he calls science. The ultimate truth, when it comes, must be able to unite these two efforts to find truth.

Moon sees one final war remaining for man—the war between democracy and communism. He believes that democracy must win though it is not presently able to do so. "Therefore, in order that God's providence of salvation might be completely fulfilled, the new truth must bring all mankind into a new world of absolute goodness by elevating the spiritualism advocated in the democratic world to a new and higher dimension, finally assimilating even materialism."[22] This new truth should be able to unite all the isms and religions of human history and bring them into one absolute system.

Moon feels that the task of the new truth is to discover how the sinful history of mankind began, what course it must follow, and in what manner it will be concluded.

The principle of creation. The principle of creation as presented in *Divine Principle* is a fundamental concept applied through all the basic Tong-il doctrine. Moon sees all of creation as the result of a reciprocal relationship between positivity and negativity both internally and in relation to other beings or things. He suggests that it is the male-female principle at work. Reciprocal relationship is the key factor. Everything exists in reciprocal relationship: inside-outside, internal-external, front-rear, left-right, and so forth. These opposite or reciprocal factors are called "dual essentialities."

One of the most basic pairs of dual essentialities existing in reciprocal relationship is that of external form and internal character. As an example, the body is the external form, the mind the internal character. The internal character governs the

21. *Divine Principle,* p. 3.
22. Ibid., p. 11.

external form. Thus the internal is the cause, the subjective position, while the external is the result, the objective position.

When applied to the relation between God and the world Moon's principle views God as the ultimate cause of all things. God is the internal, masculine subject while the universe is the external, feminine object. God is the internal character of the universe while the natural world is his external form. A further step in this view is that every object becomes an individual incarnation of truth. Man is an actual individual incarnation of truth, or the direct image of God. Every other object is a symbolic individual incarnation of truth, or God's indirect image.

Moon speaks of God as the universal prime energy—absolute and eternally self-existent. This energy provides power for the existence of all things through a "give-and-take action." The universal prime energy and the power of give-and-take action form a reciprocal relationship of cause and effect, internal and external, subject and object.

God and man were related in this give-and-take relationship before the fall of man. After the fall man's relationship centered on Satan instead of God. "True Christianity is a religion of life, through which men can restore the vertical give-and-take circuit with God by establishing, through love and sacrifice, the horizontal give-and-take circuit between men centering on Jesus."[23]

There is another step in the elaboration of relationships between God and man. This is called the "four position foundation." This four position foundation is formed by a process of origin-division-union-action. God is origin, husband and wife are division, and their offspring are union. "This is the base through which God's power is channeled to flow into all of his creation in order for creation to exist. Therefore, the formation of the four position foundation is ultimately God's eternal purpose of creation."[24]

According to Moon, man is the center of all creation and God is the center of all men. Thus Moon sees man in his dual essentiality—body and mind—revolving in a circular movement centering on God. Applying this same principle to the universe,

---

23. Ibid., p. 30.
24. Ibid., p. 32.

Moon asserts: "The ultimate center of the spherical movement of the whole universe is God."[25]

God's original plan was that man would exist in an individual four position foundation centered on God. With God as the origin, man's body and mind the division, and these together creating the union, man would then have been able to fulfill God's purpose in creating him—to return joy to God.

Adam and Eve as the first human beings were meant to play a central role in the relationship between God and the world. Perfected Adam would have been the embodiment of all the subjective elements in creation while Eve would have been the embodiment of all objective elements. Together they would have become a central body dominating the whole universe. The universe lost its center in man and is now waiting for the original nature of creation to be restored.

In the process of creation and in the period of growth, Moon sees the number three repeated again and again. Every created being goes through a process which has three aspects: existence, movement, growth. The motif of "threeness" is seen in God, Adam and Eve, and their children; the process of formation, growth, perfection; in the division of minerals, plants, animals; in the various states of matter—gases, liquids and solids; in the roots, trunk, and leaves of plants; and in the head, trunk, and extremities of animals.

Moon applies this trinary emphasis to the whole of creation. God created man as the ruler of the universe. He was to serve as the mediator and the center of harmony. And he was to be the substantive microcosm of the whole. In the fall of man the whole of creation lost its ruler. To be reinstated in his intended place in the plan of God, man must pass through a three-stage restoration—formation, growth, and perfection.[26]

The principle of creation is basic to all of Moon's thought. As he interprets the meaning of human existence, the basic content of the Bible, and the major eras in secular and Christian history, there is a constant application of this principle.

The fall of man. According to Moon, the fall of man prevented the realization of God's original intention in creation.

---

25. Ibid., p. 35.
26. Ibid., p. 53.

Specifically, he sees the fall not as the eating of fruit from a forbidden tree in response to the serpent's temptation, but rather as an immoral sex act. Adam as perfected man is represented in the tree of life. Eve as perfected woman is represented in the tree of the knowledge of good and evil. The serpent symbolizes the fallen angel Lucifer who lusted after Eve and subsequently had sexual intercourse with her. In Moon's terminology, Lucifer and Eve together formed a reciprocal base and had sexual intercourse with each other through their give-and-take action.[27] From this immoral act a line was established which descended from Satan rather than from God.

It was originally intended, according to Moon, that Adam and Eve should have become husband and wife only after reaching the perfection stage, or the third stage in human growth. However, Eve hoped that sexual relations with Adam, her intended spouse, would rid her of the guilt and fear that resulted from her illicit relations with Lucifer. Instead, relations with Adam consummated the fall.

Eve's relation to Lucifer may be seen as the spiritual fall while her relation with Adam represents the physical fall. In this way, Moon says, the blood line was established whereby all men inherit original sin. The result of the fall, therefore, is that all creation now is under the power of Satan. Nevertheless, man still has the power within himself to help begin the process of restoration.

In the tension between good and evil in man Moon finds the underlying cause of all conflicts and divisions in human history.

The consummation of human history. Moon claims that all of human history is "the period of the providence through which God intends to save fallen men and have them restore the original world of goodness."[28] It is in this struggle for goodness that Moon finds the source of all religions. He also sees all these religio-cultural spheres[29] as being in the process of formation into a world-wide cultural sphere centering on Christianity. Religion and science (corresponding to the internal and

---

27. Ibid., p. 79.
28. Ibid., p. 105.
29. He identifies four: East Asia (Confucianism and Buddhism), Hinduism, Islam, and Christianity.

external aspects of the human quest) are now involved in the tension between democracy (the ideology related to Christianity) and communism (the ideology relating to science). Moon believes that Christianity will be the inevitable victor in this conflict. Out of that victory will emerge the great unification of religion and science.

Moon identifies the "last days" with those periods when there is a transference of the world from satanic to divine rulership. There have been many periods that could be called "last days": the time of Noah, the time of Jesus, and the future coming of the Lord in his second advent. In each of the former "last days" God was unable to consummate history because of human failure. But Moon professes to see evidences that the ultimate consummation of history is taking shape in our times.

The advent of the Messiah. Moon says that the purpose of Christ's first coming to earth was to fulfill the providence of restoration. God, he believes, intended for the Jews to believe in Jesus as their Messiah. Jesus did not really come to die on a cross.[30] "Because the Jewish people disbelieved Jesus and delivered him up for crucifixion, his body was invaded by Satan, and he was killed. Therefore, even when Christians believe in and become one body with Jesus whose body was invaded by Satan, their bodies still remain subject to Satan's invasion."[31] Though Christians say Jesus came to die, actually he "came to accomplish the will of God in his lifetime, but had to die a reluctant death due to the disbelief of the people."[32]

Here Moon introduces unusual support for his new understanding of Jesus' intended work. He says, "If we ask Jesus directly through spiritual communication, we can see the fact even more clearly. When direct rapport is impossible, we should seek the testimony of someone with such a gift."[33] On several occasions throughout *Divine Principle*, allusions are made which obviously seem to refer to Moon. Since in the introduction he declares himself to be the bearer of new truth, that Moon is in direct contact with Jesus seems to follow as a natural

---

30. *Divine Principle*, p. 143.
31. Ibid., pp. 147-48.
32. Ibid., p. 152.
33. Ibid.

corollary. The allusions are made in general terms, however, and they do leave room for conflicting interpretations.

Moon does recognize that traditional Christian interpretations do not agree with his view of Jesus. He says, "We must abandon the conservative attitude of faith which has caused us to be afraid to remove old traditional concepts."[34]

Resurrection. Moon asserts that the death which resulted from the fall of man was not physical death but "the state of having fallen from the good dominion of God to the evil dominion of Satan."[35] Thus resurrection is the process of restoration of fallen man back to the dominion of God.

God's efforts to restore men pass through the three stages necessary for all growth. The first period from Adam to Abraham established the foundation for the providence of resurrection. The period from Abraham to Jesus constituted the formation stage. The period from Jesus to the present is the growth stage leading to perfection at the time of the second advent of the Lord. And the Lord of the second advent has the responsibility to find 144,000 saints who will help him establish the foundation for victory over the satanic world.

Moon declares that in the last days which are presently upon us, there are people who can communicate with the spirit world. Some of these even claim to be the Lord of the second advent but for one reason or another each in turn fails and succeeds only in creating confusion.[36] Nevertheless, co-operation is possible between those in the spirit world and those alive on earth. "Spirit men" can help earthly men by healing diseases, doing mighty works, and enabling earthly men to experience trances in which they see many features of the spirit world. They can also give earthly men the spirit of prophecy and inspire them spiritually. Through such activity "spirit men" substitute for the Holy Spirit and co-operate with earthly men to fulfill the will of God.

The whole process of restoration begins on an individual level, passes through the family level, and moves on to the national and finally a world-wide level. As mentioned above,

34. Ibid., p. 163.
35. Ibid., p. 169.
36. Ibid., pp. 117-18.

Christianity plays a central role in the unification of all religio-cultural spheres. "Therefore, Christianity is not a religion of Christians alone, but has the mission of accomplishing the ultimate purpose of all religions that have appeared in the past."[37] In a process which seems to share characteristics of the Christian doctrine of resurrection and Eastern teachings of reincarnation, "spirit men" will arrive to aid earthly men in this consummation. But the Lord of the second advent will play the leading role. When he comes all will be unified. God will abolish hell completely. The purpose of creation will be attained.

Predestination. The *Divine Principle* states that God wills the restoration of all men to their original state in creation, and that God will accomplish his purpose. God intended that Adam should remain in his original state but Adam failed. Jesus came as the second Adam. But, failing to acknowledge him as their Messiah, the Jews killed Jesus. Now God has still another central figure through whom he will realize the final restoration of man.

Moon sets forth the qualifications for this central figure of the providence of restoration.

> First, he must be born out of the chosen nation, he must be the descendant of ancestors with many accomplishments of good-ness. Then, even though he may be the descendant of ancestors with many good deeds, he must be endowed with the natural disposition suitable for the accomplishment of the will. Even if a man has these endowments, he must subsequently have good conditions in which to grow and work in his lifetime. Still, even among these persons, God would select first the individual most fully prepared at the appropriate time and place of God's need.[38]

Such a prophecy seems tailored to Moon's own professed qualifications but once again the passage does not explicitly name him. It states that God has predestined the one who is to fulfill the purpose of restoration. God's part is to "call" that man. The appointed man's part is to respond.

Christology. Under this rubric the *Divine Principle* deals with the relationship between Jesus, the Holy Spirit, and fallen

---

37. Ibid., p. 189.
38. Ibid., pp. 200-01.

man, along with such subjects as rebirth and the Trinity. Moon insists that Jesus is not God. Jesus is a man who attained the purpose of creation. Jesus is the image of God, "but he can by no means be God himself."[39]

Claiming special revelations in which these truths were disclosed to him, Moon asserts that in order for a man to be born again (as Jesus prescribed in John 3) there must be a true mother and a true father. The true mother, according to Moon, is the Holy Spirit. The true father is Jesus. Thus the Holy Spirit is the second Eve, the female principle, negativity, working in the earth. Jesus is the second Adam, the male principle, positivity, working in heaven. When we have a spiritual rebirth, it is through the love of the spiritual true parents emanating from the give-and-take action between Jesus, the spiritual true father, and the Holy Spirit, the spiritual true mother.

Moon speaks of the Trinity as Jesus and the Holy Spirit who together become one body centered on God. This is the very relationship which was originally intended for Adam and Eve, who together were to be one body centered on God. Since the fall man has been centered on Satan. Therefore, man must be born anew through the true parents of mankind, Jesus and the Holy Spirit.[40]

Carrying this one step further, the *Divine Principle* teaches that because of the death of Jesus this process of rebirth can take place presently only on a spiritual level. Consequently, Christ must come again in the flesh in order that he may be the true parent both spiritually and physically.[41]

The process of restoration. Part II of the *Divine Principle* deals in greater detail with the age of restoration. It is the application of the principle related in the first half of the book to the Bible, to the history of Christianity, and to world history in general. Moon calls this process the "providence of restoration through indemnity." Man lost his original status through the fall. Certain conditions must be established for his original position to be restored. The setting up of such conditions is called "indemnity."

---

39. Ibid., p. 211.
40. Ibid., p. 217.
41. Ibid., p. 218.

There are three ages in the course of the providence of restoration, each of which is to last two thousand years. The first was from Adam to Abraham and is described as "the age to lay the foundation on which to start the providence of restoration by setting up Abraham, the father of faith." But it was invaded by Satan and ended in failure. The next period was from Abraham to Jesus but it also ended in failure because the Jews killed Jesus. So one more period was required in order to finally realize restoration—the period from Jesus to the present. Moon is confident that we are now in the last period and it will not fail.

The importance of certain numbers becomes apparent to anyone who studies Moon's periods. The number forty derives its significance from the multiplication of ten (unity) by four (the four position foundation). Moon cites many instances of the number forty in the Bible.

The number three is important because there are three stages in the period of growth. First, the formation stage—symbolic type; then the growth stage—image type; and finally, the perfection stage—substantial type.

Other important numbers are four and twenty-one. Using these numbers in his mathematical interpretive scheme, Moon arranges all of the outstanding events of Bible history. These numbers relate in special ways. The number three, for example, is the heavenly number, the number of perfection. The number four represents the four positions on the compass—north, east, south, and west—and is the earthly number. Seven is the sum total of the heavenly number and the earthly number—thus the Bible indicates that creation required seven days.

In each "providential age" God chooses a nation through which he will work: "Having it walk the typical providential course of restoration to establish the formation to receive the Messiah, [God] directs the chosen nation to be the center of His providence and to lead the history of mankind."[42] Moon bases this teaching on parallels between Old Testament and New Testament history, as well as on the history of religion, politics, and economics.

---

42. Ibid., p. 406.

There is a further aspect of the interpretive scheme introduced in the *Divine Principle* which merits our attention. After the fall, the conditions for indemnity had to be met in order to accomplish the restoration of man to his original state. These conditions entailed the offering of a sacrifice. Adam could not offer sacrifices on his own behalf since he had already fallen and potentially become the servant of two masters. Thus Cain and Abel, his two sons, were chosen in Adam's stead.

Cain and Abel represent good and evil. Since Cain and Abel were the children of Eve, they were the fruit of her sin. There were two aspects to Eve's sin—the one revealed in her intercourse with Satan and the other in her intercourse with Adam. God determined that Cain should represent or symbolize man's relationship to Satan, Eve's intercourse with Satan being the more deplorable of the two unions. Abel represents man's relationship to God, Eve's union with Adam being the lesser of two evils because Adam was Eve's intended mate and the union was evil only in that it was premature. In keeping with this symbolism, Cain offered a sacrifice to Satan while Abel offered his sacrifice to God. For Moon, Cain is thus to be identified with Satan and Abel is to be identified with God.

Applying this symbolism to recent history, Moon sees the view of life typified by Cain as being expressed in the Enlightenment, deism, and the philosophical systems of Hegel, Feuerbach, Marx, and Engels. Finally, it has come to be expressed in communism as we know it today. The view of life typified by Abel is discoverable in religious movements which have opposed rationalism—movements like Pietism, Methodism, and Quakerism. Finally, this view is to be found in democracy. Even within democracy, however, Moon professes to see both Cain and Abel views. Cain-type democracy originated with the French Revolution and has issued in communism. Abel-type democracy is to be found in England and the United States.

The *Divine Principle* claims that the great world wars of the twentieth century have been a necessary part of the process of restoration. Furthermore, since the restoration must pass through three phases, there is yet one more world war to be fought. In fact, not only must there be three wars, but also three major nations must be involved on each side in order to fit the established pattern. In keeping with this, consider Moon's interpretation of World War II.

The Abel-type nations representing the heavenly side were the United States, England and France. The United States—the man-type nation—symbolized Adam. England—the woman-type nation—symbolized Eve. And France—an intermediate type—represented the archangel. Likewise on the satanic side, Germany represented the man—Adam; Japan, the woman—Eve; and Italy, the intermediate—Lucifer.[43]

Second advent. Since the culmination of all things and the perfecting of the process of restoration must take place at the second advent, it is appropriate that the *Divine Principle* ends with this concern. It asserts that God will speak to those who have ears to hear so that they may be enlightened by the saints concerning that which will take place.[44]

When will Christ come again? Moon concludes that now is the time. These are the last days. In what manner will he come? Not in literal clouds and not suddenly as many Christians have supposed. Rather he will come by being born on earth as a perfected man both spiritually and physically. Where then will he be born? "If Christ is to be born as a man in flesh on this earth, and not to come again in a spiritual body, he will surely be born in a certain nation of God's elect in some place of God's predestination."

What nation might this be? Not among the Jews as some suppose. They killed him. Citing Revelation 5:1, 7; 6:1, and 7:2-4, the *Divine Principle* sees "the rising of the sun" as referring to a country in the East. By Eastern nations is always meant Korea, Japan, and China. But Japan has worshiped Amaterasu Omikami. Japan has been totalitarian and has persecuted the Christians in Korea. It cannot be Japan. China, being a communist nation, is on the satanic side together with Japan.[45] "Therefore, the nation of the east where Christ will come again would be none other than Korea."[46]

There are several qualifications which must be met by the nation in which Christ is to be born again. Only Korea meets

---

43. Ibid., p. 498.
44. Ibid., p. 516.
45. Ibid., p. 520.
46. Ibid.

those qualifications. First, the chosen nation must lay a nation-wide "foundation" for the restoration by indemnity. This is a forty-day foundation which excludes Satan and enables the cosmic restoration of Canaan to occur. Thus Korea will become the "third Israel"—God's elect. The immediate descendants of Abraham were the first Israel. The Christians in the New Testament were the second Israel. Korea, as a result of her forty years of persecution under Japan, meets the necessary conditions for the nation-wide foundation for the restoration by indemnity.

The second qualification which Korea meets is that it is located on the front line between the forces of God and Satan—roughly the thirty-eighth parallel. Democracy and communism, Abel and Cain, stand facing each other in Korea.

A third qualification is that "this nation must be the object of God's heart."[47] Moon believes that Korea has walked the path of blood, sweat, and tears. It is a nation of people who are good in God's sight—loyal, filial, and virtuous. He also believes that "the Korean people are endowed with a religious gift."[48]

A fourth qualification for that nation to which Christ comes again is the existence of prophetic testimonies among its people. Moon indicates that ever since the rise of the Yi dynasty in 1392, Koreans have believed that the King of Righteousness would come. He also cites the fact that the believers of every religion in Korea are receiving revelations which indicate that their founders will come again to Korea. Moon sees all these being united in Christianity. The Lord of the second advent will be the realization of that for which all Koreans wait.

The last qualification is that all aspects of culture and civilization must bear fruit in the elect nation. Moon assures us that all aspects of civilization have been realized in Korea—there have been developments on land, rivers and seas, and even in relation to climate. All aspects of civilization have borne fruit in Korea.

The *Divine Principle* concludes by showing similarities between Jesus' day and the second advent. First, at the time of Jesus' first advent the religious leaders were so bound to au-

47. Ibid., p. 527.
48. Ibid.

thority and rites that they failed to acknowledge him. Moon predicts that Christians will react in a similar way to the second advent.

Second, just as the Jewish leaders were the first to persecute the Messiah at the first advent, so Christians will be the first to persecute him at the time of the second advent.

Third, Moon says that at the second advent the Lord will "not simply repeat the New Testament words given 2,000 years ago, but will give the new words necessary to establish the new heaven and earth." But, he continues, Christians of today are "captives to scriptural words" and thus "will surely criticize the words and conduct of the Lord of the Second Advent."[49]

Finally, just as the earlier religious leaders failed to recognize the Lord and lead people to him, Christian leaders today will also fail to recognize the Lord of the second advent and therefore will not lead their people to him.

Regretting the confusion caused by the multiplicity of languages in the world, the *Divine Principle* says, "In order that the ideal world of one great family under the Lord of the Second Advent as the True Parent might be realized, all the languages must necessarily be unified." Only then will the whole of mankind become "one people speaking one language, thus establishing one world of one culture."[50]

Methods of Propagation

Tong-il is highly organized and extremely aggressive in its methods of propagation. At the head of Tong-il in Korea is Yu Kyo Won, long-time associate of Moon. The administrative section of the organization handles the rural districts and all general, cultural, and business affairs. Those departments directly related to propagation include the Departments of Evangelism, Education, Publications, Missions, Anti-Communism, and Student, Cultural, and Academic Affairs. Each department plays a strategic role in propagating Tong-il faith.

Evangelism. Special evangelistic programs include a biannual forty-day evangelistic emphasis, itinerant evangelistic teams, and rural service evangelism. All expenses for these activities are

---

49. Ibid., p. 533.
50. Ibid., p. 536.

paid by the participants. In a pattern long followed by seminary students from major Protestant denominations in Korea, rural service evangelism is a summer program which includes participation in community development projects and other practical demonstrations of concern for members of the community. Relationships are established and further instruction is given, usually in the evenings, to those who evidence special interest.

Instruction of converts. New converts become the responsibility of the Education Department for their instruction in the basic doctrinal tenets of Tong-il. These converts are required to pass periodic examinations on the content of the *Divine Principle* in order to maintain their positions in the group. Instruction is usually conducted in rented facilities and often continues for as long as forty days.

The lecturers chosen for these forty-day special instruction sessions seem to be chosen for their personal charisma and flair as much as for their knowledge of the *Divine Principle*. With rapid tongue and quick hand lecturers put doctrinal outlines on large blackboards. Much of the content, like so much of the teaching of Tong-il, involves the use of familiar passages in the Bible, but the interpretive schema has been made to fit Moon's revisionist view.

Emphasis on students. Of the various departments, the Department of Student Affairs is among the most active. Clearly, great emphasis is placed on winning the youth of the nation. Throughout the various provincial organizations, the young people are grouped according to their level in school. Students are organized into study groups where they learn the teachings of the *Divine Principle*, and into action groups for service activities, work camps, and medical clinics. Particular focus is directed toward students at Seoul National University, Korea's leading university. There students are organized into groups of twelve, each of which has a leader appointed to guide doctrinal discussions and other activities. Similar groups are organized at Methodist Ewha Women's University, Korea's most prestigious university for women.

Anti-communist activity. Anti-communism is a major emphasis of Tong-il. Activities of this sort are undertaken in conjunction with the International Anti-Communist Association, the Anti-Communist Enlightenment, an anti-communist leadership training program, and a Korean headquarters for anti-communist activities.

Given the strong anti-communist stance of the government of South Korea, Tong-il's emphasis on anti-communism has caused some to assume that Tong-il receives covert support from the government. Reports of such support are categorically denied by Tong-il leadership. There is no doubt, however, that Tong-il has been able to capitalize on the deep anti-communist feeling of the people of the Republic of Korea and may have gained the support of some who would not otherwise accept all of its religious teachings.

Tong-il and the media. Tong-il is extremely active in the production of printed materials and very effective in the use of communication media. The regular publications include a monthly magazine, *Unification World;* a weekly newspaper called *The Weekly Religion;* an international anti-communist paper; and an international students' paper.

Tong-il seems to exert prodigious efforts with a view to making itself visible. Special events are staged to create public awareness. Large advertisements are taken in newspapers to give these events publicity. In these endeavors, Tong-il is aided by the fact that in Korea it is not uncommon to pay a reporter to cover a specific event, a plan which usually leads to a favorable report.

A recent example of this kind of activity was the World Rally for Korean Freedom held in Seoul on June 7, 1975. Nearly a million people reportedly were in attendance including a thousand "delegates" from sixty foreign countries. For weeks prior to the rally young people from Korea and other countries walked the streets of Seoul wearing hats, bands, badges, and ribbons identifying them as members of the Tong-il sect. All over the city as well as in other cities on the peninsula they zealously buttonholed passers-by urging them to join Tong-il for the salvation of Korea. Though these young people often became irritatingly persistent, their participation undoubtedly went a long way in increasing public awareness of Tong-il.

Considerable publicity for Tong-il comes from the performances of the Little Angels, a singing and dancing troupe. These young girls are used as unofficial ambassadors for Korea in the tradition of the World Vision Children's Choir, the Christian group which has become so well-known in Korea and the United States. Frequent concert tours in other parts of the world have made the Little Angels widely known and have also helped to build a positive public image for Tong-il.

Still another activity which has drawn wide public attention is the mass wedding ceremony. The first of these was held May 15, 1961, when 36 couples were married. Subsequently, the number of participants has increased. On June 24, 1962, there were 72 couples; on July 24, 1963, there were 124; on February 2, 1968, 430; on October 21, 1970, 777; and on February 8, 1975, nearly 2,000 couples were married in the largest ceremony ever. In the latter ceremony there were couples from Japan, the United States, and seventeen other countries. All of these marriages were arranged by Moon (or his representatives) from information submitted by the faithful.

These mass wedding ceremonies are not purely publicity stunts, however. Moon and his present wife (some say his fourth) are considered to be the "earth parents." The only pure blood line is from such unions. Originally the Tong-il group required a secret initiation rite involving intercourse. This was called *pikarume,* or blood separation. Mass wedding ceremonies of couples matched by Moon represent an attempt to purify the human blood line.

Tong-il makes it easy for a man to leave his wife and find another, for Moon denigrates marriages performed under existing social orders and encourages people to disregard or abandon them for alliances "perfected" by his blessing. The only requirement made of the individual is a period of service to the church *including the introduction of three new converts to the group.*

Tong-il "plausibility structure." Of considerable importance to a new religion such as Tong-il is the building of what has been called a "plausibility structure."[51] This may well be one of the main thrusts of Tong-il efforts. A favorite technique in Korea is to invite noted intellectuals and church leaders to all-expense-paid training sessions in comfortable hotels.[52] When

51. Martin E. Marty, "Say It Ain't So, Roger," *Christian Century XCII*, No. 23 (1975), 647.
52. Ibid.

reports of such meetings appear in the newspapers, great care is taken to include each man's name and position. This builds "plausibility" for the next round of invitations.

A similar effect comes from Moon's rallies in America. Reports of large numbers of Americans attending rallies in some of America's best known public auditoriums are impressive to Koreans. As a rule these rallies do not overtly seek to win converts to Tong-il on the spot. Rather, there is an appeal to some currently popular theme around which many are willing and even anxious to rally. The World Rally for Korean Freedom mentioned earlier was directed toward strengthening relations with "our allies" against the communists. Apart from the name *Unification Church* there was no mention of Tong-il doctrines or even of Moon in the advertising. At the rally itself Moon told the crowd, "We have gathered here today to warn Kim Il Sung of his self-destruction in case he tries any military provocation against the south. We three million believers of the Unification Church over the World are strongly resolved to fight against the evil dictator."[53] No understanding of the finer points of doctrine in Tong-il was required for Koreans to rally around such a strongly anti-communist speech.

In addition to the anti-communist theme, certain other emphases enhance plausibility. The expected messianic role of Korea and a Korean citizen, and the interesting mix of mathematical formulae and Oriental philosophy evident in the *Divine Principle* are especially appealing to Koreans. Many of the new religious groups in Korea suggest a similar special role for Korea and Koreans.[54]

It is conceivable that Moon's move to make America his base of operation has hurt him at the most important point, his plausibility. Korean followers of the cult may feel he has deserted them for America. Meanwhile, it is unlikely that overwhelming numbers of Americans will follow a Korean immigrant whose fundamental teaching sees not America but Korea as having the decisive role in the culmination of human history. But it can be said in regard to Moon's Unification Church that it is one of the two best known cults in Korea and certainly of

---

53. *The Korea Times,* June 7, 1975, p. 3.
54. Elder Pak and the Olive Tree Church have a similar emphasis.

indigenous Korean religious groups it is the best known outside of the peninsula.

Foreign missions.[55] Mission activity outside of Korea has been most dramatic in America where Moon's pursuits have been widely reported. Tong-il claims to have representatives in more than sixty countries. Just how active these representatives are as propagators of Tong-il is difficult to document. Activity in America is especially pronounced and deserves a separate study inasmuch as it involves propagational dynamics which are somewhat different from those in Korea.

Conclusion

It is not difficult to investigate the teachings of Tong-il, though it is a rather formidable task to achieve a full understanding of those teachings. (As a matter of fact, it is highly probable that even among adherents the number of those who are thoroughly conversant with all of its doctrines is very small.) It is even difficult to ascertain the extent of Tong-il's current growth, though the fact that it has witnessed phenomenal growth to this point cannot be gainsaid. Perhaps the most difficult task of all is to explain the reasons for this rapid growth. Nevertheless, some of the most important reasons would seem to be those that we have suggested here.

APPENDIX A
Important Dates

May 1, 1954—The founding of the Holy Spirit Association for the Unification of World Christianity, Seoul, Korea.

July 4, 1955—Moon Sun Myung imprisoned for activity in a false religion (released October 4, 1955).

July 22, 1957—National evangelistic activity. Adherents go two-by-two for forty days to 120 cities.

August 15, 1957—First publication of the interpretation of doctrine.

January 1, 1958—Four districts organized.

July 17, 1958—First missionary sent to Japan.

January 2, 1959—First missionary sent to America.

---

55. See Appendix C for a list of countries in which Tong-il has missions.

January 10, 1959—First national training institute for evangelists established.

October 4, 1960—Monthly paper established.

January, 1961—First American publication on Tong-il doctrine.

October 4, 1963—First official recognition of Tong-il by Korean government.

January 28, 1965—Moon Sun Myung commences first world tour which lasts for ten months and takes him to forty countries.

June 25, 1965—Moon visits ex-President Eisenhower.

September 9, 1968—First Christian leaders' invitational seminar on Tong-il doctrine is held.

February 2, 1969—Moon begins his second world tour requiring three months and taking him to twenty-one countries.

December 5, 1971—Moon commences his third world tour. The tour lasts for five months and takes him to fifteen countries. He lectures in nine major cities on the topic "One World Crusade."

November 21, 1972—Moon's fourth world tour begins. Eight months are required to complete it.

August 7, 1973—Moon begins a tour of America with lecture rallies in twenty-one cities over a period of four months.

November 30, 1973—The *New York Times*, the *Washington Post* and twenty-one other newspapers in America carry Moon's Watergate Statement.

February 15, 1974—Moon begins a thirty-two city tour of America.

APPENDIX B
Basic Doctrines

1. The unique Creator God is the Father of mankind.
2. The Old and New Testaments are accepted as the sacred scriptures.
3. Jesus the only Son of God is man's Savior. At the same time he is the forefather of goodness and now the restorer of the original state of the human race.
4. Jesus will return to Korea at his second coming.
5. When Jesus returns to earth he will make all peoples unite in one big family.
6. The final purpose of God's providential salvation is to rid heaven and earth of sin and hell and to establish good and heaven (Paradise).

APPENDIX C
Thirty-four Countries with Tong-il Missions

Argentina

Australia

Austria

Belgium

Canada

Cyprus

Denmark

England

Finland

France

Guiana (Ghiana)

Holland

India

Indonesia

Ireland

Italy

Japan

Luxembourg

Malta

Mexico

New Zealand

Norway

Pakistan

Paraguay

Peru

Portugal

South Pacific

Spain

Sweden

Switzerland

Taiwan

Turkey

United States

West Germany

David J. Hesselgrave

David J. Hesselgrave is director and professor of the School of World Mission and Evangelism at Trinity Evangelical Divinity School. He was born in Wisconsin and educated at Trinity Evangelical Divinity School (Dip. Theol.) and the University of Minnesota (B.A., M.A., Ph.D.). His doctoral dissertation was entitled "A Propagation Profile of the Soka Gakkai." He has served pastorates in Wisconsin and Minnesota and as a missionary with the Evangelical Free Church in Japan (1950 to 1962). He is married and has three children.

7 | NICHIREN SHOSHU SOKA GAKKAI—

The Lotus Blossoms in Modern Japan

David J. Hesselgrave

In the shadow of Japan's spectacular Mount Fuji stands a modern wonder—the Grand Main Temple of the Orthodox Sect *(Shoshu)* of Nichiren Buddhism. Reputedly the "largest temple on earth," it rivals the set of a Cecil B. De Mille spectacular— but this one is for real, constructed of solid masonry and designed to withstand the ravages of earthquakes, fire and time.[1] The temple area is twice as large as that of the Basilica of St. Peter in Rome. The temple itself is 129 meters longer than St. Peter's and the peaks of its unique roof reach skyward another 20 meters beyond the famous dome in the Vatican.[2] The temple—called *Sho-Hondo* in Japanese—was built at a cost of $115,000,000 contributed by some 8,000,000 members of the Soka Gakkai. It seats 6000 (600 priests and 5,400 worshipers), all of whom have a completely unobstructed view of the *Honzon*, the tablet inscribed by Nichiren some seven hundred years ago which is the central object of worship in this religion.

---

1. Edwardo Jachua, "The Biggest Temple on Earth Opens in Japan," *The Asian*, October 15-21, 1972, p. 8.
2. Ibid.

The *Sho-Hondo* does not stand alone. Before the visitor ascends the broad stone stairs that lead to its "Garden of the Law" he will pass building after building—many of which exhibit the unmistakable architectural contemporaneity of modern, prosperous Japan. Among them, however, he will also see those quaint wooden structures that constitute the legacy of other eras when Japan was still mired in feudalism and the Nichiren Orthodox Sect was comparatively obscure and weak.

The gap between the old and the new is almost as great as that between the ox-drawn plow and the modern tractor, for Nichiren Shoshu Soka Gakkai developed from relative obscurity to its present prominence by virtue of one grand leap forward after World War II. The Soka Gakkai itself has grown from less than 5000 families in 1951, to over 16,000,000 believers in Japan and over 300,000 additional adherents in more than thirty other countries—most of them in the United States.[3]

Seven hundred years ago Nichiren insisted that just as Buddhism had come to Japan from India via China, the "true" and "complete" Buddhism which he taught and propagated would be sent from Japan back to India. The announced mission of the Soka Gakkai is to win Japan by 1980 and after that the rest of the Orient and at least one-third of the population of the whole world.[4] The ultimate goal is the establishment of a "third civilization," that is, a peaceful world based on the law of Nichiren and geographically and religiously oriented toward Taisekiji (the Great Stone Temple)—the large estate at the foot of Mount Fuji which has been headquarters for Nichiren Shoshu since Nichirenism split into two main divisions shortly after Nichiren's death. The technical term epitomizing the Gakkai goal is *kosen-rufu* (proclamation and perpetuation)—a term connoting both method and accomplishment. In keeping with the vision of becoming a truly universal religion, the foundation

3. Soka Gakkai membership statistics are difficult to evaluate. The figure 16,201,488 is taken from Kenneth J. Dale, *Circle of Harmony* (Pasadena, CA: William Carey Library, 1975), p. 14. It is based on reports published by the Ministry of Education in Japan. *Time* gives the 1975 membership as 10,000,000 in Japan and 200,000 in the United States (January 13, 1975), p. 26.
4. "The Super Missionary," *Time*, January 13, 1975, p. 26.

of the Mystic Sanctuary of the new temple is reported to contain stones contributed by believers in 135 nations.[5]

The Historical Background

The Soka Gakkai (Value-Creation Society) is commonly thought of as one of the "new religions" in Japan, but is more correctly seen as the lay auxiliary of Nichiren Shoshu (the Orthodox Sect of Nichiren Buddhism). Two men, Tsunesaburo Makiguchi and Josei Toda, were largely responsible for the inception and early growth of the society.

Makiguchi was an educator who worked temporarily with the Education Ministry of the Japanese government. Objecting to Japan's authoritarian policies, he left the Education Ministry and became an elementary school teacher and principal in Tokyo. In 1930 he organized the Soka Kyoiku Gakkai (the Value-Creation Study Society) and published a work which became the theoretical basis for the organization. It was basically a utilitarian approach to pedagogy but was pedagogically significant only because it was written in a milieu of strict authoritarianism. Josei Toda became a devoted disciple of Makiguchi while serving as a teacher in the same school.

Two years before the organization of the Soka Kyoiku Gakkai, Makiguchi had been converted to the Nichiren Shoshu faith. Toda followed him into the new faith after becoming disenchanted with certain other religions including Christianity. The religious commitment of the two leaders gradually changed the complexion of the new movement. Increasingly they became preoccupied with the reformation of the daily lives of the adherents and with the religious implications of the Nichiren faith. Nichirenism had a new ally—not simply one or two new converts, but a new lay auxiliary which, though not of its own making, would lift it from provincial obscurity to international prominence.

By 1942 the organization had grown to about 3000 adherents, but difficult days were in the offing. Makiguchi's opposition to authoritarianism now expressed itself in a disavowal of state Shinto and Japanese chauvinism. He and other leaders of the sect refused the talismans from shrines and openly blamed defeats in war upon the Shinto evil and the failure of Japanese

---

5. Daisaku Ikeda, "Main Temple Completed After Eight Years," *The Japan Times*, October 16, 1971, p. 1.

leaders to embrace the Lotus Sutra. Makiguchi, Toda and twenty-one others were incarcerated in 1943 for *lese majesty*.

Makiguchi died in Sugamo Prison in 1944 thus furnishing the Soka Kyoiku Gakkai with a martyr. Most of the other leaders renounced the society, but Toda continued steadfast, reading the Nichiren Shoshu literature, the writings of Nichiren, and the Lotus Sutra incessantly. He also reports that he repeated *Namu Myoho Renge Kyo* ("homage to the wonderful law of the Lotus Sutra") over two million times, thus attaining enlightenment.

After he was released from prison in 1945 Toda began the task of reconstruction. Since the main goal was to bring peace and happiness to all mankind, the word *kyoiku* (education) was dropped from the name of the society, making it simply Soka Gakkai. The official publication was called the *Daibyaku Renge (Great White Lotus)*. Concurrent with the election of Toda to the presidency in 1951 another publication was undertaken called the *Seikyo Shimbun (Holy Teaching Newspaper)*. Gradually the society began to attract national attention. At the time of Toda's inauguration in 1951 the membership had grown to between 3000 and 5000 families. When he died in 1958 it had increased to over 750,000 families. Many predicted the collapse of the sect, but Toda had trained an able successor in the person of Daisaku Ikeda. By the time Ikeda assumed the full presidency in 1962 membership had increased to approximately 2,500,000 families. Subsequently it continued to grow until it became one of the most phenomenally successful religious groups in the world.

There is no understanding of the blossoming of the Nichiren Shoshu Soka Gakkai "lotus" apart from an examination of its rootage in the uniquely fertile soil of feudal and modern Japan.

The religious strain. The thirteenth-century Buddhist prophet Nichiren was profoundly disturbed by the proliferation of sects in Buddhism and the apparent inadequacy of any to make an impact on the governing families of his day. He taught that the true Buddhism is that which is based on Buddha's teachings in the Lotus Sutra (Sanskrit, *Saddharma Pundarika Sutra;* Japanese, *Hokekyo*). Though in Japan the essence of that truth was to be found in Tendai Buddhism, the incorporation of Amidism into that school had resulted in corruption and decay.

Instead of practicing *nembutsu* (invoking the name of Amida) true faith involved calling on the Buddha of the Lotus Sutra with the words *Namu Myoho Renge Kyo*.

Nichiren became a fearless opponent of the *nembutsu* and a vigorous preacher of orthodox truth as he saw it. Forced to leave the Tendai Sect in 1253 he became a kind of *persona non grata*, but though he suffered banishment, malignity and the sentence of death (from which he escaped) he never ceased to admonish religious and political leaders and appeal to the common people. The wrath to which Nichiren was never a stranger was occasioned by his exclusivism, vituperaticn, and wholesale condemnation of other sects and teachings. His opinion of them is summed up in the oft-quoted words: "The Nembutsu is hell; the Zen are devils; Shingon is natural ruin; and the Risshu are traitors to the country."

Concerning him Masaharu Anesaki wrote,

If Japan ever produced a prophet or a religious man of prophetic zeal, Nichiren was the man. He stands almost a unique figure in the history of Buddhism, not alone because of his persistence through hardship and persecution, but for his unshaken conviction that he himself was the messenger of Buddha, and his confidence in the future of religion and country. Not only one of the most learned men of his time, but most earnest in his prophetic aspirations, he was a strong man, of combative temperament, an eloquent speaker, a powerful writer, and a man of tender heart. He was born in 1222, the son of a fisherman, and died in 1282, a saint and prophet.[6]

In addition to passionate iconoclasm, the Nichiren legacy includes numerous writings and the all-important *Honzon* which the Nichiren Shoshu claims to have enshrined in the Grand Main Temple at Taisekiji.

Our repeated mention of the Orthodox Sect of Nichirenism warrants some explanation at this point. At the time of his death, Nichiren had six leading disciples named Nisho, Nichiro, Nikko, Niko, Nisshin and Nitcho. Historical concensus seems to indicate that Nichiren did not select any one of them for a special position of leadership but determined that they should

6. Masaharu Anesaki, *Nichiren the Buddhist Prophet* (Cambridge, MA: Harvard University Press, 1916), p. 3.

rotate in assuming the responsibility for attending his grave and the custodianship of his temple at Minobu.

There are various versions of the break that came after Nichiren's demise. The explanation offered by Nichiren Shoshu Soka Gakkai is that Nichiren had actually transmitted the secrets of the "true Buddhism" to Nikko—his finest disciple. The feudal lord Minobu, however, refused to listen to Nikko's teaching and submit to his religious authority. As a result, Nikko simply packed up the *Honzon* and other relics and treasures, and took them to Taisekiji where he established his own temple. Thus the true priestly succession passed from Minobu (the headquarters of one of the rival sects of Nichiren Shoshu) to Taisekiji, where it has been maintained in a direct line down to the present high priest.

The basic religious teaching of the Orthodox Sect is that various buddhas are revealed in their proper historical ages in order to teach the law that is relevant for those ages. Sakyamuni (Gautama Buddha), for example, was the Buddha of his time and taught the Buddhism that was relevant for that period. In the present age of *mappo* (the "age of the deterioration of the law"), however, the Buddha and teaching revealed in the Lotus Sutra are relevant and supreme. And these turn out to be, as one would expect, Nichiren and his law as preserved and propagated at Taisekiji.

The philosophical strain. The second strain discoverable in the Soka Gakkai is a philosophical one. At the heart of Makiguchi's pedagogy was the contention that happiness is the goal of education and that educators are to give guidance in the ways to achieve "benefit," good and beauty for the individual and society. Makiguchi claimed to have exposed, for the first time, the contradiction which exists in the philosophy of Immanuel Kant. The main Kantian categories are, of course, truth, good, and beauty. Indeed, human thought, learning, and education have trifurcated human values in this manner from time immemorial until the present day. But, according to Makiguchi, this is a misconceived division which is characterized by both inconsistency and a glaring omission. Good and beauty are values which immediately affect man's happiness. Truth, on the other hand, is not a value and is not directly related to happiness. Truth is objective and unchanging. Values are subjective and relative. Truth simply *is* while values are *created*. Makiguchi proposed that truth be supplanted by *ri* (benefit, advantage, gain, profit). This value is created by scientifically controlling the relationships between the external world and the life of the individual (considered in its entirety) and the community, and affecting those relationships in a manner that will bring "benefit" to all.

Soka Gakkai Leadership

The Soka Gakkai furnishes us with a classic example of Eric Hoffer's typology of leadership as propounded in his book *The True Believer*.[7] Hoffer believes that timing and leadership are indispensable ingredients of any mass movement. Leaders will accomplish little unless the time is ripe. On the other hand, no movement will be markedly successful without the right kinds of leaders no matter how opportune the time. Furthermore, leaders do not necessarily have to be characterized by exceptional intelligence, noble character, or even originality. "The most decisive [characteristic] for the effectiveness of a mass movement leader seems to be audacity, fanatical faith in a holy cause, an awareness of the importance of a close-knit collectivity, and, above all, the ability to evoke fervent devotion in a group of able lieutenants."[8]

Hoffer elucidates a succession of three types of leaders: the men of words, the fanatics, and the practical men of action. These are not mutually exclusive types. One man may possess qualities that fit more than one pattern. But Hoffer thinks that the ground is best prepared by a man of words, the hatching of a movement requires a fanatic, and consolidation is the work of a man of action.

Our disagreements with Hoffer may be many and profound. But that should not blind us to his insights. Indeed, the first three leaders of the Soka Gakkai so perfectly fit into the Hoffer pattern that once these leaders have been characterized the "fit" seems almost contrived.

Tsunesaburo Makiguchi—the man of words. Makiguchi was an educator before he became a believer in Nichiren Shoshu.

7. See Eric Hoffer, *The True Believer* (New York: Harper & Row, Inc., 1951; Mentor Book, 1958).
8. Ibid., p. 106.

He had formed his pedagogical society before he converted it to a religious movement. As an educator he was possessed by an overpowering passion to lead Japan out of the absolutism and authoritarianism inherent in the Imperial Rescript on Education. But as a believer he reintroduced absolutism through the back door of religion by insisting that Nichiren Shoshu Soka Gakkai was the true religion.

Makiguchi was more a student and theorist than a scholar. He was a man who was always thinking, and always writing down his thoughts. He wrote the year around. He was truly the man of words. As Saki and Oguchi note: "He was a man who ordinarily could not be quiet and still. . . . He was always reading something, talking, or taking out a piece of paper to write something down. When he sat down he would vigorously move around on the *zabuton* [pillow one uses when sitting on the floor], and there were times when he would end up tearing it."[9]

Josei Toda—the fanatic. As we have noted, Makiguchi in dying at the right time furnished the Soka Gakkai with a martyr. When Toda heard that Makiguchi had died in prison, he vowed: "What do they mean, letting a man of the calibre of Makiguchi *Sensei* die in prison! All right I'll show them! Toda will take up the mission of Makiguchi *Sensei*. Toda will see that the world hears this teaching!"[10]

Makiguchi had set the stage. Toda emerged on the stage and with reckless abandon and untiring energy worked to bring the scattered remnant of the Soka Gakkai together. By the time he became the second president of the society, he was in absolute control. He *was* the Gakkai. He organized, he wrote, he lectured, he assailed his enemies. Of the abbots of the Tendai Sect he said, "The bonze who brazenly recites such useless *kyo* (sutras) for pay and lives on this pay is a wicked man and a swindler of non-productive existence. Japan today has no reserve energy to spare to support such. Therefore, we loudly advocate,

---

9. Akio Saki and Iichi Oguchi, *Soka Gakkai* (Tokyo: Aoki Shoten, 1957), pp. 70-71.
10. Noah Brannen, *Soka Gakkai—Japan's Militant Buddhists* (Richmond: John Knox Press, 1968), p. 76.

'Cast out the Bonzes, or put them to hard labor!' "[11] He challenged his audience to convert to the *Honzon*. To an audience of four thousand in Tokyo he said:

> Nichiren Daishonin is in the state of Nirvana so even if you say He lies, you cannot bring complaint against Him. However, Josei Toda is alive. I am only conveying to you the Daishonin's words, "Happiness can absolutely be attained by praying to the Dai-Gohonzon." If it doesn't work out, however, you are free to kill or assault me as you please. Don't hesitate to come over and see me. Accuse me, saying, "Scoundrel, you have told a lie." However, it isn't a good idea to come after me without first experimenting.[12]

Noah Brannen says of him,

> His keen administrative ability, charismatic personality, and bellicose spirit, his struggle up through the ranks by sheer hard work, his aggressiveness and masculinity coupled with a keen sensitiveness, a sense of humor and an astute mind—all these qualities added up to "charisma" and an irresistible leader. He was the kind of man postwar, insecure, disillusioned Japan could follow.[13]

Daisaku Ikeda—man of action. In 1960 the young, dapper, practical protégé of Josei Toda was inaugurated as the third president of the Gakkai—a position he still holds today. Ikeda gives the impression of the confident, "man-of-the-world" Japanese entrepreneurs who have fashioned a new place for their country in the world economy. The son of a Tokyo seaweed vendor, he has become a citizen of the world. By the time he had been president for five years he had journeyed abroad six times. Subsequently he has met with such leaders as Alexsei Kosygin, Chou En-lai, and Kurt Waldheim. Under his leadership there has been a great increase in the variety of Soka Gakkai activities, an extension of the frontiers, the formal inauguration of a successful political arm, the establishment of a university (Soka Daigaku near Tokyo) and an incessant flow of propaganda. He has campaigned for nuclear disarmament, a world

11. Josei Toda, *Essays on Buddhism*, trans. Takeo Kamio (Tokyo: The Seikyo Press, 1961), p. 24.
12. *The Sokagakkai* (Tokyo: The Seikyo Press, 1960), p. 109.
13. Brannen, *Soka Gakkai*, p. 78.

food bank and world peace. To use the humorous expression of Nittatsu, the sixty-sixth high priest of Nichiren Shoshu, he always "moves on before his seat gets warm."[14]

Ikeda has partially abandoned the harsh line of Toda. He almost invariably closes his addresses in a very typical Japanese manner: "I heartily wish you will give my best regards to . . . !"; "Let us fight the good fight . . . ever encouraging each other . . ."; "I want you to grow up with devout faith . . . with this heartfelt wish, I close my address"; "I am anticipating victory in your vigorous and vital struggles."

He is indeed "made to order" for an organization seeking recognition outside the strict confines of Japanese society and temperament. To many he is a reincarnation of Nichiren himself.

Worth noting is the contribution of loyal, able, forceful, disciplined lieutenants whom these leaders have always had around them. They bear out the theses of Hoffer that able leaders produce good lieutenants. Their contribution to the advance of the society is perhaps one of the most significant aspects of its growth.

Soka Gakkai Organization

The basic organization of the Soka Gakkai was a legacy from Josei Toda. It has been elaborated and extended under Ikeda but remains basically the same. It is an organization well conceived to initiate and consolidate change.

The General Headquarters in Tokyo reminds one of a giant corporation. At the top are the President, the Board of Directors (with a Chief Director), and the Administrative Section. The single most powerful individual in the hierarchy is the President. The Board of Directors is the highest policy-making body. And the Administrative Section is made up of various departments with their General Managers: Planning, Publishing, Education, Finance, Information, Public Relations, and Culture.

The individual departments require numerous officers to staff the many subdivisions which supervise activities that are carried on throughout the entire movement. The Culture Department, for example, includes divisions of public opinion, education, science, art and economics. As activities and involve-

---

14. Nittatsu, quoted in Daisaku Ikeda, *Lectures on Buddhism*, four volumes (Tokyo: The Seikyo Press, 1962), I, Preface.

ments increase, new divisions and heads are added. As of 1970 there were "Twenty-five General Managers, fifty-seven Vice-Chief Directors, 558 members of Directors and 591 members of Assistant Directors, bringing the total number to 1,232."[15]

Under the General Headquarters there are also large organizations based on age and sex—Men's, Women's and Youth Divisions. It is said that the Youth Division numbers almost one-half of the entire Gakkai membership![16]

But this does not exhaust Soka Gakkai organizational machinery by any means! If one begins out in the local areas, the basic unit (called *kumi*) is made up of five to ten local households (the *honzon* is enshrined only in households, not entrusted to individuals as such). Fifteen to thirty families constitute a group *(han)*; 150 to 300 families a district group *(chibu)*; approximately 1000 families a chapter *(shibu)*; several chapters combine to form a general chapter *(so-shibu)*; and general chapters combine under a joint headquarters in a horizontal "block style" organization which makes it possible to mobilize people readily for political or other reasons.[17]

Several aspects of this organization are worthy of special notice. First, there is a direct line of authority from the President to the family units. This is maintained through the officials of the intermediate groups, through publications, and by careful utilization of the members of the Youth Division and Education Department. The members of the Youth Division, for example, are directly under the President and thought of as his *hatamoto* (i.e., vassals, as of a feudal warlord). Members of the Youth Division will often attend small group meetings in the local areas.

Second, the whole organization is geared to enlist every member in the program of propagation of the faith. The Soka Gakkai seems to be excellent proof of the thesis that organizations succeed to the extent that they are successful in enlisting every member in a program of propagating their faith. One of the master strokes of Soka Gakkai strategy is the absolute refusal to bifurcate between belief and action, between "converted" and "converting." Everything that *faith* secures is also

---

15. Hirotatsu Fujiwara, *I Denounce Soka Gakkai*, trans. Worth C. Grant (Tokyo: Nisshin Hodo Co., 1970), p. 43.
16. Ibid., p. 42.
17. Ibid., p. 41.

secured by *propagating the faith*. The result is that all believers study the *Shakubuku Kyoten (The Manual of Coercive Propagation)* and most of them put its arguments and methods into practice. Members often say that "nothing moves 'for free' except earthquakes and the Gakkai."

Third, there is a vertical mobility for all members of the society. By disciplined study and passing a series of examinations, members can rise to the positions of assistant lecturer, lecturer, assistant professor, or professor with an ever-widening circle of prestige, responsibility and influence. Thus the door of advancement is never closed to believers who are highly motivated. Their promotions are by means of self-effort and are not simply left to the vagaries of chance recognition or machine politics.

Fourth, the Soka Gakkai is so organized that every member will find groups which appeal to him on the basis of sex, age, and special skills and interests. Male and female, young and old, musician, gymnast, artist—all can find groups within the organization that will invite their participation, sharpen their skills, and utilize their energies and abilities in the achievement of Gakkai goals.

Fifth, within the organizational structure there is one level that has come to play such an important role in Soka Gakkai propagation that it merits special attention. The *zadankai* (small discussion group) has been a key to success since the middle of the 1950s. We will elaborate on it after a closer examination of that distinctively Gakkai approach to propagation called *shakubuku*.

The Shakubuku Approach to Propagation

The success of Josei Toda and his associates in postwar Japan was not immediate. Until 1951 the Soka Gakkai made but very modest gains in its reconstruction. It stirred the surface, as did numerous other ideologies, but it failed to touch the deepest spirit of the masses which had responded so enthusiastically to the intransigent summons of Shinto imperialism. With the introduction of the Great *Shakubuku* Advance (*Shakubuku Daikoshin*) by Toda in 1951, the situation changed and changed radically. Adherents were numbered in the thousands, then in the tens of thousands, then in the hundreds of thousands, and finally in the millions.

Shakubuku theory. The word *shakubuku* refers to an extremely aggressive means of propagating the Nichiren Shoshu Soka Gakkai faith and involves making new converts by vehemently attacking competing beliefs, insisting on Nichiren Shoshu Buddhism as the true faith, and exerting every possible pressure to secure the worship of the *Honzon* of Taisekiji. The word *shakubuku* is a compound of two Chinese characters which mean "to bend" or "to break down," and "to make prostrate" or "to make submissive" the opposition. It is usually translated as "forced conversion" and this certainly does no violence to the term—the implication is that submission may be secured by means of physical force. The translation "coercive propagation" seems preferable for two reasons. In the first place, "coercive" is as suggestive of ideological "browbeating" as it is of physical violence. Though the term *shakubuku* allows for the use of physical force, it also applies when the situation does not demand or permit the use of force. Secondly, "propagation" seems to be a better choice of words than "conversion" because it relates the word *shakubuku* more directly to the approach or method of spreading the message and by so doing does not focus exclusively on the object of the process.

The *shakubuku* concept is often contrasted with *shoju*, which has reference to propagating the doctrine by mild persuasive methods so that the potential convert receives the new faith willingly and apart from pressure of any sort. However, in the present age people in general are held to be "malicious" in their attitude toward the true law. For this reason the only way to turn men from their folly is to follow the example of the great Nichiren in adopting the harsh, severe, iconoclastic methods of *shakubuku*. This involves a radical methodology in which one is made to see the evil and falsehood of all other religious beliefs and caused to embrace Nichiren Shoshu.

The practice of *shakubuku* admittedly results in misunderstanding, slander and hatred of the one who practices it. It is, however, an act of mercy by which one can both help others and change his own karma. It brings enlightenment, riches, success and happiness. Toda said, "If you never neglect your daily worship and convert one person a month for a year, the difficulties you face will surely be surmounted."

The Manual of Coercive Propagation. "I earnestly hope that by using this book our members will become devoted to the practice of coercive propagation."[18] With these words, Josei Toda closes his preface to this volume (hereafter simply called *The Manual*) which has been mastered by hundreds of thousands of ordinary believers throughout Japan and around the world since its publication in 1951.

Because of its singular importance an overview of *The Manual* might be in order.[19] It is made up of 445 pages and is divided into two main sections—the "General Treatise" and a "Special Treatise." The first part is concerned with fundamental teachings of the society, an apologetic, and a polemic against other Buddhist sects and religions. For example, it is asserted that there are three types of proof demonstrating the superiority of the Nichiren Shoshu Soka Gakkai religious faith: (1) literary proof stemming from the Buddhist sutras and especially the Lotus Sutra; (2) rational proof stemming from logical, philosophical and scientific verification of Gakkai faith; and (3) experiential proof that is evident in the everyday life of believers. This section closes with a discussion of *shakubuku*, and the difficulty and importance of propagating the faith.

The second section of *The Manual* contains directions on how to deal with six types of people who will be encountered by those who practice *shakubuku*—the unconcerned, the antagonistic, those "satisfied with other Buddhist faiths," seekers of faith, believers in Nichiren Shoshu who are not members of the society, and believers in non-Buddhist religions and popular faiths. Adherents are told to argue against Christianity by insisting that it does not have the power to save from the sufferings of life, it teaches absurd doctrines, it is hopelessly divided, it has persecuted those who would not submit to its teachings, and so forth.

18. *Shakubuku Kyoten (The Manual of Coercive Propagation)*, comp. Soka Gakkai Education Department, Josei Toda, supervisor, revised edition (Tokyo: Soka Gakkai, 1958), p. 2.
19. The edition summarized here is the revised edition of 1958. To the author's knowledge no English translation of *The Manual* has ever been published though some of the included material has appeared in other English Soka Gakkai publications.

The importance of *The Manual* becomes apparent to anyone who has traveled widely in Japan and encountered Soka Gakkai propagandists. From Hokkaido to Kyushu, Gakkai propagandists can be expected to make the same case, repeat the same arguments, and even use the same phrases. There is abundant evidence that many believers have done their homework in this textbook on propagation.

The Honzon—A Happiness Machine

Makiguchi's "philosophy of value" finds its embodiment in the *Honzon*—a tablet on which Nichiren inscribed the "sacred title" *Namu Myoho Renge Kyo* in 1279. There is no little dispute among calligraphers as to the genuineness of the inscription, but adherents are convinced not only of Nichiren's authorship but also that it is the supremely valuable object in the universe. The sutra referred to is the Lotus Sutra, which is said to disclose the true and final teaching of the Buddha. The sacred title, when uttered in faith, both epitomizes that teaching and constitutes the ultimate in reverential homage.

There are, in fact, three *Honzon:* the *Honzon* just described which is enshrined in the new Mystic Sanctuary; the *Honzon* for the emperor's use when he is converted; and the *Honzon* for lay people—those objects of worship to be found in the possession of believers around the world. Believers are assured that if they worship the *Honzon* and repeat the sacred title:

> No prayer is unanswered
> No sin unforgiven
> All good fortune will be bestowed
> And righteousness will be proven.[20]

The way to "create value (benefit, advantage)," therefore, is to worship the *Honzon;* this leads directly to enlightenment. The evidence of enlightenment *(jobutsu)* in this life is absolute happiness which consists of a vital life-force, a transformation of character, and enduring material and spiritual blessings. At the time of death, the corpse is said to exhibit physical proofs of enlightenment: fair-complexioned cheeks, half-opened eyes, slightly parted lips, and the complete absence of *rigor mortis* and the odor of death.

---

20. *The Sokagakkai*, p. 72.

In an effort to discover which appeals and arguments were most effective in winning new believers to Soka Gakkai, I made an analysis of 422 testimonials which appeared in the *Holy Teaching Newspaper* at the height of Gakkai success in 1960-61.[21] Of the 422, some 163 mentioned their previous religion. Of these, 161 noted that they were disappointed with those religions. The overwhelming majority were disappointed on practical rather than theoretical grounds. (This indicates the persuasive value of linking failures and discouragements with religious faith. Every such reversal seems to reinforce the notion that one's religion is the cause of such failures; at the same time the individual is absolved of responsibility.) The appeals that were most effective in securing the conversion of these subjects, and the number of subjects who mentioned them were as follows: (1) physical and emotional (almost entirely the need for physical health, but some mentioned mental or physical health)—235; (2) ethical and spiritual (in the sense of the need for reforming one's life, or the need for such reform in the case of another individual, betterment of home relationships, etc.)—144; (3) economic and practical (finding work, job promotion, business success, money, etc.)—122. Very few (3) mentioned the persuasiveness of theoretical and logical appeals or the utopian ideals of building a new society, though these appeals loom large in the propaganda. This does not necessarily argue for the unimportance of the latter types of appeal, but would seem to indicate that immediate practical considerations are most significant in effecting conversion.

It is evident that for these people the *Honzon* indeed constitutes a "happiness machine" par excellence!

From Confrontation to Dialogue

In the days following the war, Soka Gakkai propagandists placed a great reliance on confrontation. Gakkai experts would challenge Shinto and Buddhist priests of "aberrant" sects to open debate. Ordinary believers would invade the homes of prospects and threaten them with dire consequences if they did not convert, or would simply assert that they would not leave

---

21. David J. Hesselgrave, "A Propagation Profile of the Soka Gakkai" (Ph.D. dissertation, University of Minnesota, 1956), pp. 204-26.

until the prospects embraced the *Honzon*. Needless to say, such coercive tactics aroused the ire of many, and after a few years gave evidence of becoming counterproductive.

Since 1956 the small discussion group *(zadankai)* has been Gakkai's major means of propagation. At that time a general meeting of 60,000 members from all over Japan was held in Korakuen Stadium in Tokyo, and three points relating to the future policy of the society were elaborated: (1) the authority of the group leader should be fostered: (2) the *zadankai* should be understood as a battlefield where *shakubuku* is carried on; (3) there should be more concentration on guiding the members of the society, taking the idea of devotion as a basic principle.

The small local meetings advocated in the second point have proved to be the means of converting millions to the faith. Meetings are informal with singing, testimonials, and discussion of important items in Soka Gakkai publications. Special attention is always focused on newcomers with a view to persuading them to enter the society. Periodically and at critical times a representative of the headquarters will be in attendance in order to make sure that the group is getting the proper instruction and proceeding according to the lines laid out by Gakkai leadership. When the group grows to a point where the average small Japanese home can no longer provide sufficient space, it simply divides into two parts, one part going to the home of another believer to provide a new base for propagation.

Soka Gakkai does hold giant extravaganzas periodically with large-scale parades, gymnastic exercises, folk dances and fiery speeches. These rallies attract tens of thousands and qualify in every way for the term *spectacle*. But they are for believers and are conceived to keep them moving together in the causes espoused by the society. The primary means of propagation is not the mass rally but the small group meeting. It is these small groups that constitute islands of camaraderie and belonging in the depersonalized ocean of modern industrial society in Japan. They go a long way to explain the success of the society. The verdict of J. A. C. Brown has been borne out in the history of the Gakkai: "One of the most successful means used today to bring about attitude change is the creation of a group in which the members feel belongingness since in these circumstances the individual accepts the new system of values and beliefs by accepting belongingness to the group."[22]

The Use of the Media

Perhaps because of a reluctance of Japanese radio and television stations to sell time to Soka Gakkai propagandists or perhaps because of a studied policy on the part of society leadership, media use has been restricted to the society's own printed publications from the very early days. And an ingenious and effective use it has been! In addition to a number of books including titles by Nichiren, Makiguchi, Toda, Ikeda and several others, the society has placed great reliance on periodicals and the newspaper mentioned previously. They are available throughout Japan. The three most important publications include: (1) *The Seikyo Graphic (The Holy Teaching Graphic)*, a monthly (later bimonthly) pictorial magazine concentrating on the national and international activities of the Soka Gakkai, testimonials of the type we have studied, and material which is best characterized as religious and social criticism; (2) *The Daibyaku Renge (The Great White Lotus)*, a more sophisticated bimonthly magazine emphasizing theory, but also devoting significant space to serial stories (related to Soka Gakkai) and other material of higher reader interest; (3) the *Seikyo Shimbun (The Holy Teaching Newspaper)*, formerly a biweekly newspaper and now a daily with a circulation of some 4,500,000 copies.[23] Traditionally the *Seikyo Shimbun* has been both a newspaper and propaganda sheet, with much of its space devoted to Soka Gakkai activities, advertising, and testimonials. The author made an analysis of the contents of the three publications over a period of time in the early 1960s. The results were revealing.

(1) The material was surprisingly equal in the emphasis given to theory, criticism, testimonials, general interest items, and advertising with but one exception—almost twice as much space was given to Soka Gakkai activities as to any other type of material. The appeal most often used was to "get on the bandwagon."

---

22. J. A. C. Brown, *Techniques of Persuasion: From Propaganda to Brainwashing* (Baltimore: Penguin Books, 1963), p. 67.
23. "The Super Missionary," *Time*, January 13, 1975, p. 26.

(2) Almost one-fourth of the space devoted to the activities of the sect was given to reporting activities of an international character. This indicates that Soka Gakkai propagandists have capitalized on the sensitivity of the Japanese to overseas conditions and opinion. There is propaganda value in this type of material. The fact that there are active groups of Soka Gakkai believers in the West reassures believers in Japan since the Japanese have tended to look in that direction for leadership. Moreover, the reports of activities throughout the Orient reinforce a kind of religious chauvinism which *may* be a reflection of the political variety of chauvinism which formerly pertained.

(3) The fact that Soka Gakkai propagandists assume that a majority of their potential converts have a Buddhist orientation is reflected in the fact that little of their theoretical material was directed toward a Buddhist apologetic or polemic. Persuasion was rather geared toward an insistence on the correctness of the Nichiren Shoshu position in its dispute with other branches of Buddhism.

(4) It is significant that very little criticism was directed toward education (the major interest of the society originally, and an area of high current interest), or politics (another major interest of the society). Rather, problems in these areas were superficially linked with the prevalence of "false religions." Critical material was directed toward the general social scene and other religions. This approach is analogous to the effort to link all personal disappointments with mistaken religious loyalties. Too much emphasis on precise theory may have the effect of nullifying the persuasive effect of generalized criticism, and may also lead to schism within the group.

The contribution of these (and other) publications to the growth of the Soka Gakkai can hardly be overestimated. Not only are they of the highest quality, they are also widely read and wisely used by adherents. They are not distributed on a gratis basis as a rule. They are costly to produce and command a certain price or subscription fee. Members will sometimes give them to a prospect without charge, but it is usually made clear that the distributor is in effect making a donation.

The use of the media in propagation of society beliefs is indeed sophisticated. International and national happenings are given an official interpretation. There is something for every age and interest group. The printed materials become the basis for discussion in the *zadankai* all over the country. In this way the mass media message is relayed and reinforced by local leaders.

Summary and Conclusion

Much more could be written. As mentioned previously, the society formed their own political party, the *Komeito* or Clean Government Party, in 1964. The rise of the party was rapid. A surprisingly high percentage of Gakkai candidates were elected at every level of government. Nationally the *Komeito* has become the third most powerful political party in terms of number of members in the Japanese Diet. As of January, 1975, the *Komeito* had twenty-four representatives in the Upper House of the Diet and thirty in the Lower House. The political party is organizationally independent of the Soka Gakkai, but believers constitute about 90 per cent of the *Komeito* membership.[24] It purports to champion the causes of the little man in modern Japan.

The goals of the society can be ultimately realized only by political power. It is not believed that the nation can be won and the "third civilization" ultimately established by *shakubuku* alone. Rather, the goal is to win a plurality to the faith and then establish Nichiren Shoshu Soka Gakkai as the national faith by "democratic" process. This is the significance of the national altar and the emperor's *Honzon* at Taisekiji. It is highly questionable whether *shakubuku* as currently practiced can result in the conversion of that many people in Japan or anywhere. Growth has slowed somewhat already. Nevertheless, the Soka Gakkai has already proved to be one of the most successful religious movements ever conceived in the Land of the Rising Sun. By virtue of a combination of right timing, outstanding leadership, salable doctrines, and studied strategy, the lotus has indeed blossomed in modern Japan!

---

24. Ibid.

PART FOUR

The Middle East

Merlin W. Inniger

Merlin W. Inniger is Principal of the Missionary Language Board at Murree (Pakistan) Language School. In addition to studies at Indiana University and Moody Bible Institute, he has received the B.A. degree from Wheaton College and the M.A. from Wheaton Graduate School. Mr. Inniger is the author of numerous articles in missionary and anthropological journals. Among these has been "Mass Movements and Individual Conversion in Pakistan," which appeared in the May-June 1963 issue of Practical Anthropology. *He has also published various theological materials in the Urdu language. From 1954 to 1974 he served with the International Christian Fellowship in Iran and Pakistan. He was Principal of Pakistan Bible Training Institute in Hyderabad from 1966 to 1972.*

8 | THE AHMADIYA MOVEMENT:

Islamic Renewal?

Merlin W. Inniger

One of the many ancient Islamic traditions quotes the prophet Muhammad as saying that with the passing of time, the true religion would decline. With the beginning of every century, however, a *mujaddid,* or renewer of religion, would arise, calling straying Muslims back to the pure, original Islam.

In 1889, early in the first decade of the fourteenth century of the Muslim calendar, Mirza Ghulam Ahmad of Qadian first announced that he had received a new revelation from God—authorizing him to accept *bay'at.*[1]

The appearing of a "Renewer" in Indian Islam took place against a background of uncertain hopes and a feeling of insecurity and instability in Muslims of the subcontinent. The mutiny of 1857 had been unsuccessful in driving the British out of India. Furthermore, Muslims were outnumbered and overshadowed by the Hindus, who threatened to keep them permanently in a place of subjugation, especially if the ruling British should depart. The Muslim who desired the well-being

---

1. *Bay'at* is the oath of allegiance which was sworn to the caliphs. This claim, therefore, amounted to the assumption of the caliphate by Mirza Ghulam Ahmad.

of his people felt frustrated between the call by the conservative *maulvis* to return to traditional orthodoxy and the reforming spirit of men like Sir Syed Ahmad Khan, who urged adoption of Western thought and ways.

Another phenomenon in mid-nineteenth century India which was to have a telling effect upon the thought and attitudes of the Renewer was the thrust of Christian missions into northwestern India. One of the early centers of Presbyterian missionary work in the Punjab was the city of Sialkot, where Mirza Ghulam Ahmad spent several of his early years in government service.

Ghulam Ahmad was born into the leading family of Qadian, a village in Gurdaspur district of the Punjab, in the year 1839.[2] The title *Mirza,* which usually accompanies his name, relates to the family's connections with the Mughal conquerors of sixteenth-century India. Ghulam Ahmad's father, Mirza Ghulam Murtaza, a physician of some learning and repute, had set an example of loyalty to the ruling British in the days of the 1857 mutiny. He coveted for his son a life of security and honor in government service.

The education which Ghulam Murtaza provided for his son was largely traditional, and contained very little Western influence. Tutors were provided to teach the lad Persian and Arabic, and he gained exceptional facility in the latter. Ghulam Ahmad was studious and reflective, preferring books and meditation to business and politics.

His father insisted, however, upon securing employment for him. Consequently, Ghulam Ahmad served for four years in a subordinate capacity in the district courts at Sialkot. It was during these years that the young man became acquainted with some Church of Scotland missionaries in that city. This contact with Christian missionaries and the hours spent in religious discussion were to become extremely important in the formation of Ahmadiya doctrine.

It became evident soon enough that the mundane affairs of the courts were not to young Ahmad's liking. He returned

---

2. This is the generally accepted date of his birth as given by biographers. The *Munir Report* on the Punjab disturbances (Lahore, 1954), gives his birth date as February 13, 1835.

to Qadian, where he assisted his father in connection with some lawsuits arising out of the family estate. In these efforts, his lack of business acumen and his distaste for this-worldly pursuits were revealed. Evidently his father came to realize that he could do no more to secure some measure of worldly advancement for the young man, for Ghulam Ahmad himself later admitted, "He gave up all hope of me and regarded me as little better than a guest who ate his bread and did nothing for him."[3]

The struggle to please his father and to regain lost family property gave way to a life of meditation and religious study. There are differing accounts of Ahmad's various eccentricities, his propensity for hearing voices, seeing visions and dreams. Fainting spells were frequent, and all his life he suffered from diabetes and vertigo. One thing is certain: as he neared the crucial age of forty,[4] he became convinced that he was destined to receive special revelations from God and to be the Renewer of Islam at the beginning of the fourteenth century.[5]

Between 1880 and 1884 Ghulam Ahmad wrote his first and most celebrated work, the four-volume *Barahin-i-Ahmadiya (Ahmadiya Proofs)*. This was well received among orthodox Muslims, even though the seeds of his later, unique Ahmadiya doctrines can be found throughout the work.

The focal point of his career came shortly afterward, on March 4, 1889, with the announcement of a divine revelation giving him the right to accept homage and an oath of allegiance from his disciples. This marked the real beginning of the Ahmadiya sect as independent from orthodox Islam, and a group came into being whose members accepted Mirza Ghulam Ahmad as their guide in all things spiritual and religious.

The line of demarcation between the new sect and the larger world of Islam became sharp and irrevocable with another startling declaration made by Ahmad in 1891. He announced that he was both the promised *masih* (Messiah) and the *mahdi*

---

3. *The Review of Religions II* (1903), 63, quoted by Phoenix in *His Holiness* (Lahore: n.p., 1958), p. 6.
4. It was at the age of forty that Muhammad first began to receive the Quran in the cave outside Mecca.
5. The year 1882-83 corresponds to 1300 A.M., the beginning of the fourteenth Muslim century.

expected by the Muslims. In orthodox Islamic eschatology, these are apparently two distinct persons. The *masih* is *Isa Ibn-i-Maryam* (Jesus Son of Mary), who will descend from heaven in the end time to preach Islam. *Al-mahdi* is the one who will come just before the end of time to lead Muslims in restoring the faith and exposing the *dajjal* (False One or Anti-Christ) by the force of the sword. Hereafter, the storm of controversy broke suddenly and continued not only through Ahmad's lifetime, but throughout the twentieth century, shaking the modern state of Pakistan to its foundations.

Originally, the controversy raged on three fronts. (1) It involved, above all, orthodox Muslims, who understood Mirza Ghulam Ahmad to be not a Renewer of the Faith, but rather a heretic and a threat to the solidarity of Islam. A number of important mullahs in India secured a *fatwa* (legal pronouncement by an authority on Muslim law) excommunicating Ahmad and his followers from Islam, and declaring that according to the "law of apostasy" in orthodox Islam, they deserved to be destroyed.

(2) Because Ghulam Ahmad felt the force of the growing Christian missionary movement in India, Christianity received more than its share of his attention. His aim was to completely discredit the Christian faith in the eyes of Indian Muslims. To achieve this he sought to persuade Muslims that their time-honored beliefs about *Hazrat Isa* (Jesus) were unfounded. Consequently Ahmadiya propaganda has seemed, at least to Christians, to be largely an anti-Christian polemic. The points of controversy between orthodox Islam and Christianity will be dealt with more fully later in this chapter.

(3) Inevitably, Ghulam Ahmad's quarrel was also with Hinduism. Much in the *Barahin-i-Ahmadiya* was meant to combat Hindu philosophy and preaching. His attack was primarily focused upon the Arya Samaj, a reformed Hindu movement which was gaining popularity at the end of the nineteenth century. His bid for acceptance by the Hindu community was based upon his claim to be the *avatar* (incarnation) of Krishna.

In these years of controversy, Mirza Ghulam Ahmad offered several signs of divine revelation. Twelve of his "fulfilled prophecies" are explained in the Urdu language *Ahmadiya*

Ta'limi Pocket Book[6] which many Ahmadis in Pakistan carry with them to convince doubters and persuade inquirers. One prophecy concerns the Arya Samaj preacher Lekh Ram, of whom Ahmad predicted in 1893 that he would meet his end within six years under mysterious circumstances. Lekh Ram was indeed murdered in 1897. Another prediction concerned the well-known American evangelist and faith healer, John Alexander Dowie, who founded Zion, Illinois. Ahmad challenged Dowie's faith and claims, and predicted a shameful end for Dowie. When Dowie's fortunes crumbled and he died more or less in accordance with Ahmad's prediction, the Renewer could claim that Allah was indeed putting his seal upon his claims, and thousands of his countrymen were persuaded that this indeed was the case.

There is doubtless a tendency to dwell upon the bizarre in Ghulam Ahmad's character and the extravagant in his writings. Indeed, in a society where high value is placed upon the strange, the numinous, the *pir* (spiritual guide), and the *sadhu* (ascetic), this eccentric element in the founder's character has inevitably turned out to be an asset in gaining converts to the movement. If the Western reader is not particularly attracted by the extraordinary claims of Ghulam Ahmad, his fulminations against enemies or his attacks against the Bible, the reader must remember that for many in the Indian context these provided a powerful argument for acceptance of the Renewer. Men of stature were attracted to him—men such as Maulvi Muhammad Ali, who in his early days with the sect edited the English monthly *The Review of Religions* and later became a leader of the Lahore branch of Ahmadiya. At least two early members proved their loyalty by giving their lives in Afghanistan, where they were stoned to death.[7]

Mirza Ghulam Ahmad died suddenly in Lahore on May 26, 1908, while attending a religious conference. He was buried in his native Qadian, in a tomb which had been previously prepared.

6. (Rabwah, Pakistan: Anjuman Ahmadiya Publishers, n.d.).
7. The execution of one of these, Maulvi Abdul Latif, in accordance with orthodox Islamic law, is described in an account in H. A. Walter, *The Ahmadiya Movement* (Calcutta: n.p., 1918), p. 70. It took place on July 14, 1903. Three other Ahmadis suffered the death penalty in Afghanistan in 1924.

New Departures

Are Ahmadis true Muslims?[8] This question has been implicit in the movement from the beginning, although it has been only very recently that modern Pakistan has felt its explosive significance. Ahmadis would reply that their community in fact embodies the only form of Islam, revitalized and informed by the revelations given to Ghulam Ahmad. The basics — the unity of God, Muhammad as the prophet of God, the Quran as the revelation given through Muhammad—are indeed held in common with the larger world of Islam. But there are at least four important departures from the orthodox faith, and these gave the followers of Ghulam Ahmad their distinctive character as a new sect, provided them with adequate content for polemic and persuasion, and made them self-assured and confident in their encounter with Islam and Christianity.

Inspiration. Orthodox Islam distinguishes two levels of inspiration. *Ilham* is the lower level of inspiration thought by many to be granted to saints and holy men as well as prophets. It is knowledge given by direct illumination rather than received through a man's efforts. Because of the subjective element in *ilham*, it is not always reliable. *Wahy*, on the other hand, is the inspiration of the Quran. It is granted only to a true prophet, who is certain that it comes from God. *Wahy* is external, objective, infallible.

In writing about the message of God given to him, Ghulam Ahmad quite consistently uses the word *ilham*. H. A. Walter notes that "although he claimed to be a prophet with evidentiary miracles, he made no claim to *wahy*, so far as I can discover."[9] The force which Ahmad gives to *ilham*, however, makes the reader feel he is actually speaking of *wahy*. In his *Teachings of Islam*, Ahmad explains, "What is *ilham* then? It is the living and powerful Word of God in which he speaks to or addresses one of his servants whom he has chosen, or intends to choose

---

8. The adherents of this sect are called either *Ahmadis* or *Ahmadiyas*, though the latter word is actually an abstract noun. The words *Qadiani* and *Mirzai* are also used to designate members of the sect, although the latter is felt to be a term of derision.

9. Walter, *The Ahmadiya Movement*, p. 55.

from among all people."[10] W. C. Smith believes the claim of Ahmad includes both *ilham* and *wahy*[11] and modern Muslims assert that he actually makes no distinction between the two. A contemporary Islamic scholar, Fr. M. Geijbles, agrees that Ahmad often claims to be the recipient of *wahy*, and at least once in his writings uses the word itself.[12]

Finality of prophethood. In the view of orthodox Muslims, this issue above all others separates the Ahmadis from the true believers. A key and extremely sensitive doctrine of orthodox Islam is that although many prophets have been sent for the guidance of mankind, the Holy Prophet of Islam is the last of this series.[13] Prophethood *(nabuwwat)* ceased with the death of Muhammad, and no new prophet *(nabi)* shall appear after him. This doctrine is deduced from several Quranic verses, especially Sura 33, verse 40, "Muhammad is not the father of any of your men, but [he is] the Apostle of God, and the Seal of the Prophets and God has full knowledge of all things." Commentaries on this and other verses, as well as several traditions, contend that no prophet shall arise following the *Khatm-an-Nubuwwa*.[14]

That Ghulam Ahmad claimed to be a prophet *(nabi)* is beyond dispute, and according to orthodox Muslims this is enough to put him completely outside the pale of Islam. He himself refused to regard others as genuine Muslims unless they acceded to his claims. "I am a prophet of God and he who does not believe in me is a *kafir* (infidel)."[15] Here the gulf seems to be fixed and impassable. In later years, however, Ahmad's followers themselves became divided over the precise

---

10. (London: n.p., 1910), p. 178, quoted by Walter in *The Ahmadiya Movement*, p. 55.

11. "Ahmadiya," *The Encyclopedia of Islam*, Vol. I (Leiden: E. J. Brill, 1960), p. 301.

12. Fr. Geijbels is with the Christian Study Center, Rawalpindi, Pakistan. This comment was made in his lecture "Prophecy as a Contemporary Issue," given in Murree, Pakistan, on August 14, 1974.

13. A generally accepted tradition states that the number of prophets is 124,000. Some of these are mentioned in the Bible, including Jesus.

14. Or, in Persian and Urdu, *Khatm-i-Nabuwwat*. *Khatm* can mean either "seal" or "conclusion," "termination."

15. Quoted by Zafar Ali Khan in the foreward to Phoenix, *His Holiness*, p. viii.

interpretation of prophethood, and some rejected the term *nabi* in favor of *mujaddid* (renewer).

Christology. We have already referred to Ghulam Ahmad's declaration that he was the promised Messiah. By this he did not mean that he was the original Jesus of Nazareth who descended to earth as a sign of the approaching day of resurrection. The doctrine of Jesus himself returning to earth is a delusion which Ahmad felt must be removed from Muslim thinking. Not Jesus himself, but another person with the attributes of Jesus was to be expected. Now he had come—Mirza Ghulam Ahmad—in the "spirit and power" of Jesus![16]

To make good this claim, it became necessary for Ahmad to attack the belief about Jesus held by most Muslims. Quranic verses concerning *Isa Ibn-i-Maryam* are obscure and may admit different interpretations, but the one most often quoted, on which orthodox belief seems to rest, is Sura 4, verses 157-158:

> They said (in boast), "We killed Christ Jesus the son of Mary, the Apostle of God";—but they killed him not, nor crucified him but so it was made to appear to them, and those who differ therein are full of doubts, with no certain knowledge, but only conjecture to follow, for of a surety they killed him not;—Nay, God raised him up unto himself; and God is Exalted in Power, Wise.

The majority of Muslims hold that this passage clearly indicates that through some divinely ordered optical illusion Jesus was delivered from the wrath of his persecutors, and completely escaped the cross. Thereupon, God raised him up to the "fourth heaven," where he is still alive and from where he will personally descend before the day of resurrection.

Jesus was actually crucified, Ahmad alleged, but he did not *die* on the cross. He merely swooned away, and in this condition was placed in the rock-hewn tomb. The coolness of the tomb, together with the application of *marham-i-Isa* (the Jesus ointment), the formula of which was divinely revealed to the disciples, brought resuscitation and complete healing to Jesus.[17]

---

16. *The Review of Religions* II, (1903), 192, quoted in Walter, *The Ahmadiya Movement*, p. 88.
17. The followers of Ahmad at Qadian claimed to possess the formula for this miracle-working ointment, and sold it for its healing qualities.

Jesus left Palestine after forty days and traveled east on a mission to the ten lost tribes of Israel who had settled in Afghanistan and Kashmir. In that part of the world he died at the venerable age of 120, and was buried in Srinagar, the capital of Kashmir. Ahmadis proudly publish reports and pictures of his tomb, located in Khan Yar Street in the capital.[18]

With this "proof" of a Jesus dead and buried, Ahmad hoped to end for all time Muslim and Christian expectations of a Messiah yet to come. He believed the Christian edifice would crumble like a house of cards, and Muslims would be ready to accept the newly manifest "mahdi-messiah." In *The Call of Islam* Maulana Muhammad Ali made the link between a dead Jesus and Ahmadiya propagation very clear:

Propagation of Islam was the *mujaddid's* sole mission, but he had also to remove the obstacles that there were in the way. It was impossible to meet Christianity or to propagate Islam amongst the Christians, unless Jesus were kept to his proper place—a prophet among the prophets of God, eating and drinking like them, subject to other human needs like them, changeable in his physical condition and also dead like all the rest of them.[19]

A Friday sermon delivered in 1959 by Mubashshir, an Ahmadiya *amir* in Ghana, illustrates how Ahmadiya Christology is presented to West African Muslims:

I will tell you about the works of the Promised Messiah. The first of these was to declare the death of Jesus. The orthodox view of Jesus is not in the Quran . . . the idea that Jesus is in the sky was brought to Islam by Christian converts, who deluded the original Muslims (just as West Africans bring into Ahmadiyah certain corrupting influence, such as funeral customs).[20]

Concerning other aspects of Jesus' life and character, there are many contradictions in Ahmadi writings. Ghulam Ahmad accepted the traditional Muslim belief that Jesus was a prophet

18. The tomb, which Ahmad said was miraculously revealed to him, bears the inscription of one Yus Asaf. To establish his claim, Ahmad made the deduction that Yus was a corrupted form of Yesu, the Urdu name for Jesus.
19. *The Call of Islam* (Lahore: Ahmadiya Anjuman Ishiat-i-Islam, n.d.), p. 42.
20. Quoted in H. J. Fisher, *Ahmadiyah: A Study in Contemporary Islam on the West African Coast* (Oxford: Oxford University Press, 1963).

sent from God, and yet he and his followers have spared no efforts in attacking the virgin birth (which orthodox Muslims accept), belittling his miracles, and challenging every aspect of his character and work. It was as if the person of Jesus Christ presented an insoluble enigma to them, and the preaching of him as crucified and risen presented a barrier which must be removed at all costs.

Jihad. According to H. A. Walter, the conception of *jihad*, or holy war, was the point of sharpest divergence between the faith of Ahmad and that of the majority of Muslims.[21] Numerous Quranic passages, particularly Sura 2, verses 190-194,[22] form the basis of the orthodox doctrine that it is the duty of every Muslim to spread and defend Islam by force of arms. This tension between the *Dar-ul-Islam* (Abode of Islam) and the *Dar-ul-harb* (Abode of War) will exist until the coming of the *mahdi* who will lead the host of Islam in a universal and altogether victorious *jihad*.

Ahmad's revelations were to the effect that this conception is altogether in error. He declared unequivocally that he had come with a commandment that "henceforth *jihad* by sword is forbidden."[23] Islam was to be preached and propagated with reasoning and heavenly signs. In their presentation of Ahmadiya to the West, Ahmad's followers have emphasized this strongly. They realized that the idea of the propagation of Islam by the *mahdi* at the point of the sword could not produce anything but disgust in men's hearts. "Not steel, but rational persuasion and spiritual signs, could captivate the heart of humanity."[24]

The main contention of the Muslim *ulema* (scholars or theologians) was that Ahmad was not expounding a Quranic doctrine but was repealing an existing law of the Quran. Ahmad's enemies insisted that by laying down a new doctrine either superseding or modifying the original doctrine in the Quran, he was claiming to be a prophet with authority to isssue new teaching. This claim clearly violated the sacred doctrine of *Khatm-i-Nabuwwat!*

---

21. Walter, *The Ahmadiya Movement*, p. 71.
22. This passage begins as follows: "Fight in the cause of God those who fight you, but do not transgress limits. . . ."
23. Quoted in *Munir Report*, p. 193.
24. M. Muhammad Ali, *The Call of Islam*, p. 42.

Given these unresolvable differences, the cleavage between orthodox Muslims and the followers of Mirza Ghulam Ahmad proved to be irreconcilable. The die was cast. The new sect was barred from using ordinary mosques. Henceforth Ahmadis would pray under the leadership of Ahmadi *imams* only. Qadian became the center of a movement which would take the message of a renewed Islam to the ends of the earth!

Propagation: Multiplication by Division

Shortly before his death in 1908, Ahmad boasted of 500,000 followers. Objective estimates, however, allow for only about one-tenth of that number.[25]

After the passing of the founder, the direction of the movement passed into the hands of Hakim Nur-ud-Din, one of the first disciples, an industrious, intelligent man. He became known as Khalifah-ul-Masih.[26] And during his years as successor to Ghulam Ahmad the movement saw considerable growth. Societies were formed to care for the administrative and educational needs of the community, and for the propagation of the Ahmadiya message. Qadian became the Mecca for the faithful, and a great conference was held each December at which as many Ahmadis as possible would gather. From the beginning, education for girls was emphasized and as a result there has been a comparatively very high female literacy rate among Ahmadis. A college for training missionaries was also maintained at Qadian. Despite his gifts, Nur-ud-Din was not able to reconcile growing differences within the movement concerning the founder's status, succession, and relationship with other Muslims.

Following Khalifah Nur-ud-Din's death in 1914, a group of Ahmadis who were convinced that leadership and authority should remain within the founder's family, elected Ghulam Ahmad's son, Mirza Bashir-ud-Din Mahmud Ahmad, as *khalifah*. This quickly brought differences into the open, a few members who disagreed with this election seceded, and, along with others who shared their views, formed a new society with headquarters at Lahore.

---

25. Walter, *The Ahmadiya Movement*, p. 112.
26. In Islamic history, the *khalifah* (caliphs) were the successors of Muhammad. Ahmadis were playing on the sentiments of orthodox Muslims, many of whom wanted to see the *khalifat* re-established.

The seceding group, led by Khwaja Kamul-ud-Din and Maulvi Muhammad Ali, opposed the election of a *khalifah* on the grounds that the affairs of the community should be in the care of the society, or committee, which had been formed for that purpose. They insisted that a *khalifah* would tend to become diotatorial and a son of the founder would presume too much upon his family relationship.

This schism did not mean the end of the Ahmadi movement but instead brought two groups into existence, each with its own distinct emphases and methods. Both groups had a missionary zeal for propagation unknown to orthodox Islam.

Jama'at-i-Ahmadiya (The Ahmadiya Community). This group, popularly called the Qadiana party, continued the disciplined community life centered around Qadian (later Rabwah) for which the sect has become famous. Other aspects which distinguished the Qadiani party were stricter adherence to the founder's original doctrines, and a reverence for his successor, Bashir-ud-Din, the second *khalifah*. They insisted that Ghulam Ahmad must be regarded as a prophet *(nabi)*, even though this drove them even farther from orthodox Islam.

Qadianis had enjoyed security and freedom for their activities under the British rule in India. Ghulam Ahmad had written often and enthusiastically in support of the British *Raj,* and its policy of religious toleration. Inevitably his enemies branded the movement as a handmaid of the British. Just as inevitable, however, was the day of withdrawal by the British from the Indian subcontinent and the partition of the land into two sovereign states, India and Pakistan. Qadian found itself on the Indian side of the border and, in the confusion and hatreds of 1947 India, it became necessary for the Ahmadis to leave Qadian and find a new home in Pakistan. This must have been with some trepidation, since Ghulam Ahmad had warned his followers against involvement in the activities of the Muslim League, and thus Qadianis had not been involved in the demand for a separate Islamic state.

The Ahmadis migrated from Qadian to a barren tract of land located ninety miles southwest of Lahore, and set about to prove that rugged will and patient labor could make it habitable. Out of this has emerged Rabwah, an exclusive Ahmadiya town with its own internal judiciary, a central advisory council, largely elected, and a strong central secretariat containing various departments such as foreign affairs, public affairs, publication and propaganda. Authority is ultimately vested, however, in the *khalifah*, who for more than fifty years was Bashirud-Din Mahmud Ahmad. The Rabwah group as it exists today can be said to be largely his creation. After Bashir-ud-Din's death in 1965, the *khalifat* passed to his son, Mirza Nasir Ahmad, who is the present head of the Rabwah Ahmadis. Thus the succession has remained within the founder's family.

This strong and centralized organization has made possible well-planned and vigorous missionary work throughout the world. The training college for missionaries begun in Qadian has been continued in Rabwah. Trainees are expected to master Arabic and English as well as the language of the country in which they will spread the Ahmadiya message. The Bible and Christianity are studied for polemical purposes; a well-trained Ahmadiya knows how to use the Bible as well as the Quran in "proving" the doctrines of the Messiah of Qadian. Attention to physical discipline is not neglected. The trainee is expected to prove his ability to ride a bicycle for long distances under a hot sun, and to live on simple fare. When the time comes for an Ahmadiya missionary to go abroad, he knows that he cannot expect to take his wife and children with him—they stay in the community at Rabwah—and he will not see them again until his term of service (sometimes as long as ten years) is completed. Faithful Ahmadi members support this program by giving 10 per cent of their salary, and are expected to give above this to special offerings for charitable purposes.

Today Rabwah can boast of Ahmadi congregations from Indonesia to the Arab world with small bands of converts in the large cities of Europe and the United States, and a mission (of all places) in Israel! Rabwah's greatest success, however, has been in West Africa where Pakistani missionaries have established Ahmadi congregations in Ghana, Nigeria, and Sierra Leone. There the Ahmadis have freely borrowed methods used for decades by Christian missionaries, and they may be found establishing schools in villages, preaching and distributing literature at bazaars and fairs, and utilizing their persuasive arguments to win Muslim, Christian and pagan. H. J. Fisher, in his study of the Ahmadiya movement in West Africa, points out the difficulty of telling precisely how many followers of the sect there are in the area.[27] Rabwah claims 45,000 Ahmadis in Ghana, despite the insistence of the *amir* in charge that there are between 18,000 and 28,000. Fisher's own estimate in 1963 was a total of about 35,000 Ahmadis in the three countries of Ghana, Nigeria and Sierra Leone.

Dr. Kenneth Cragg sees such propagation efforts of the Ahmadis as having inaugurated a new tradition in Islam. Such a specific, organized mission sustained by offerings of the community and carefully directed and planned with personnel, literature, schools, and clinics indeed knows no parallel among Muslims. Dr. Cragg further states, "Ahmadiya initiative in this way has been in part a factor in arousing similar projects of dissemination on the part of venerable bodies like Al-Azhar, either in emulation or correction of its zeal."[28]

The Rabwah group claims to have approximately one million followers world-wide, about half of these being in Pakistan.

Ahmadiya Anjuman Isha'at-i-Islam *(Ahmadiya Society for the Spread of Islam).* Having rejected the *khalifat* of Mirza Bashir-ud-Din the Lahore Ahmadis gradually moved somewhat closer to orthodox Islam. They dissociated themselves completely from the idea that Ghulam Ahmad was a prophet *(nabi)* who had brought new truth, and insisted that he was called by God only as a *mujaddid* of the faith. Muhammad Ali sought to emphasize this in his writings: "Let us be clear at the very outset as to the true mission of such reformers *(mujaddid).* They come with no new truth, no new principle, no new rule of conduct. The Holy Quran is a complete code.... All they do is rally the Musalmans, fallen away from the true Islamic path, once more to the standard of Islam."[29]

In contrast to the Qadianis, the Lahoris further asserted that it is not forbidden to join other Muslims in saying their prayers and that Ahmadi daughters may be given in marriage to non-Ahmadis. Also they were unwilling to designate non-Ahmadi Muslims as *kafirs* (infidels) though the Qadianis continued to do so.

---

27. Fisher, *Ahmadiyah*, p. 155.
28. Kenneth Cragg, *Counsels in Contemporary Islam* (Edinburgh: University Press, 1965), p. 160.
29. M. Muhammad Ali, *The Call of Islam*, p. 9.

In other ways, however, the Lahore Ahmadis have retained the stamp of the founder. They have continued to be a thorn in the side of the conservative *ulema,* have retained the "spiritualized" interpretation of Islamic teachings such as *jihad* and animal sacrifices, and have surpassed even the Qadianis in their insistence that Jesus is dead and buried.

Because of a more sophisticated, intellectual approach, the Lahoris have been able to make a greater impact upon the West, and the English-reading public in general. Both leaders, Khwaja Kamal-ud-Din and Maulvi Muhammad Ali, were educated at Lahore's Forman Christian College, and throughout their long careers both published many works intended to commend Islam to Western readers. Muhammad Ali was the leader of the Lahore movement until his death in 1951. His English translation of the Quran has had wide acceptance in the West despite its anti-Christian bias in the notes. Ahmadis have in fact been the leaders in translating the Quran and thus making it available to the world outside Islam. Before he died, Muhammad Ali had written: "We would be seriously neglecting our duty to the Word of God and to humanity if we do not make the Holy Quran accessible to the peoples of the world in at least a hundred languages within the next twenty years."[30]

Khwaja Kamal-ud-Din is best known for his long service in England as the *imam* of the Ahmadi mosque in Woking, Surrey. Although this center has attracted mostly converts from Muslim backgrounds, there have been a few notable accretions from British society, the earliest and most prominent being Lord Headley, an Irish peer.[31]

Kamal-ud-Din's *The Sources of Christianity*[32] illustrates how he attempted to commend Islam to Westerners. In the book he seeks to prove that modern Christianity has arisen from heathen practices and superstitions. He also makes extensive use of the higher criticism which was influential in Germany and England during the growing years of Ahmadiya.

Lahore Ahmadiya publications best known to English readers are *The Light,* a weekly published in Lahore, and *The Islamic Review,* the official monthly of the Woking Mosque. These pub-

---

30. Ibid., p. xi.
31. Walter, *The Ahmadiya Movement,* p. 153.
32. (Woking, England: The Bashir Muslim Library, 1924).

lications contain articles complimentary to Islam by European authors like Carlyle and Toynbee, the testimonies of Christians won to Islam, the repudiation of Christian doctrines, and fairly enlightened social views.

Not infrequently in the literature of the Lahore Ahmadis one finds the doctrine of equal opportunity for all—Hindus, Buddhists, Christians, and Muslims—to practice and preach their faiths. Ahmadis in Pakistan are most zealous in opposing the Bible and Christian teaching, and yet they insist that Christians should have the fullest freedom to propagate their faith. The Quranic "no compulsion in religion," they maintain, is meant for all. Freedom of religion is not a one-way street as the conservative Maulana Maudoodi wished to make it. An Islam linked with tolerance and progressive views was bound to appeal to many Muslims weary of mullahism and ultraconservatism. Ahmadis could also claim to have solved the problem of a Jesus alive and in heaven, a doctrine which is often more of an embarrassment than a living hope to orthodox Muslims.

Innumerable Muslims who have never identified themselves with the movement doubtless have been influenced by Ahmadiya arguments. The Lahore group has remained small in numbers. They have been satisfied to harness their zeal and vitality in propagation on behalf of Islam in general. Yet, strangely, they too were counted outside the fold of Islam by the nation of Pakistan when the great test for the Ahmadiya movement came.

Elements in Ahmadiya's Success

Before considering the challenge to the Ahmadiya movement in modern Pakistan, it may be helpful to summarize some of the principal elements in the success of Ahmadiya propagation throughout the ninety years of the movement's existence. Some of these elements were more relevant in the early days of the movement, particularly the first two points to be mentioned. Other elements are more relevant to Ahmadiya propagation in the West.

(1) From the beginning, the drawing power of the movement was found in the charismatic or the numinous aspect of the founder's character. For his followers, Ghulam Ahmad was a prophet who was in touch with Allah. His courageous challenges put his enemies to flight and his predictions concern-

ing them were fulfilled. In an age of uncertainty, change and political upheaval in the subcontinent, such a figure inevitably gained a following. It is noteworthy that the Rabwah group, which has grown much faster than the Lahore section, has retained its devotion to the founder and his family.

(2) Because of the Ahmadi practice of giving through the community for charitable purposes, the Ahmadis have been able to give substantial financial aid to needy families who have joined the movement. This appears to have been a factor in drawing adherents throughout the history of the movement. One Ahmadi from a Hindu background interviewed by the author spoke warmly of the compassion shown by the community to his grandfather at a time of great need.

(3) Ahmadiya has provided an alternative for Muslims to ultraconservatism and mullahism. It is not the only alternative, to be sure, and great numbers of Muslims continue in orthodox Islam. Ahmadiya has offered an Islam with modern views of freedom, a humanitarian view of holy war, a more scientific outlook (even acceptance of a form of evolution), stress on women's education, and the translation of the Quran into many languages.

(4) Ahmadiya provides its own answer to the "problem" of Jesus. It is noteworthy that in dealing with Muslims and Christians alike, the Ahmadiya approach begins with the "life and death" of *Isa Ibn-i-Maryam*. This is the first argument advanced in the *Pocket Book* guide issued by the Rabwah group for propagandists. Muslims must be persuaded that Jesus is not alive in the "fourth heaven." The only Messiah is Mirza Ghulam Ahmad. Christians must see that the resurrection of Christ is merely a legend, and that he is actually dead and buried in Kashmir. In either case, this teaching is the door to becoming an Ahmadi.

(5) Particularly in the Rabwah group, there is a high degree of discipline and organization for propagation. It is truly remarkable that a small sect with its center in a poor, developing country in the Third World has established missions in no less than sixty countries! This surely is a tribute to the discipline and thorough training given at the Rabwah college, and to the willingness of Ahmadi members to sacrifice for what they believe to be the truth.

In research for this chapter, no sociological study of the movement has been made. Such a study would surely reveal interesting facts as to how far the movement has spread as a result of family structures and relationships. Some knowledgeable Ahmadis interviewed deny that the movement has grown largely along family lines. They maintain and passionately believe that the motivating thrust of the movement has been the dynamic of the truth revealed through Mirza Ghulam Ahmad, and that minds open to the truth have chosen and will continue to choose Ahmadiya.

Controversy, Persecution, and Growth

Kenneth Cragg has written, "Not seldom in the history of religions a divergent community serves to precipitate issues of an importance out of all proportion to its own numbers or the quality of its inner achievement. Its presence proves a catalyst whereby implicit questions take explicit shape and become themes of public controversy with a sharpness and provocation they might otherwise lack."[33]

The emergence of Pakistan as an Islamic state in 1947 provided the occasion for the surfacing of such important issues as Dr. Cragg mentions. Those who pressed for the Islamic state could scarcely have imagined the problems and the inner ambiguities which the new Pakistan would experience! "What is an Islamic state?" An even more basic question was: "What is a Muslim?" These were some of the unresolved questions which suddenly took explicit, even menacing, shape when Pakistani Muslims realized the existence in their midst of a proselytizing sect claiming to be the true Islam, and yet denying the finality of the prophethood of Muhammad.

As early as 1949, within two years of Pakistan's creation, members of the Ahrar (a quasi-political party) demanded that Ahmadis be declared a non-Muslim minority in the new state. The significance of this demand is worth noting. If the state should make an official distinction between Muslims and non-Muslims, then the latter would be reduced to second-class citizens and barred from high offices. This would completely distort the vision of the founder of Pakistan, Quaid-i-Azam, Muhammad Ali Jinnah, who had said that the new state would

---

33. Cragg, *Counsels of Contemporary Islam*, p. 155.

be a modern democracy, with all members of the nation having equal rights of citizenship regardless of religion, caste or creed.[34]

Agitation against the Ahmadis continued, and by 1953 many other *ulema* in the country had joined in the demands first made by the Ahrar. Chaudri Zafrullah Khan, an Ahmadi who was Pakistan's Foreign Minister at the time, became the chief target of these demands. This internationally known and respected figure was abused and vilified in speeches and street processions, and his removal from office demanded.

The situation deteriorated to the extent that in March, 1953, there were serious disturbances in the country, particularly in Lahore, and these eventually resulted in the fall of the government and imposition of martial law.

Following the disturbances, a court of inquiry was set up to assess responsibility and determine the causes of the trouble. The report subsequently published by this court must surely be regarded as required reading for anyone desiring to understand Islam in Pakistan. In order to determine the position of non-Muslims in an Islamic state, the court summoned a number of leading *ulema* and asked them to give their definition of a Muslim. In the words of the report:

> Keeping in view the several definitions given by the *ulema*, need we make any comment except that no two learned divines are agreed on this fundamental? If we attempt our own definition as each learned divine has done and that definition differs from that given by all others, we unanimously go out of the fold of Islam. And if we adopt the definition given by any one of the *ulema*, we remain Muslims according to the view of that *alim* (scholar) but *kafirs* (infidels) according to the definition of everyone else.[35]

The Ahmadis had been spared, so to speak, by the disagreement of the *ulema* and by the heavy hand of martial law. In years to follow, through the "strong man" government of President Ayub Khan, and later the preoccupation of the country with two life and death struggles with India, the sect continued to propagate and grow steadily.

In the democratic government of Prime Minister Z. A. Bhutto,

---

34. From his speech to the Constituent Assembly of Pakistan, August 11, 1947, as quoted in the *Munir Report*, pp. 201f.
35. *Munir Report*, p. 218.

however, anti-Ahmadi forces again found their opportunity. In May, 1974, an incident at the Rabwah railway station sparked anti-Ahmadi demonstrations and violence throughout the country. The conservative forces again pressed their demands that Ahmadis be declared a non-Muslim minority in Pakistan, and all Ahmadis in key posts be deposed. Both the Rabwah Ahmadis and the Lahore Ahmadis were explicitly included in these demands. To these demands a new one was added, that Rabwah, the new "Qadian" in Pakistan, be declared an open city.

Prime Minister Bhutto's government, already beset by trouble in the western border regions, was shaken and threatened with disaster. Finally, in an action unprecedented in modern history, the Bhutto-controlled National Assembly on September 7, 1974, unanimously passed an amendment to the constitution which defined a non-Muslim in the following terms:

> Any person who does not believe in the absolute and unqualified finality of the Prophethood of Muhammed (peace be upon him), the last of the prophets, or claims to be a prophet, in any sense of the word or any description whatsoever after Muhammed (peace be upon him), or recognizes such a claimant as a prophet or a religious reformer, is not a Muslim for the purposes of the Constitution or law.[36]

For the time being, it appeared that the *ulema* had won. A modern democratic state had bowed to their wishes and had, in effect, declared the Ahmadis to be a non-Muslim minority in Pakistan. It was not immediately apparent whether high-ranking Ahmadis would indeed be relieved of their positions in the army and in the government.

During the long summer of 1974, Ahmadis in Pakistan were unusually quiet. Many of their mosques and shops lay in ruins, burned or looted during the disturbances. Reports circulated that many of them had adopted orthodox Islam, and some were shown concern and sympathy by Christians, with whom they now shared minority status.

Will this political setback temper the zeal and dynamic of these aggressive reformers of Islam? Or will it provide the impetus for Ahmadis outside Pakistan to make Ahmadiya a truly world-wide faith, even as Mirza Ghulam Ahmad declared it would some day surely be? Time alone will tell.

---

36. Quoted in the *Pakistan Times*, Rawalpindi, September 8, 1974.

PART FIVE

North America

Wilton M. Nelson

Wilton M. Nelson is a native of Nebraska and a graduate of Wheaton College and of Dallas, Southern Baptist (Louisville) and Princeton seminaries. He received his doctorate in theology from Princeton. He is an ordained minister of the Evangelical Free Church. Since 1937 he has been a professor at the Latin America Biblical Seminary (founded by the Latin America Mission) located in San Jose, Costa Rica, teaching in the field of church history. He served as president of the seminary from 1958 to 1968 when he was succeeded by a Latin American. Dr. Nelson has also been active in evangelistic and general missionary service. He has served as pastor of Templo Biblico, the largest evangelical church in Costa Rica. He is past editor of the Mensejero Biblico. *He has written a number of books including* A History of Protestantism in Costa Rica, Manual de Historie Eclesiastica, *and* Los Testigo de Jehova Quienes son y lo que Creen (The Jehovah's Witnesses, Who They Are and What They Believe). *Dr. and Mrs. (Thelma Agnew) Nelson have two sons and four grandchildren.*

Richard K. Smith

Richard K. Smith is a native of Steubenville, Ohio, where he was born December 1, 1937. He received his education at Asbury College (B.A.), Nyack College (B.S.) and the School of World Mission and Evangelism, Trinity Evangelical Divinity School (M.A.). From 1960 to 1962 he served as associate minister of the Christian and Missionary Alliance Church of Fairmont, West Virginia. Since 1963 he and his family have served with the Christian and Missionary Alliance in Indonesia, first on the island of Sumba, then on Timor, and presently on Sulawesi where Mr. Smith is on the faculty of the Jaffray School of Theology. His dissertation at Trinity was concerned with the propaganda methods of the Jehovah's Witnesses.

9 | JEHOVAH'S WITNESSES

Part I The Background

Wilton M. Nelson and Richard K. Smith

When the membership of a religious movement increases from 3,868 believers in one nation in 1918 to 2,021,432 members located in 210 nations within a fifty-five year period, there would seem to be good reason for inquiring into the background and growth of the movement. Jehovah's Witnesses have achieved this rapid growth and they are, therefore, a deserving subject for our present inquiry.[1]

Origin and History

The history of this flourishing sect falls clearly into three periods, each of which coincides with the tenure of important leaders.

Charles Taze Russell (1852-1916). The first period was dominated by the founder of the Witnesses—Charles T. Russell. One of the earliest sobriquets of the sect was "Russellites." A haber-

---

1. *Britannica Book of the Year, 1975* (Chicago: Encyclopedia Britannica, Inc., 1975), p. 551; *Britannica Book of the Year, 1976* (Encyclopedia Britannica, Inc., 1976), p. 590.

dasher from Pittsburgh, Russell was successively a Presbyterian and Congregationalist, but while yet a youth, he became dissatisfied with historic Protestantism and was even plagued with unbelief.[2] The doctrines of the Trinity and hell particularly troubled him.

A casual visit to a humble Adventist hall quickened his wavering faith. There, apparently for the first time, he heard an exposition of the doctrine of the second coming of Christ which provoked in him a permanent enthusiasm for the subject.[3]

About 1872, while still a lad of twenty years, Russell began holding Bible studies apart from the established churches, concentrating on the subject of the return of Christ. Abandoning "human creeds and systems of misrepresentation of the Bible" (including Adventism), Russell struck out on his own to formulate a "true" doctrinal system which centered on the second coming of Christ.[4]

As a result of his studies—especially of the Books of Daniel and Revelation—Russell came to the conclusion that Christ would set up the millennial kingdom in 1914, but that prior to the establishment there would be a forty-year period of preparation (1874-1914) which would herald the "day" of the millennium. This period was called the "millennial dawn," which explains another early nickname of the sect: "millennial dawnists."

Due to his strong personality, apparent adherence to *sola Scriptura*, notable use of visual aids, and the innate curiosity in people concerning the things of the future, Russell gained an increasing number of followers. In 1884 the Zion's Watchtower Tract Society was officially organized. By 1888 the society had attained a missionary character with representatives in England, China, India, Turkey and Haiti.[5]

In 1879 Russell launched a magazine called *Zion's Watchtower*, with an original edition of 6,000 copies. This organ

---

2. *Jehovah's Witnesses in the Divine Purposes* (Brooklyn: Watchtower Bible and Tract Society, 1959), pp. 14-15 (hereafter referred to as *JWDP*); Herbert Stroup, *The Jehovah's Witnesses* (New York: Columbia, 1945), pp. 5-6.
3. Ibid.
4. *JWDP*, pp. 26-27; Stroup, *Witnesses*, p. 8.
5. Ibid.

became, and continues to be, one of the chief instruments of propaganda for the sect. By 1970 each fortnightly printing of the *Watchtower* had reached approximately 6,800,000. Its companion periodical *(Awake!)* came a close second with a bi-monthly edition of 6,600,000 the same year.[6]

"Pastor" Russell was a prolific writer and an indefatigable speaker and traveler. It is said that he traveled a million miles, preached 30,000 sermons, and wrote 50,000 pages.[7] His *magnum opus* was the six-volume *Studies in the Scriptures* (otherwise called *The Divine Plan of the Ages*) written between the years 1886 and 1906. In it he expounded his eschatology, anthropology, Christology and soteriology. By the time of his death in 1916 some 15,000,000 copies of these volumes had been distributed. These books became a "second Bible" to his followers. They were considered to be indispensable for a proper understanding of the Bible.

The year arrived for the establishment of the millennium. Ironically, instead of millennial peace, the year 1914 brought the worst war that the world had ever known to that time. Two years later Russell died, thus bringing to an end the first period of the history of Jehovah's Witnesses.

Joseph Franklin Rutherford (1869-1942). The nonfulfilment of the major prophecy of Russellism and the death of its founder were terrible blows to the sect, almost occasioning its demise. Why didn't it disappear? The reason is found in the contribution of another man, Joseph F. Rutherford, Russell's Elisha, who initiated and dominated a new period in the history of the sect.

Joseph Rutherford's parents were Baptist farmers in Missouri. Joseph became a lawyer and for a short time was judge in a lower court; hence he laid claim to the prestigious title of "Judge." In 1906 he identified himself with the Russellites and became the organization's lawyer. The year after Russell's death (1917) he was elected president of the tottering society.[8] He saved it from dissolution by making some adjustments in its

---

6. Royston Pike, *Jehovah's Witnesses* (New York: Philosophic Library, 1954), p. 13; *Yearbook of the Jehovah's Witnesses,* Spanish edition (Brooklyn: Watchtower Bible and Tract Society, 1973), p. 42.

7. Pike, *Witnesses,* pp. 13-14; *JWDP,* p. 62.

8. *JWDP,* pp. 65-66; Stroup, *Witnesses,* p. 8.

eschatology and providing it with a new organizational structure and practical methods of propagation.

Rutherford's major problem was how to explain the failure of Russell's prophecy. He explained it as follows: The world (age) *did* come to an end in 1914—legally. Christ was enthroned and the kingdom did begin that year, but only in heaven. There is a short transitional period between the enthronement of the King and the full establishment of the millennial reign. The forces of evil are aware of the shortness of their time and therefore are battling furiously with the forces of righteousness. The "wars and rumors of war" since 1914 are evidence of the fury of that battle. The iniquitous world moves precipitously toward Armageddon which will bring to a close the transitional period and usher in the full establishment of the kingdom.

As mentioned above, Rutherford reorganized the society into a smoothly working machine and instituted effective methods of evangelizing. He initiated the custom of annual world assemblies which did much to inspire his followers and give them an *esprit de corps*. Within a few years of his rise to leadership, the moribund sect was revived, on its feet, and advancing.

Since the death of Russell the movement had been suffering from somewhat of an identity crisis. But at the 1931 assembly held in Columbus, Ohio, Rutherford told the 15,000 who were in attendance that their name henceforth would be Jehovah's Witnesses.[9] The new name gave adherents a tremendous psychological boost, a sense of purpose and mission, and even a messianic complex. Attendance at the assemblies increased until in 1941, the year before Rutherford's death, 115,000 gathered for the assembly in Detroit.[10]

The literary contribution of Judge Rutherford eclipsed that of Russell by at least twenty times. The huge Watchtower presses in Brooklyn churned out more than 300,000,000 copies of the one hundred titles authored by Rutherford. They were printed in some seventy-eight languages.[11] Titles included *Millions Now Living Will Never Die* (1920), *The Harp of God* (1921), *Our*

---

9. *JWDP*, p. 125; Marley Cole, *Jehovah's Witnesses* (New York: Vantage, 1955), p. 101.
10. Pike, *Witnesses*, p. 95.
11. Stroup, *Witnesses*, p. 18.

Lord's Return (1928), *Reconciliation* (1927), *The Final War* (1932), *Jehovah* (1934), *Angels* (1934), *Enemies* (1937), *Religion* (1940), and *Children* (1941).

On January 8, 1942, Rutherford died, leaving the organization which was dying when he had inherited it well established and burgeoning. But the kingdom had not yet come in its fullness and Armageddon was still "just around the corner."

Nathan Knörr (1905-1977). Nathan Knörr, a Pennsylvanian, renounced his Reformed Church membership and joined the Russellites when but a youth of sixteen years. He rose rapidly in the organization's hierarchy and in 1940 was named its vice-president. Just five days after the death of Rutherford he was elected to be his successor, a step which inaugurated the third period of the Russellite movement—a period which continues to the present.[12]

During this third period there has been little doctrinal change. The major difference has been that there has not been the charismatic leadership that characterized the first two periods. One indication of this change is the fact that books published since 1942 have no indication as to their author or authors, though new titles are constantly appearing: *The Kingdom Is at Hand* (1944), *The Truth Shall Make You Free* (n.d.), *Let God Be True* (1946), *New Heavens and a New Earth* (1953), *You May Survive Armageddon* (1955), *The Truth That Leads to Eternal Life* (1968), and so forth.

Notwithstanding the lack of a powerful leader the sect has grown phenomenally during the present period. The enthusiasm which now characterizes it is not due to an inspired leader but to an inspiring cause, the "theocratic kingdom," now in its precursory stage but at any moment to be established in all of its fullness and glory.

Teachings

Regarding the Bible. The Jehovah's Witnesses appear to be biblicists in the extreme. Their books are peppered with Bible references. One commentator has dubbed them as "Bible dizzy." Nevertheless, the Jehovah's Witnesses maintain a bibliology similar to that of the old Church of Rome: the Bible must be understood according to the official interpretation of the or-

---

12. *JWDP*, p. 194.

ganization. Russell claimed that his *Studies in the Scriptures* was indispensable to a correct understanding of the Scriptures.[13] The same claim is made for current books published by the sect.[14]

In each of the three historical periods there has been an outstanding study book which in reality has served as a second Bible. During the first period it was Russell's *Studies in the Scriptures*, in the second Rutherford's *Harp of God*, and in the third it has been the anonymous *Let God Be True*.

In 1950 the Witnesses published their own version of the New Testament and in 1961 of the entire Bible, which they call the *New World Translation of the Holy Scriptures*.

Regarding the Trinity. The sect rejects the doctrine of the Trinity, declaring it to be of pagan origin. Only the Father is truly God. Jesus Christ is held to be a created being, the first creation of God. Witnesses agree with Arius that he was pre-existent but not eternally pre-existent. The *New World Translation* of John 1:1 reads: "Originally the Word was and the Word was with God and the Word was a god." In reality Jehovah's Witnesses have two gods: a supreme and absolute God, Jehovah, and an inferior, created and finite god, Jesus Christ.

Concerning the Holy Spirit they not only deny his deity but also reject the idea that he has personality. The second edition of *Let God Be True* declares: "The holy spirit *[sic]* is the invisible active force of Almighty God which moves his servants to do his will" (p. 108).

The incarnation is denied. The 1921 edition of *The Harp of God* declares, "The incarnation is scripturally erroneous. Indeed, if he [Christ] had been an incarnate being, he could never have redeemed mankind" (p. 101). Witnesses teach a total *kenosis*, that is, Christ had been a spiritual being, but on coming to this world he ceased being such and became nothing more than a perfect man. According to the second edition of *Let God Be True*, "God's justice would not let Jesus, as a ransom, be more than a perfect man. So he could not be the supreme God Almighty in the flesh" (p. 106).

13. *Watchtower* (Nov. 15, 1910), cited by Walter R. Martin and Norman H. Klann, *Jehovah of the Watchtower* (New York: Bible Truth, 1953), pp. 22-23.
14. *Watchtower* (Oct. 15, 1953), p. 620.

Their concept of Christ of course affects their doctrine of the atonement. If it was only a perfect man who died on the cross, the value of that death is clearly limited. This undoubtedly explains why Jehovah's Witnesses place little emphasis on the atoning work of Christ. In reality they do not conceive of him as a Savior from sin but as a Messiah and King about to free them from the present wicked world and set up a new social order.

Moreover, in consonance with their anthropology, "the man Jesus is dead, dead forever."[15] Thus the bodily resurrection of Christ is denied. His resurrection was spiritual and not corporeal. At his death, Christ again became a spiritual being.[16] How then do Witnesses explain the empty tomb? What happened to his body? Russell conjectured that it might have been dissolved into gases[17] and Rutherford believed that God removed it miraculously and has it preserved somewhere in the world for exposition during the millennial age.[18]

The doctrine of the spiritual resurrection of Christ naturally relates to the doctrine of his second coming. This brings us to the subject of eschatology.

Concerning the second coming and the kingdom. Manipulating numbers found in Daniel and Revelation, and the dates of certain historical events, Russell and Rutherford elaborated a prophetic program, much of which has been ignored or reconstructed by the present leadership.

According to their calculations the "time of the end" (Dan. 11:40) began in 1799. In 1874 (approximately the time when Russell began his public Bible studies) Christ came (spiritually, of course) to supervise the closing period of this age. Russell called these closing days "the harvest of the Gospel Age," and declared that it would last to 1914, the year which would usher in the millennial kingdom. The parables in Matthew 13:24-30

15. Charles T. Russell, *Studies in the Scriptures*, vol. V, p. 454, as cited by Martin and Klann, *Jehovah of the Watchtower*, p. 31.

16. Joseph F. Rutherford, *Harp of God* (Brooklyn: International Bible Students, 1921), p. 168; *Let God Be True* (Brooklyn: Watchtower Bible and Tract Society, 1952), p. 116.

17. Russell, *Studies in the Scriptures*, Vol. II, pp. 129-30, as cited by Algernon Pollock, *Millennial Dawnism Briefly Tested by Scripture* (London: Central Bible Truth, 1917), p. 12.

18. Rutherford, *Harp of God*, p. 170.

and 24:31 were held to be prophecies of this "harvest." It was expected that in 1914 the entire political and religious order of the "present age" would be overthrown and that the millennial kingdom in all its glory would be inaugurated.[19] We have already pointed out the explanation given of the strange fact that the year 1914 brought war instead of peace.

The fact that the Russellites continued to "harvest" (i.e., continued proselyting) when the "harvest age" was past needed explanation. Rutherford handled the problem neatly by saying that, just as in olden times there was a time of gleaning which followed the harvest (e.g., Ruth 2), so after the "harvest of the Gospel Age" there would be "for a time a gleaning work going on in which a few Christians would be gathered in."[20] Those "few" now sum up to almost 2,000,000! The gleaning has produced some one hundred times more grain than the harvest itself! However, the fact is that Russell's doctrine of a forty-year harvest period has long since been abandoned by the theologians of the movement.

It is also claimed that in the spring of 1918 Jesus again appeared to the world, this time to fulfill the prophecy of Malachi 3:1-3. He came in that year to "cleanse the temple" of the Witnesses, which had become "filthy" after the death of Russell in 1916. Also in that year the "rapture" prophesied in I Thessalonians 4:13-17 took place. This resurrection, however, was a spiritual one in which the first members of the elite 144,000 who form the celestial part of the kingdom arose from the dead.[21] (More will be said of this later on.)

One more event must occur before the (full) establishment of the kingdom, namely, the battle of Armageddon. When will this take place? The Witnesses do not know. The unhappy ex-

---

19. Russell, *Studies in the Scriptures*, Vol. II, pp. 99, 103, 170, 245, as quoted by C. E. Putnam, "Are Russell and Rutherford God's Prophets?" *Moody Monthly*, (April 1939), pp. 434-35.

20. Rutherford, *Harp of God*, p. 236.

21. Joseph F. Rutherford, *Jehovah* (Brooklyn: Watchtower Bible and Tract Society, 1934), pp. 48-49.

22. Nevertheless, former Jehovah's Witness, W. C. Stevenson, wrote in 1967 that some Witnesses set the date for Armageddon in the autumn of 1975. He wondered if the sect could survive the failure of another prophecy. See W. C. Stevenson, *The Inside Story of Jehovah's Witnesses* (New York: Hart, 1967), p. 194.

periences suffered in attempts to fix dates for visible events have discouraged the practice of date-setting.[22]

Regarding the church. The Jehovah's Witnesses are extremely sectarian. They identify the kingdom of God with their movement. All other religious groups, Christian as well as non-Christian, are outside. The seventh volume (posthumous) of *Studies in the Scriptures* declares that "in 1878 the stewardship of the things of God, the teaching of Bible truths, was taken away from the clergy, unfaithful to their agelong stewardship, and given to pastor Russell" (p. 386), who "in 1881 . . . became God's watchman for all Christendom" (p. 387). "The clergy's God is plainly not Jehovah but the ancient deity, hoary with the iniquity of the ages—Baal, the Devil himself" (p. 410).[23] Rutherford taught the same, claiming that religion is a "racket" (*Enemies* [Span. ed.], p. 137) and that all the established Christian churches form part of "Satan's organization" (*Juicio de los Jueces,* p. 27).

The obsession that they constitute the true kingdom of God has created a form of megalomania within the sect. *Let God Be True* (p. 257) claims that the League of Nations was instituted in 1919 as a substitute for the kingdom of God which had been set up by the followers of Russell in 1914. The world opted for the League of Nations. The League failed and was kicked into the abyss. However, at the end of World War II this hated organization was resurrected in the form of the United Nations and the world again chose it rather than the theocratic kingdom of the Witnesses.[24]

A very curious aspect of the ecclesiology of Jehovah's Witnesses is the division of their faithful into two categories: the heavenly and the earthly. The 144,000 of Revelation 7:4 represent the former group and the "great multitude" (7:9) the latter. The 144,000 are an elite group. They alone are the "bride" and "body" of Christ, the "living stones" which make up his temple, the "priests" and "kings" who will reign with him. They are to reign as spiritual beings with Christ in heaven ruling over the new earth. The "great multitude" are the "other sheep" who will experience a physical resurrection and inhabit a renewed world.

23. Quoted in B. H. Shadduck, *The Seven Thunders of Millennial Dawn* (Rogers, OH: Homo Publishing Co., 1928), pp. 7-8.
24. *Watchtower* (Sept. 15, 1953), pp. 562-63.

They constitute the subjects of the kingdom who will be ruled by the 144,000 kings reigning in heaven.[25]

The former group originated in 1918 when the first resurrection or the rapture took place (see above). Their number is being completed little by little because every time a member of this group dies, he is at once resurrected spiritually and is translated into heaven.[26]

This two-category division is in evidence right now. Only the "heavenly" have a right to participate in the "Lord's evening meal" (Lord's Supper), which takes place annually. Others are observers. Every year the number of participants becomes less, indicating that the number of 144,000 is slowly being filled up.[27] Exactly how one can become a member of this elite group is not clear from the literature. But, according to *Let God Be True* (pp. 298-303), it involves a special consecration and dedication. Membership in this elite group confers a special status in the society which is similar to that of the clergy in the classical liturgical churches or to the *perfecti* of the Albigenses of the thirteenth century.

Life and Work

The Witnesses come almost entirely from the lower socio-economic classes of society. A report in 1946 indicated that "less than one per cent of the Witnesses have a college education and comparatively few of them have completed high school."[28] There is little reason to believe that their educational level has risen significantly since then. They simply are not interested in education.

Their public gatherings have little of the traditional character of worship and seem to many to lack evangelical warmth. Their "services" are composed of spiritless singing, doctrinal lectures, and classroom-style studies based on lessons found in the *Watchtower* magazine. There seems to be little for the heart—all is naively rationalistic. Their meeting places are called "Kingdom Halls" and evidence little aesthetic sense.

---

25. Rutherford, *Let God Be True*, pp. 130, 136-39, 231-32.
26. Ibid., p. 129.
27. *JWDP*, p. 292; *Yearbook of the Jehovah's Witnesses* (1964), p. 39; *Yearbook of the Jehovah's Witnesses* (Span. ed., 1973), p. 31.
28. Bill Davidson, "Jehovah's Travelling Salesmen," *Collier's*, (November 2, 1946), p. 75.

The one consuming concern, the only ministry of the Jehovah's Witnesses, is to gain more adherents. Every believer is
obliged to be involved in the task of winning them. *Let God Be
True* (p. 224) affirms that "each Jehovah's Witness is a minister of the Gospel." Baptism, therefore, is not merely the introduction into the organization but also induction into service.
This service is called "publishing," which means going from
door to door selling literature and catechizing prospects. The
Witnesses are carefully instructed on how to approach the
prospects, catechize them and do follow-up work.

In spite of its lack of mystique, few sects have been so successful in instilling zeal for their cause. It would be difficult
to find members of any other group who work as hard at their
religion as do the Witnesses. But propagandizing is the total
of their work. They have no interest in social services, save
for what they might do for their own members. This attitude
agrees with the highly apocalyptic character of their theology.
Why apply a few bandages or give a few aspirins to this rotten
old world which is destined to be destroyed at any moment,
and then gloriously rebuilt by the Lord?

The Jehovah's Witnesses have selected two targets for special attack: the established churches and present-day governments. This appeals to many in Latin America, where political
and social corruption has been pandemic. The utopianism of the
Witnesses also has an appeal to some, especially to those who
have become pessimistic as to the possibility of any betterment
in the present order. Socially, however, they subscribe to a form
of escapism and a "balcony" type of religion (to borrow a term
from John A. Mackay) in which one sits and watches the
drama of the tragedy of the world and even rejoices in it,
instead of making some effort to alleviate it. The coming utopia
is proclaimed by the Witnesses, but it will be produced by
the Lord.

9 | JEHOVAH'S WITNESSES

Part II Their Mission

**Wilton M. Nelson and
Richard K. Smith**

The messenger. The Jehovah's Witnesses hold that Jehovah God was the founder and organizer of his witnesses on earth.[1] They trace their roots all the way back to Abel who they say was the first of a long line of witnesses.[2] Jesus Christ is referred to as the "Chief Witness" who has designated others to continue testimony of the kingdom.[3] Jesus Christ is set forth as Jehovah's leading witness for the kingdom since he was the most faithful and exemplary preacher of it.[4] The commission and ordination of Jesus, the leader of all Christian preachers (that is, the Jehovah's Witnesses), were from Jehovah God. The Witnesses

1. N. H. Knorr, "Jehovah's Witnesses of Modern Times," in *Religion in the Twentieth Century*, ed. Vergilius Ferm (New York: The Philosophical Library, 1948), p. 381.
2. Jan Karel Van Baalen, *The Chaos of Cults* (Grand Rapids: Eerdmans, 1942), p. 262.
3. Knorr, "Witnesses of Modern Times," p. 381.
4. *The Kingdom Is at Hand* (Brooklyn: Watchtower Bible and Tract Society, Inc., 1944), p. 223.

point out that this did not come through any kind of religious ceremony. Christ dedicated himself to do God's will and was immersed in water to so symbolize. God accepted his self-dedication and anointed him with the "holy spirit."[5]

Following the example of Jesus Christ, the believer is required to dedicate himself unconditionally to do the divine will of God. The believer must do this with full faith in Jesus Christ as the ransom sacrifice by which his sins against God can be forgiven and canceled. One's dedication to do God's will is properly symbolized by being immersed in water.

To make good his salvation to everlasting life the believer must be a preacher in this world.[6] Every true Witness is considered a minister and is dedicated to give his time and his life, if need be, to the fulfilment of Jehovah's work.[7] Witnesses consider themselves to be ambassadors of God's kingdom. Therefore they expect the same rights and exemptions that officials of secular governments enjoy. They consider themselves aliens even in the country where they were born and raised. Therefore, as aliens they refuse to give allegiance or assume political obligations of any sort. They will not vote, salute the flag or be drafted into the armed forces of their country. On occasion such a policy brings the Witnesses into conflict with governmental authorities.[8]

The method. Jesus is set forth by the Witnesses as an example of the method that they should follow in performing their ministries. They point out that Christ preached everywhere —in the cities and villages, in homes and in public places—taking the message of the kingdom directly to the people.[9] They also point out that there were no buildings erected or bells rung to call people to come and hear Christ preach. Rather, Christ went to the homes of the people where he built up an interest

5. *This Means Everlasting Life* (Brooklyn: Watchtower Bible and Tract Society, Inc., 1950), p. 136.

6. Ibid., p. 137.

7. Marcus Bach, *Strange Sects and Curious Cults* (New York: Dodd, Mead & Co., 1961), p. 116.

8. Bryan Wilson, *Religious Sects* (New York: McGraw-Hill Book Co., 1970), p. 114.

9. *The Truth That Leads to Eternal Life* (Brooklyn: Watchtower Bible and Tract Society, Inc., 1968), p. 184.

in the kingdom. He then made "revisits" or "back calls" to these homes.[10]

The work of the Witnesses is to be done in the very same manner as Jesus did it—namely, from house to house, city to city, province to province, and publicly. Faithfulness must be shown by performing their commission to preach in spite of any and all opposition. It is in this manner that they like Jesus prove their trustworthiness.[11]

The message. The first aspect of the message is to declare the name and the kingdom of Jehovah or theocratic government. The Witnesses boldly announce the supremacy of Jehovah, making it possible for those who hear and obey to find protection and salvation. Jehovah is said to extend his mercy toward those practitioners of religion who have been deceived and held as prisoners in the religious organizations, and who unwittingly have walked with religionists.[12]

The Witnesses regard their preaching work as having been foretold by Jesus in Matthew 24:14. They preach the good news that God's kingdom was set up in heaven in the year 1914 when God installed his Son Jesus Christ as King of the new world. Witness concerning God's kingdom must be given to all the nations before the world's end comes at Armageddon.[13]

Witnesses believe that since 1919 Jehovah has revived his Witnesses and made them his watchmen to cry out the warning of the sword of Armageddon's war.[14] The Witnesses offer the opportunity to live through the impending battle of Armageddon and help repopulate the new world. This climactic battle between good and evil, Jehovah God and Satan, they say, may begin at any moment. People are therefore urged to align themselves with Jehovah and his kingdom.[15]

---

10. *The Kingdom Is at Hand*, p. 223.

11. *Let God Be True* (Brooklyn: Watchtower Bible and Tract Society, Inc., 1946), p. 132.

12. *Children* (Brooklyn: Watchtower Bible and Tract Society, Inc., 1941), pp. 208-09, 226.

13. *From Paradise Lost to Paradise Regained* (Brooklyn: Watchtower Bible and Tract Society of New York, Inc., 1958), pp. 185, 248.

14. *New Heavens and a New Earth* (Brooklyn: Watchtower Bible and Tract Society, Inc., 1953), p. 292.

15. William J. Whalen, *Armageddon Around the Corner* (New York: John Day Co., 1962), p. 15.

Reconciliation to God is mentioned but not explained as to what it involves.[16] The Watchtower Society does not speak of any spiritual relationship such as "being in Christ." Although it urges that a person must put faith in Jehovah God and in Christ Jesus, the recurring stress is on the importance of being dedicated to faithfully carrying out God's will whereby men will be awarded everlasting life.[17]

The main teaching of the group may be stated rather simply. The kingdom of heaven is at hand. The end of the age is near and Armageddon is just around the corner, when the wicked will be destroyed and the theocracy, or rule of God, will be set up on the earth.[18]

An Apologetic and Polemic

The Jehovah's Witnesses base their apologetics on a belief in God and in the authority and infallibility of the Bible. Watchtower publications make few attempts to persuade the agnostic who rejects belief in both God and the Bible.[19]

Nowhere do the society's writings try to "prove" the existence of Jehovah God as does St. Thomas Aquinas in his five proofs.[20] For the Witnesses, the Bible teaches that there is one God, who in the Old Testament is called Jehovah.[21] God must be known under his proper name, Jehovah, in order that he be distinguished from false gods. In Watchtower publications God appears to possess all those attributes which are ascribed to him in the Bible. But the stress appears clearly to lie upon the side of his power and his inexorable justice rather than upon the side of his love and forgiveness. He is a jealous God who requires submission.[22] His supremacy has been challenged by Satan who caused the rebellion in Eden and who puts the integrity of all men to test. God's primary purpose is the vindication of

---

16. *Things in Which It Is Impossible for God to Lie* (Brooklyn: Watchtower Bible and Tract Society of New York, Inc., 1965), p. 404.
17. *Let God Be True,* revised edition (Brooklyn: Watchtower Bible and Tract Society, 1952), p. 279.
18. Charles Samuel Braden, *These Also Believe* (New York: Macmillan Co., 1949), p. 370.
19. Whalen, *Armageddon,* p. 99.
20. Ibid.
21. Gustave Weigel, *Churches in North America: An Introduction* (Baltimore: Helicon Press, 1961), p. 96.
22. Braden, *These Also Believe,* p. 371.

his supremacy.[23] He is a jealous God who requires submission and exaltation of his name. Those who blaspheme it must be brought low.[24] Those who reject the truth of Jehovah will be utterly destroyed by fire and those who are loyal to Jehovah will live forever.[25] God is, to be sure, Father, or Life-Giver, the giver of every good and perfect gift. But this side of his nature is not emphasized in Watchtower writings.[26]

The Witnesses believe in the Bible's complete inspiration and divine authority.[27] They insist that the Bible and the Bible alone is the source of their beliefs.[28] They maintain that the Bible is the full and accurate record of Jehovah's revelation of himself and of his plans for the world and man.[29] As for the authority of the Bible, the Witnesses say that its inner harmony and the loftiness of its message guarantee its inspiration.[30] Because the Bible is regarded as the infallible word of God, the Witnesses hold that its words must be taken literally and at face value.[31] To quote a passage of Scripture in support of any teaching is considered sufficient to establish the truth.[32]

Though Jehovah's Witnesses have never resorted to violence or illegal means in defense of their beliefs, they have been outspoken against those doctrines and religious practices which they do not believe are supported by the Bible. They rely entirely on the Bible as an offensive weapon.[33] Thus the Bible is not only their apologetic but also their polemic.

The Witnesses travel from city to city, preaching vigorously and attracting attention by assurances that "there is no hell"

---

23. Milton G. Henschel, "Who Are Jehovah's Witnesses?" in *Religions in America,* ed. Leo Rosten (New York: Simon & Schuster, 1963), p. 96.
24. Braden, *These Also Believe,* p. 371.
25. Weigel, *Churches,* p. 97.
26. Braden, *These Also Believe,* p. 371.
27. Ibid., p. 379.
28. Weigel, *Churches,* p. 96.
29. Walter B. Stuermann, "Jehovah's Witnesses," *Interpretation* 10 (July 1956), 332.
30. Whalen, *Armageddon,* p. 99.
31. Louis Cassells, *What's the Difference?: A Comparison of the Faiths Men Live By* (Garden City, NY: Doubleday & Co., 1965), p. 172.
32. Braden, *These Also Believe,* p. 379.
33. A. H. Macmillan, *Faith on the March* (Englewood Cliffs, NJ: Prentice-Hall, 1957), p. 162.

and that "millions now living will never die."[34] They claim that they have "discovered" and can interpret the real meaning of Christianity.[35] They will generally point to the calamitous world conditions of our time, placing the responsibility for all existing evil upon Christendom, which is equated with Babylon, or Satan's organization. Failure to bring better times to the world is blamed on Christendom as a whole. Such an approach appeals to hard-pressed people who are desperately looking for any straw which might be grasped in order to save the world from going to its destruction.[36]

Methods of Propagation

Attitude towards other religious bodies. The Jehovah's Witnesses strongly deny that their movement is religious.[37] Rutherford said that religion is doing anything contrary to the will of God and that it is of the devil.[38] They call it Babylon.[39] Over against religion stand the Jehovah's Witnesses—announcers of the gospel of the kingdom, and the coming of the theocracy, or the rule of God.[40]

The Witnesses are quite hostile toward the churches for church members are "religionists" and "teach religion." Witnesses attack the teaching, organization and ministry of both Protestantism and Catholicism. Watchtower publications refer to Protestantism as the offspring of the great harlot. Following devilish wisdom, the offspring is as dead as she is.[41] Its clergy are accused of trying to keep the message of truth from the people.[42]

---

34. Elmer T. Clark, *The Small Sects of America* (New York: Abingdon Press, 1949), p. 44.
35. Walter R. Martin, *The Christian and the Cults* (Grand Rapids: Zondervan, 1956), p. 62.
36. Albert Muller, "Jehovah's Witnesses Call," *Homiletic and Pastoral Review*, May 1963, p. 680.
37. Braden, *These Also Believe*, p. 358.
38. *Religion Reaps the Whirlwind* (Brooklyn: Watchtower Bible and Tract Society, Inc., 1944), p. 58.
39. *Enemies* (Brooklyn: Watchtower Bible and Tract Society, Inc., 1937), pp. 66, 71.
40. Braden, *These Also Believe*, p. 358.
41. William J. Schnell, *Thirty Years a Watch Tower Slave* (Grand Rapids: Baker, 1956), p. 184.
42. *Preservation* (Brooklyn: Watchtower Bible and Tract Society, Inc., 1932), p. 66.

Under Knorr's presidency and leadership the Jehovah's Witnesses have been given a thorough public relations face lifting and as a consequence they now have a more sophisticated look. Witnesses are now trained to be proficient and to avoid being abrasive. Propagation methods, although forceful and effective, are not as high-pressured as in the past. Watchtower publications are now more positive and much less prone to attack others. The attacks on religion, the churches and clergy, made largely during Rutherford's presidency, have not been retracted. But in present-day Watchtower publications such attacks are made in a more diplomatic style. The Witnesses still do not recognize any other body within Christendom. They boldly proclaim that the truth can be found only in their movement.

Public forums. Jehovah's Witnesses believe that they must preach the kingdom message around the world before this generation passes away because the end of the age is fast approaching. They use all possible ways of getting the message out.[43]

In 1945 Knorr instituted a method of getting the message out by directing local congregations to sponsor regular public meetings on selected Sunday afternoons.[44] The one-hour talks are usually well advertised by means of house-to-house canvassing and handbills. To insure uniformity of presentation the society provides new topics and outlines for these talks each year. The speakers are either adult male witnesses of the local congregations or visiting representatives of the society.[45]

The Witnesses have used circuit assemblies, district assemblies, and national and international conventions in furthering their work.[46] At some of the conventions important doctrinal pronouncements have been made. Not only do these conventions receive much space in press, radio and television, they also give an ostentatious display of organizational unanimity, discipline, and drive. The conventions also are calculated to stimulate the members so that they will increase their propa-

43. Henschel, "Who Are Jehovah's Witnesses?" p. 102.
44. Whalen, *Armageddon*, p. 71.
45. Edmond Charles Gruss, *Apostles of Denial* (Nutley, NJ: Presbyterian and Reformed Publishing Co., 1970), p. 245.
46. Ibid.

gation efforts.[47] Often there are reports of converts joining the ranks during some of the conventions for while Witnesses hold their conferences they also witness from door-to-door.[48]

The printed page. Without question the most important phase of the propagation of the Jehovah's Witnesses is their vast publishing enterprise.[49] The printed page is extremely important to the growth of the society.[50] Perhaps no other religious body has used the printed page so extensively and so successfully.[51] Under Knorr's administration the Watchtower presses have turned out an average of more than one new book each year.[52] The great modern printing plant in Brooklyn annually turns out an amazing amount of printed matter for circulation all over the world.[53] The immense circulation of the Watchtower publications dwarfs that of most other religious periodicals.[54] It is even claimed that their total output exceeds that of all Catholic publishers in the United States combined.[55] Numerous Watchtower books have reached millions of copies. During 1974, 18,239,169 booklets and 51,663,097 Bibles were printed.[56]

The *Watchtower,* first issued in July, 1879, and *Awake!* have a total monthly circulation of almost 40,000,000. The *Watchtower* is published in seventy-nine languages and *Awake!* in thirty-one languages. The magazines are usually used to gain entrance into the home of prospective converts.[57] To sustain interest in the message of the impending disaster of this world the Witness tries to leave copies of various books and magazines in the hands of all those he contacts. The magazine *Awake!* is a most effective tool in this regard. Its front cover features some of the subjects to be dealt with on the inside. These subjects are usually of current interest or of a controversial nature in order to arouse reader curiosity. There is always a section (and often a main

47. Muller, "Witnesses Call," p. 680.
48. Bach, *Strange Sects,* p. 122.
49. Braden, *These Also Believe,* p. 369.
50. Gruss, *Apostles,* p. 240.
51. Braden, *These Also Believe,* p. 360.
52. Gruss, *Apostles,* p. 240.
53. Braden, *These Also Believe,* p. 369.
54. Whalen, *Armageddon,* p. 17.
55. Muller, "Witnesses Call," p. 679.
56. *1974 Yearbook of Jehovah's Witnesses* (Brooklyn: Watchtower Bible and Tract Society of Pennsylvania, 1975), p. 259.
57. Gruss, *Apostles,* p. 240.

article) devoted completely to an exposition of Witness theology or the tearing down of other beliefs. The *Watchtower*
magazine could be termed the cult's religious journal.[58]

In Watchtower parlance the Witnesses are known as "publishers." They buy their literature at a small discount and must
dispose of a set quota each month. Witnesses often lose money
on these transactions because they give away many publications
(particularly the magazines) to prospects who do not make a
donation.[59]

The door-to-door appeals. In the total missionary program of
the Jehovah's Witnesses the two factors that are likely to contribute most to rapid growth are the prolific use of the printed
page and the aggressive door-to-door witnessing. Witnesses are
given assigned territories that are their missionary responsibility.
They try to make at least two calls a year on every household
in their assigned areas. The Witness probably averages at least
ten homes a week. All hours spent in doorstep preaching,
return or back calls on interested prospects, and the organiz-
ing and conducting of home Bible studies are carefully tabu-
lated in the local Kingdom Hall and reported periodically to
Brooklyn headquarters.[60] In 1975 the total hours of such door-
to-door witnessing and other types of missionary work throughout the world reached a staggering 382,296,208 hours.[61]

Sometimes Witnesses will go from door-to-door alone but
usually two Witnesses work together as a team. They are prepared to talk at the door if not invited to enter the home. They
proceed to a discussion marked out along definite lines, for the
supposedly extemporaneous Bible discussion is in reality a
carefully planned Watchtower missionary outline, well studied
and rehearsed. As we have seen, Witnesses will often carry
copies of some of the key Watchtower books which they attempt
to sell to interested prospects. They may quote liberally from
these "authoritative" publications. When the Witness departs,
the latest edition of *Watchtower* and *Awake!* magazines will
be left behind for a small donation, or at his own expense.[62]

---

58. Ibid., pp. 240-41.
59. Whalen, *Armageddon*, p. 17.
60. Ibid., pp. 16-17.
61. *Watchtower*, January 1, 1976, p. 23.
62. Martin, *The Christian and the Cults*, p. 62.

The Witnesses' approach is generally to present their message of the theocratic kingdom first and then to make a diplomatic attack on the cardinal teachings of historic Christianity.[63] Until a person is deeply committed to their "theocratic movement" the Witnesses make no mention of controversial matters such as their refusal of blood transfusions.[64] They capitalize on the respect most persons have for the Bible by quoting voluminously from the Scriptures, often in violation of the context. Witnesses are hostile toward the fundamentals of Christian theology and utilize many Bible quotations to "establish" their objections.[65] They are prepared to discuss doctrines upon which they place special emphasis. They make extensive use of both their own translations of the Bible, and their own textbooks, to which they appeal as being completely authoritative.

The Witness is taught that one of his first objectives is to gain entrance to the house of the prospect. If it is snowing or raining he uses the discomfort of the householder to suggest that it would be better if he stepped inside to explain his purpose. If a man answers the door the discussion might begin with some remark about the worsening world situation. The conversation may gradually move on to the battle of Armageddon. If a woman answers, the "publisher" may begin more directly with a religious message. He may seek agreement to the proposition that it is a shame that people do not read and study the Bible as much as they should. He always tries to get several affirmative answers to maneuver the prospect into a mood of agreement.[66]

After a few minutes the Witness will explain the nature of the literature he is selling. The Witness is urged to convince people that the literature is a product of careful research, not a compilation of individual opinions and interpretations. He is instructed to ask for a contribution and to try to get the householder to accept one of his books. If the "publisher" makes a sale he is supposed to tell the buyer that he is now entitled

---

63. Ibid., pp. 63-64.
64. Alan Bestic, *Praise the Lord and Pass the Contribution* (New York: Taplinger Publishing Co., 1971), p. 232.
65. Martin, *The Christian and the Cults*, pp. 63-64.
66. Whalen, *Armageddon*, p. 114.

to a free private lesson on the contents of the book. The ideal is to set a specific date and time for the back call immediately.[67]

The Witnesses ask questions and attempt to get the prospect to commit himself. They do not tell the "person of good will" (one who is receptive to the Watchtower message) that he will be required to quit his religion if he accepts the message. This will be the case, of course, but at the outset many people are given the impression that the Witnesses are representative of some Christian Bible society rather than the agents of one of the world's best-organized iconoclastic cults.[68]

As indicated previously, as calls are completed, Witnesses must fill out detailed reports concerning their door-to-door work. At the end of each month each Witness must submit a field service report listing the hours spent in doorstep preaching, the total number of books and magazines sold, the subscriptions obtained, and the back calls made.[69] This door-to-door missionary work is done at the Witnesses' own expense. There are, however, numerous Witnesses who preach and teach full-time in isolated areas. In 1974 there were 1,102 full-time missionaries of the society and 13,629 special "pioneer publishers." The latter spend a minimum of 150 hours each month going from house to house and conducting home Bible studies. These full-time workers are assisted with accommodations, meals, travel, and clothing expenses. In 1974 the Society spent $8,812,-245.60 to help such workers carry on their work.[70]

The seven-step program. Witnesses do not stalk converts in a haphazard or hit-and-miss fashion. They follow a systematic seven-step program to bring others into the Watchtower Society.[71] Once this program has run its course, the candidate seldom reverts.[72]

(1) The first step is to get a Watchtower book or magazine into the hands of the householder. Each doorstep sermon concludes with an offer of a Watchtower publication. The price is small, possibly no more than fifty cents for a book of medium

---

67. Ibid.
68. Ibid.
69. Ibid., pp. 111-12.
70. 1975 Yearbook, p. 258.
71. Whalen, Armageddon, p. 110.
72. Gruss, Apostles, p. 247.

size. Copies of *Watchtower* and *Awake!* magazines are always left behind whether purchased by the prospect or given gratis by the Witness.

(2) The second step is the "back call" which is designed to encourage the purchaser to read and study the book(s) he has received. The Witness makes comments designed to create more interest in the book(s). Dramtic events are often related to whet the prospect's appetite. There is also an attempt to dislodge any and all of his loosely held ideas on religion and religious practices.

(3) As a third step the Witness tries to get the prospect to agree to attend a weekly home Bible study session on the book(s) in question. The course has little to do with the Bible as such because the main textbooks are Watchtower publications designed to implant new ideas, that is, the society's beliefs. The "person of good will" is strongly encouraged to subscribe to *Watchtower* and *Awake!* as part of his study.[73]

(4) The fourth step is to invite the prospective convert to join one of the area study groups.[74] The territory of each local congregation is divided into areas, and studies under direct congregational supervision are held in each area. Leaders are referred to as "study conductors."[75] Homes selected for the studies are designated "service centers."[76] There the prospective convert meets additional active Witnesses and is engaged in a carefully controlled dialogue.[77] At the close of each study coming activities and plans of the local congregation are announced.[78]

(5) The fifth step is to invite the new candidate to attend the "Watchtower Study" in a Kingdom Hall.[79] This meeting, which generally follows the Sunday public talk, is the most important meeting of the week. It is important because it is believed that the *Watchtower* is the channel through which God gives additional light on His word. The study session is led by the "study conductor." Members are expected to study the magazine before coming so they will be prepared to partici-

73. Ibid., p. 132.
74. Whalen, *Armageddon*, p. 111.
75. Schnell, *Watch Tower Slave*, p. 133.
76. Gruss, *Apostles*, p. 244.
77. Whalen, *Armageddon*, p. 111.
78. Gruss, *Apostles*, p. 244.
79. Whalen, *Armageddon*, p. 111.

pate in a controlled but open discussion.[80] Potential converts are warmly welcomed by the believers and are shown how they themselves have learned. By this time candidates may have come to regard their former church home (if any) as simply part of Satan's empire.[81]

(6) As a sixth step the new candidate is asked to help bring in other people by calling on his neighbors even as someone called on him. To do this preaching effectively and in harmony with the "plan of God," the candidate must join with the Jehovah's Witnesses as they prepare and plan their preaching work.[82] This is done in the "service meeting" which is held one night each week. Better methods and means of presenting the message and literature of the Witnesses are discussed at that time. The order of this service is outlined in the monthly publication, *Kingdom Ministry*.[83]

(7) The seventh and final step is to encourage the convert to be regular in his attendance at the various meetings, and to convince him that he must dedicate himself to God's service through water baptism. Baptism officially inducts the candidate into the organization of Jehovah's Witnesses as a "kingdom publisher" or "minister."[84]

Organization for Propagation

The Watchtower Society is well organized to effect the program we have outlined. The highest official is the president. Twelve directors serve under him. At the helm in each country where Witnesses work there is a "branch servant" who is assisted by regional, district, circuit, zone and congregation servants.[85] It is the responsibility of these servants to stimulate the Witnesses and their congregations, to see that they distribute their quota of literature, to audit the local books, and to hold zone assemblies and district conferences. Appointed over the local companies are the "company servants" or "service directors" who correspond to the local pastors of Protestant churches.[86]

---

80. Gruss, *Apostles*, p. 244.
81. Whalen, *Armageddon*, p. 111.
82. Gruss, *Apostles*, p. 248.
83. Ibid., pp. 244-45.
84. Ibid., pp. 248-49.
85. Muller, "Witnesses Call," p. 678.
86. Braden, *These Also Believe*, pp. 365-66.

These leaders are considered to be on the same level with regular members, however, because Russell viewed the clergy-laity distinction as pagan.[87]

Every member is considered a minister and all are required to give generously of their time and money in proclaiming their faith and teachings. These rank-and-file members or ministers are divided into two groups: "publishers" and "pioneers." The publisher devotes an average of about fifteen hours a month to preaching the kingdom.[88] He holds a full-time secular job, attends four or five classes a week in Kingdom Hall, participates in a Bible study group, and tries to devote his spare hours to doorstep preaching.[89] While encouraged to live and eat at a decent level, he is invited to turn over any surplus wealth or income to the movement. (The Witnesses neither tithe their incomes nor pass the collection plate in their services. Members drop their contributions in a box at the rear of each local Kingdom Hall.[90])

The second group of ministers constitutes the elite of the organization. These "pioneers" are divided into "general pioneers" and "special pioneers." General pioneers are expected to give a minimum of one hundred hours of service a month which may be in a place of their own choosing. They do not receive any financial support from the society though members of the congregation will voluntarily give them a little help on occasion. Generally, they live very frugal lives.[91]

Special pioneers are supposed to give a minimum of 150 hours of service and make not less than fifty back calls each month. They are sent to smaller towns where there are no regular companies. They may help weaker companies in other communities, however. They receive a monthly allowance from headquarters.

Women may serve as ministers in the society but male supremacy is maintained in the congregations. No woman may hold a teaching post, deliver public lectures, or direct the activi-

87. Macmillan, *Faith on the March*, p. 159.
88. F. S. Mead, *Handbook of Denominations in the United States* (New York: Abingdon Press, 1961), p. 119.
89. Whalen, *Armageddon*, p. 118.
90. W. J. Whalen, *Separated Brethren* (Milwaukee: Bruce, 1958), p. 180.
91. Bestic, *Praise the Lord*, p. 236.

ties of the men; women are not to argue with, contradict, or give instructions to men.[92]

The society believes that even children may participate as ministers of the gospel. Some sell magazines on the street corners. Some accompany their parents or older Witnesses on the door-to-door calls. They also participate in all the meetings in the Kingdom Hall.[93]

Conclusion

The Jehovah's Witnesses is one of the most successful religious movements of the twentieth century—successful in terms of marshaling its members and their resources, ordering its priorities and arguments, and utilizing its opportunities for face-to-face and mass communication. Critics of the movement may have many misgivings when evaluating its precepts and propagation, but most of them will also have much to learn in the latter category.

---

92. Whalen, *Armageddon*, p. 117.
93. Ibid.

Jerald and Sandra Tanner

Jerald and Sandra Tanner were both raised in the Mormon faith, and are descendants of prominent Mormon pioneers. Sandra is a great-great-granddaughter of Brigham Young. After diligent research they gave up Mormonism and turned to Christ. Since 1964 they have spent full time in research and writing to bring the factual history of that religion to light and point its adherents to Christ. They have published numerous pamphlets and books, including a most comprehensive work, Mormonism—Shadow or Reality? *In the October 8, 1966, issue of* The Evangelical Beacon, *Dean Kenneth Kantzer of Trinity Evangelical Divinity School referred to the Tanners' research as "the definite, fully-documented, utterly devastating case against the divine authority and truthfulness of the foundational documents upon which the Mormon religion is based."*

10 | MORMONISM

Jerald and Sandra Tanner

Who could have predicted 150 years ago that one branch of a North American-based church not yet founded would succeed in marshaling a missionary force of 23,000 and gathering a membership of over 3,500,000 in less than a century and a half? Yet, on May 7, 1976, *Christianity Today* reported the 1975 world membership of this movement as 3,570,000 and notes that the figure represents an increase of almost 50 per cent over a ten-year period. (The membership figure projected for 1982 is 6,000,000.)

This record of growth, of course, belongs to the Church of Jesus Christ of Latter-day Saints which began in 1830. In that year the Mormon prophet Joseph Smith published the *Book of Mormon*—a book which purports to be a history of the "former inhabitants of this continent." The same year he organized a church in the state of New York. Today, there are two main groups which claim to base their teachings on Joseph Smith's writings. They are the Church of Jesus Christ of Latter-day Saints and the Reorganized Church of Jesus Christ of Latter-day Saints. The larger of these is the Utah-based Church of Jesus Christ of Latter-day Saints—the religious movement with which we are concerned in this study.

Understanding Mormonism

Joseph Smith's call. When Joseph Smith was a young man, his family moved from Vermont to New York. He claimed that in the spring of 1820, at the age of fourteen, he went out into the woods to pray for wisdom concerning church membership. At that time God the Father and Jesus Christ appeared to him as two separate, distinct beings and told him not to join any church "for they were all wrong; and the Personage who addressed me said that all their creeds were an abomination in his sight; that those professors were all corrupt."[1]

Then, in 1823, an angel appeared to Joseph to tell him of an ancient record hid in a nearby hill. The next day Smith uncovered the gold plates, and, if his story is true, he made one of the greatest discoveries in the history of archaeology. These plates contained "an account of the former inhabitants of this continent, and the source from whence they sprang." More important than this, however, they contained "the fulness of the everlasting gospel." According to the Mormon leaders the *Book of Mormon* is far superior to the Bible because it contains the "pure" words of Christ. The Mormon Apostle LeGrand Richards claims:

> "The "everlasting gospel" could not be discovered through reading the Bible alone . . . this is the only Christian church in the world that did not have to rely upon the Bible for its organization and government; . . . if we had no Bible we would still have all the needed direction and information through the revelations of the Lord "to his servants the prophets" in these latter-days.[2]

Joseph Smith, as God's prophet, seer, and revelator, claimed to restore Christ's true church in 1830. Many of his revelations are printed in *The Doctrine and Covenants,* a volume of Mormon scripture. In 1835 Joseph bought some Egyptian mummies and rolls of papyrus. He claimed one of the rolls contained the writings of Abraham while in Egypt. This was incorporated in another volume of Mormon scripture, *The Pearl of Great Price.* This work also contains the *Book of Moses* and Joseph Smith's

---

1. *The Pearl of Great Price* (Salt Lake City: Church of Jesus Christ of Latter-day Saints, 1950), p. 46.
2. LeGrand Richards, *A Marvelous Work and a Wonder* (Salt Lake City: Deseret Book Co., 1966), p. 41.

personal history of the founding of Mormonism. The main sources of Mormon doctrine are *The Doctrine and Covenants* and *The Pearl of Great Price*.

During the first fourteen years of Mormonism, Joseph Smith was able to expand the ranks of his church to 35,000 members. Today it is one of the twelve largest churches in the United States. Approximately one out of every one hundred United States citizens is a Mormon.

Unique beliefs. While traditional Christianity maintains God is absolute, man is basically sinful, and salvation is by God's grace, Mormonism boldly asserts that God is a progressive being, man is a god in embryo, and salvation is by works.

In one of Joseph Smith's last sermons he stated,

> First, God himself, who sits enthroned in yonder heavens, is a man like unto one of yourselves, that is the great secret. . . . I am going to tell you how God came to be God. We have imagined that God was God from all eternity . . . God himself; the Father of us all dwelt on earth the same as Jesus Christ himself did. . . . Jesus said, as the Father hath power in himself, even so hath the Son power; to do what? Why what the Father did, that answer is obvious; in a manner to lay down his body and take it up again. Jesus, what are you going to do? To lay down my life, as my Father did, and take it up again. . . . You have got to learn how to be Gods yourselves; to be kings and priests to God, the same as all Gods have done; by going from a small degree to another, from grace to grace, from exaltation to exaltation. . . .[3]

The Mormons also have a unique concept of the fall. They believe Adam made the right choice in eating of the fruit in the garden. By this act he became mortal and thus capable of fathering the human race. Bruce R. McConkie, a Mormon apostle, explains that,

> according to the foreordained plan, Adam was to fall. . . . Adam was to introduce mortality and all that attends it, so that the opportunity for eternal progression and perfection might be offered to all the spirit children of the Father.
>
> In conformity with the will of the Lord, Adam fell both spiritually and temporally.[4]

---

3. *Times and Seasons* 5 (Aug. 15, 1844), 613-14.
4. Bruce R. McConkie, *Mormon Doctrine* (Salt Lake City: Bookcraft, 1966), p. 268.

According to Mormonism the result of the fall was mortal death, not a fallen nature. Thus the atonement of Christ was to provide release from mortal death by giving resurrection to all men. When Mormons speak of salvation by grace they are generally referring to universal resurrection. They believe all men will be saved (resurrected), but whatever one receives beyond this is by good works.

The priesthood. The Mormon Church has no paid ministers other than those referred to as "General Authorities." Apostle Hugh B. Brown defines this term as follows:

> The presiding authority of the Church is the First Presidency, consisting of three high priests, a president and his two counselors. Associated with them and next in authority are twelve apostles who have twelve assistants, . . . also a Patriarch to the church. . . . .
>
> Also numbered among the General Authorities of the Church is the First Council of The Seventy. . . . Next in order is the Presiding Bishopric, three high priests. . . .
>
> These presiding quorums in the Church are made up of men from various walks of life. . . . When men are called into this ministry they give up their activities and devote themselves exclusively to Church work.[5]

Apostle Brown goes on to explain that the Mormon priesthood has two divisions—the Melchizedek and Aaronic—each with its own responsibilities. The former directs all the affairs of the church (general, stake, ward and mission). It has its various quorums, namely, the High Priest's Quorum, the Quorum of the Seventy, and the Elder's Quorum (in descending order of authority). The responsibilities of the Aaronic order are apparent in the names of its various quorums—the Priest's, Teacher's, and Deacon's Quorums. Every male member of the church who is over twelve years of age (except a Negro) has the privilege of being ordained to some office in the priesthood, if he lives "worthily."

A bishop presides over a congregation of about 400 to 1,000 members, known as a ward. He continues to work at his regular employment, performing his duties as bishop in his free time. The many responsibilities attached to directing a ward are

5. Hugh B. Brown, *Mormonism* (Salt Lake City: Deseret News Press, 1963), p. 13.

L.D.S. CHURCH ORGANIZATION

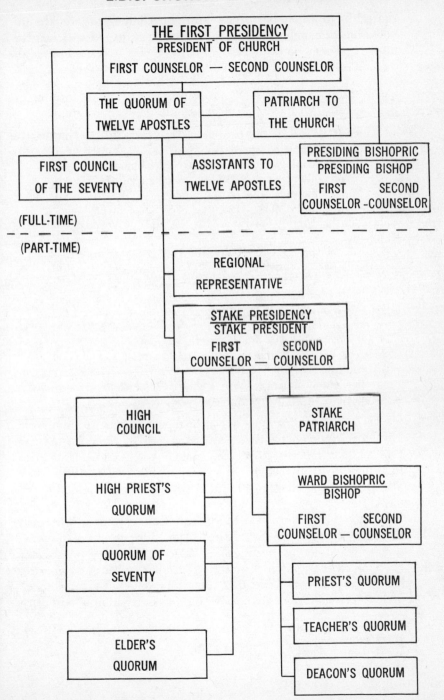

shared by the members. The Mormon Church, seeking to involve all its members, has a ratio of one officer or teacher for every 2.65 members.

The Missionary Program

Every six minutes someone joins the church, according to the Mormon *1974 Church Almanac*. It goes on to state:

> When 1971 ended, the church had passed the three-million-member milestone by more than 90,000, and, since that time, nearly 240 people per day have received membership.
>
> In July, there were 3,218,908 members of the church. . . .
>
> The greatest majority of the members—2,525,279—reside in the United States. The remaining 693,629 members, who live outside the United States, are in the area of greatest church growth.
>
> Membership growth outside the United States since 1960 is up 350 per cent, while inside the country, the growth is a slower, but still impressive, 77 per cent. . . .
>
> South America, with 134,383 members . . . is the largest of nine divisions of church membership outside the United States.
>
> Rapid growth also has been seen in other areas of the world, including the South Pacific with 98,558 members . . . Mexico, 92,108 members . . . Great Britain, 71,638 members . . . and Europe, 62,097 members. . . .
>
> In Central America there are 35,449 members . . . while Canada has 55,532 members.[6]

The *Salt Lake Tribune* recently reported that Mormons are currently experiencing their fastest growth in London.[7] At the time of that report (1974) the church had 1,600 missionaries in Britain, more than twice the number they had in 1960. They also claimed 250 chapels in Britain with a new one added every week!

Of the more than 6,000 Mormons on the continent of Africa, the majority live in South Africa. The Mormons have no missionary work among the blacks of Africa, although a few blacks have joined the church. Bruce R. McConkie, a Mormon apostle, has stated: "Negroes in this life are denied the priesthood; under no circumstances can they hold this delegation of authority

---

6. *Deseret News 1974 Church Almanac* (Salt Lake City: Deseret News, 1974), p. 116.
7. *Salt Lake Tribune*, November 26, 1974, p. 25.

from the Almighty. The gospel message of salvation is not carried affirmatively to them."[8] The Mormons once tried to establish a work in Nigeria but were refused visas because of this racial policy of denying priesthood to blacks. At home or abroad the Mormons proselyte primarily among people with a Christian background. In 1973 they made their very first Moslem convert in Beirut, Lebanon. The *1974 Church Almanac* states that Fahman Fatafitah was "apparently the first Moslem to join the church in the Middle East. Though other Arabs had joined the church, they had been of a Christian background."[9]

The training program. Generally, a Mormon missionary is between nineteen and twenty-one years old and will serve for two years. Young women, twenty-one or older, may also serve on missions, but for only eighteen months. Each missionary is responsible for his expenses while on his mission assignment and the church pays his entire return fare.

Mormon youth are prepared for future missionary work through the seminary program. This entails high-school level classes in religious instruction which meet off campus for one hour five days a week (during the school term). The four-year course covers the Old Testament, New Testament, *Book of Mormon*, and history of the Mormon Church. There are over 170,000 students enrolled in this program currently. At the college level there is a similar program called the Institute of Religion, with approximately 62,000 students currently enrolled.

Before a missionary goes to a foreign language area he takes an eight-week language course in one of the Mormon schools. In order to meet the growing demand for missionaries the Mormons now plan to build a new Language Training Mission Complex on their Brigham Young University campus in Provo, Utah. The Brigham Young alumni paper reported:

> It's a profound combination: Take BYU and add a multi-million dollar language center designed to teach at least 20 languages to 22,250 missionaries each year. The result is, as one observer conjured [sic], the "language center of the world.". . .
> Currently, 20 languages are being taught to missionaries in widely separated locations of Provo, Ricks Colleges and BYU-

8. Bruce McConkie, *Mormon Doctrine* (Salt Lake City: Bookcraft, 1958), p. 477.
9. *Deseret News 1974 Church Almanac*, p. 45.

Hawaii Campus. They include Afrikaans, Spanish, French, German, Italian, Portuguese, Tahitian, Navajo, Dutch, Norwegian, Swedish, Danish, Japanese, Korean, Cantonese, Mandarin, Thai, Samoan and Tongan. . . .

The new complex, scheduled to go into operation in 18 months to two years, will accommodate 1250 missionaries every eight-week period in the first phase of operation. It will be designed to allow expansion for 1800 missionaries and long-range building plans provide for dormitories, eating facilities and study space for 3,750 missionaries each eight-week period.[10]

Spencer W. Kimball, President of the Mormon Church, has given the following 1974 statistics on the Mormon missionary force:

It may be of interest to you brethren, some of you, to know that of the 17,564 missionaries, as of last week 9,560 are teaching the gospel in English, which is about 55 per cent of all the missionaries, and these are in the United States, Canada, Great Britain, Australia, New Zealand, and the Philippines. About 8,000 missionaries are learning languages in the language training missions. These 45 per cent are training in the three language schools—about 17 per cent or 3,000 in Spanish, about 1,000 in German, about 1,000 in Japanese, about 400 in French, and about 600 in Portuguese, and substantial numbers in Danish, Finnish, Dutch, Norwegian, Swedish, Chinese, Italian, Korean, Thai, Samoan, Afrikaans, and Navajo.[11]

The special training of the missionary lasts for five days and is held at the Salt Lake Mission Home. He will arrive on Saturday and depart for his assigned area Wednesday afternoon or Thursday morning. Those going to a foreign language area will spend an additional eight weeks in language study. While in Salt Lake the young missionary will participate in the Mormon temple ceremonies twice, attend numerous training sessions, purchase books and supplies, and try to memorize at least the general concepts of each lesson in the missionary handbook. Every missionary uses the same lesson plan and is expected to memorize it. The handbook contains over two hundred pages of instruction and sample dialogues.

---

10. *Brigham Young University Today,* August 1974, pp. 1, 8.
11. *The Ensign,* October 1974, p. 8.

Upon arrival at his mission area, the new missionary will be assigned to train with a missionary who has already served several months on the field. A typical day for a missionary would be as follows:

6:30 A.M.	Out of bed
7:00-7:30 A.M.	Eat breakfast and clean up
7:30-8:30 A.M.	Individual study
8:30-9:30 A.M.	Study lessons with companion
9:30 A.M.-9:30 P.M.	Proselyting (one hour off for lunch and one for dinner)
9:30 P.M.-10:30 P.M.	Study and make out reports
10:30 P.M.	To bed

After following this schedule for a week he and his companion (Mormon missionaries always go in twos) should have spent at least twenty-five hours in "tracting," sold twelve copies of the *Book of Mormon*, conducted six discussion sessions, and contacted three hundred people. If they conducted no discussion sessions that week they should have spent fifty to sixty hours in tracting instead of twenty-five. The missionaries are given Monday off to take care of their shopping and laundry, with possibly some time for recreation.

A missionary manual. In 1973 the Mormon Church adopted a new eight-lesson missionary program entitled *The Uniform System for Teaching Families*.[12] The lessons are briefly outlined below:

(1) The family at home. This lesson has no doctrinal discussion but emphasizes family togetherness and suggests ways for a family to spend one night a week together sharing in songs, games, devotions and prayer. It provides a basis by which Mormon missionaries can gain entrance into a home so they can introduce the doctrinal lessons in the weeks following their first visit. They are instructed to introduce themselves as follows:

Missionary: Good afternoon. We are representatives of The Church of Jesus Christ of Latter-day Saints. We would like to share a successful family program with you and your family,

---

12. *The Uniform System for Teaching Families* (Salt Lake City: Deseret Press, 1973).

without any obligation on your part and with nothing to buy. May we come in for a moment? . . . (If he says he already has his own religion, say:) . . . Wonderful. Our message is for families of all faiths. May we come in?[13]

(2) The restoration. (a) The Father and the Son appeared to Joseph Smith. (b) Joseph Smith was told to join none of the churches. (c) The *Book of Mormon* is the word of God. (d) Peter, James, and John gave the authority of the priesthood to Joseph Smith. (e) Like the original church, the restored Church of Jesus Christ is directed by twelve apostles and a living prophet. (f) The family can receive the full blessings of the kingdom of God. (g) The family will read the Joseph Smith pamphlet, read and ponder the assigned pages from the *Book of Mormon,* and pray sincerely to know the truthfulness of the gospel. (h) God and Jesus Christ are separate and distinct persons; each has a glorified and perfected body of flesh and bones.

(3) Eternal progression. (a) We all lived in a premortal existence, as spirits, with our Father in heaven. (b) Mortality is a probationary period during which we prepare to meet God again. (c) The gift of the resurrection will come to all men because of the death and resurrection of Christ. (d) We will all be resurrected to varying degrees of glory, depending on our individual faith and obedience to the Lord's commandments. (e) Our Heavenly Father has provided for all his children to hear the gospel before the resurrection. (f) Those who die without hearing the gospel can receive its full blessings through the faithful works of those who accept it in this life. (g) Little children cannot sin and are saved without baptism through Christ's atonement.

(4) Continuing revelation and individual responsibility. (a) God spoke to his prophets in ancient times. (b) God continues to speak to his prophets today. (c) Jesus Christ is the head of his church today, and he directs it by revelation to his prophets. (d) Scriptures are divine truths that God has revealed to his prophets. (e) All authority and knowledge necessary for our salvation are found in the Church of Jesus Christ of Latter-day Saints. (f) We receive blessings by following the counsel of

---

13. Ibid., p. B5.

Church leaders. (g) Each person grows spiritually by accepting responsibility in the Church.

(Baptismal challenge. This section may be given whenever the missionary feels the contact is ready, preferably in conjunction with the fourth lesson. The manual says:

> If you do not feel they are ready after you have given them four discussions, seek special divine direction on how to proceed. Do not be afraid to challenge people to be baptized. Remember that baptism is the only gate through which they can enter the Kingdom of Heaven. Set the baptismal date for just a few days after you expect to give the final lesson.)

(5) Truth versus error. (a) The truth leads to freedom from sin, guilt, and unhappiness. (b) Mankind's rejection of the gospel resulted in the loss of gospel truth and authority from the earth, a condition which existed at the time of Joseph Smith. (c) Christ restored truth and authority to the earth through the prophet Joseph Smith. (d) Our Heavenly Father knows all truth and has provided ways for us to learn the truth. (e) The Light of Christ is the influence that helps us discern truth from error. By responding to it, we show our faith in Christ. (f) Total repentance requires effort. Those who repent sincerely can have their sins forgiven completely. (g) We can communicate with God through prayer to learn truth. (h) The Scriptures teach us principles of truth and righteousness. (i) Proper baptism is essential to our salvation. (j) The Holy Ghost will guide us to all truth and strengthen our conviction of it. (k) The Holy Ghost is our access to truth. (l) The leaders in the Savior's church receive inspiration to guide us to truth.

(6) Bestowal of the Lord's blessings by obedience to his commandments. (a) The commandments of God are given to show us how to achieve eternal life and to enable us to become like him. (b) Through obedience to the law of tithing we learn to be unselfish, we gain material and spiritual blessings, and we participate in promoting the growth of the Lord's kingdom. (c) Obedience to the law of chastity helps us strengthen our family ties. (d) Obedience to the Word of Wisdom brings both physical and spiritual blessings. (e) Observance of the Lord's day will help us remain unspotted from the world and gain a greater knowledge of the gospel. (f) The Ten Com-

mandments were given as guidelines for all aspects of living.
(g) Every blessing from the Lord comes as a result of obedience to one of his commandments.

(7) Our relationship to Christ. (a) We can have a personal
relationship with Jesus Christ. (b) Jesus Christ, in his premortal spirit state, created the earth and everything on it. (c)
Jesus Christ overcame death and thus brought to pass the
resurrection of every person. (d) In the atonement, Jesus Christ
took upon himself the suffering that provides for redemption
from our sins, if we repent and keep his commandments. (e) We
begin to make the Savior's atonement effective in our lives by
repenting and being baptized. (f) Jesus Christ will be our judge.

(8) Membership in the kingdom. (a) Through the atonement of Jesus Christ we can receive a remission of sins by
obeying the principles and ordinances of the gospel. (b) After
baptism, we must remain obedient to the commandments of
God in order to enter his kingdom. (c) We must live the law
of tithing. (d) We must continue to live the Word of Wisdom.
(e) We must obey the Ten Commandments. (f) As we are
faithful in our priesthood callings, we can be a blessing to
our families. (g) Church members must set a good example
for their associates, both members and nonmembers.

The instructions at the front of the manual suggest that the
missionary

> memorize the discussions exactly as they appear. As you use
> them more, you may be more comfortable and effective using
> your own words. . . . Be careful not to change the spirit or intent
> of the questions. . . . Plan to give each of the families you teach
> two or three discussions per week depending on how rapidly the
> family is progressing. Between the regular discussions you will
> want to make supplementary visits to them. No more than two
> days should go by without their having a visit from you or other
> members of the Church. . . . The discussions call for your testi-
> mony in many places. Both you and your companion should
> testify as inspired by the Spirit.[14]

Periodically throughout the lessons, missionaries are reminded
of this responsibility to testify. For example, in the lesson on
the restoration there are eleven places where the missionaries

---

14. Ibid., pp. A1, A3.

are instructed to testify that they know what they are teaching is true.

Special programs at home and abroad. The church has proved itself to be unusually resourceful in inaugurating appealing programs for propagating its faith around the world.

(1) A very effective missionary tool is the Mormon school program. According to *The Ensign,* "A worldwide membership has created the need for establishing a number of school systems to serve members in areas where adequate schools may not otherwise be available. Church schools are presently administered in New Zealand, Tonga, Fiji, Samoa, Chile, Bolivia, Paraguay, and Mexico."[15] For instance, in Mexico, with about 92,000 members, the Mormons have over 8,000 students enrolled in their schools. They maintain thirty-five elementary schools and six secondary schools. *The Ensign* reports: "Unquestionably Church schools in Mexico have blessed the lives of thousands of members in that country and have contributed significantly to the growth of the Church in Mexico."[16]

There are over 3,000 students enrolled in elementary and secondary schools in South America, with Chile having the largest enrolment (2,638). In the Pacific islands there are over 5,000 students enrolled. The two largest schools are on Tonga, with 1,722 students, and Western Samoa, with 1,956 students.[17]

(2) The church has been unusually successful in its use of radio. Spencer W. Kimball, President of the Mormon Church, gives a high priority to this medium of communication in the Mormon program of propagation:

> I am confident that the only way we can reach most of these millions of our Father's children is through the spoken word over the airwaves, since so many are illiterate. We have proved the ability of our young men to learn other languages. . . . Just think what can be accomplished when we broadcast our message in many languages over numerous radio stations, large and small, around the world, and millions of good people listening on their transistors are being indoctrinated with the truth.[18]

15. *The Ensign,* July 1974, p. 21.
16. *The Ensign,* September 1972, pp. 34, 36.
17. *Deseret News 1975 Church Almanac* (Salt Lake City: Deseret News, 1975), p. F37.
18. *The Ensign,* October 1974, pp. 10-11.

The Mormon Church has recently produced a series of thirty-and sixty-second spot announcements dealing with family unity which are aired as a public service on CBS Radio. Each message ends with the words, "A thought from the Church of Jesus Christ of Latter-day Saints—the Mormons." Mormons are greatly appreciative of the potential of these spot announcements, as is apparent from a recent article in *The Ensign:*

> The series reaches beyond the United States. It is being accepted in Australia and New Zealand, and we are preparing "Homefront II" in Spanish and Portuguese for distribution in South America. Approximately 200 stations in Brazil used our first "Homefront" series.
>
> We are reaching more people with "Homefront" than with any of our other programs. For instance, CBS Radio told us that in 1973 they broadcast our message 179 times on their network and it had a combined listening impression of 210 million. What is impressive is that this is only 10 per cent of the total exposure "Homefront" receives. . . .
>
> Compared with other Church-oriented programs, the "Homefront" series is a relative newcomer to the airwaves. The Tabernacle Choir has been broadcasting since 1929, and the present format of "Music and the Spoken Word" has been on the air since 1936.
>
> General conferences receive worldwide exposure through radio and television, and "Sunday Evening from Temple Square" featuring music and talks, has been broadcast since 1932 and now is carried by 370 radio stations.[19]

(3) The famous Mormon Tabernacle Choir is a most successful missionary tool. The *1974 Church Almanac* reports:

> The Tabernacle Choir provides more than just beautiful music while on tour. Although the musical impact is great, the choir's missionary impact is equally, if not more, potent. . . .
>
> Thousands attended the concerts because of their love for good music. In so doing, they became familiar with the church, if nothing more than the name "Mormon." Such familiarity made future contact by missionaries easier and, at the same time, provided members of the audience with the program information and the introduction of the choir, which included a message from President Lee.[20]

19. *The Ensign,* July 1974, p. 68.
20. *Deseret News 1974 Church Almanac,* pp. 35, 38.

(4) The Mormon Church uses every opportunity to build its public image by means of cultural attractions. In Laie, Hawaii, the Mormons have built a huge Polynesian Cultural Center. In the *1974 Church Almanac* we read:

> The center was built in 1963 as a means of helping students at the Church College of Hawaii earn their way through school. Located on 19 acres adjacent to the college, it is one of the most popular paid attractions in Hawaii. It preserves the best aspects of the colorful heritages of Hawaii, Samoa, Tonga, Maori New Zealand, Fiji, Tahiti, and other Pacific areas.[21]

A free tram ride is offered from the center to the Church College of Hawaii and the Hawaii Temple Visitors Center. "Here the passengers dismount and spend 45 minutes at the temple site before reboarding the tram to complete the round trip."[22]

Every year some 150,000 people attend the Hill Cumorah Pageant in Palmyra, New York. The pageant depicts the history of the people in the *Book of Mormon* from 600 B.C. to A.D. 421.

Another favorite attraction is the Southern California Area Dance Festival in Pasadena. In 1973 some 55,000 people attended the festival, which was held in the Rose Bowl. Six thousand Mormons took part in the performance.

Every year thousands of tourists pass through the Visitor's Center built at Nauvoo, Illinois, where many of the old Mormon homes and shops are being restored. In fact, part of the recent musical, "The Adventures of Huckleberry Finn," was filmed in Nauvoo.

The Mormons maintain a fifteen-member shop to build exhibits for fairs and expositions, the best known being their exhibit at Expo '74 in Spokane, Washington.

The most widely known tourist attraction, however, is Temple Square in Salt Lake City, Utah. A growing favorite for visitors to Salt Lake is the free summer play, "Promised Valley," at the Mormon-owned Pioneer Playhouse.

At all the visitor centers and displays the Mormons encourage people to sign the guest register. Then begins one of the best follow-up programs of any church. Every day the names and addresses are sorted out and mailed to missionaries in the

---

21. Ibid., p. 106.
22. Ibid., p. 60.

area of the visitor's home. Within a few weeks someone will make a house call to further introduce the family to the church.

Evaluation of Mormon Missionaries
and Missionary Work

After ministering in Utah for some time, a Lutheran pastor gave the following evaluation of the Mormon missionary program and approach:

The Mormon missionary has many things going for him. One of these is the glorified saga of how the persecuted Mormons made their way into the wilderness of the West and made it blossom like the rose. People, generally, are enthralled by this religious Horatio Alger-type story. It is the most effective ear catcher of all that is said during the temple grounds tour.

The almost unlimited operating budget of the Mormon Church, which is carefully and wisely used, permits an almost unbelievable program of expansion in all departments of the church's work.

Social solidarity may be due to several factors, but the fact is that the Mormons show an externally united front to the rest of the world.

Perhaps the greatest strength of the Mormon Church lies in its policy of wholesale participation on the part of all members. Since it is a "lay church," it must depend on its general membership for spiritual, as well as material, strength. Every Mormon boy and girl is motivated from early childhood to accept eagerly the call from the church leadership to spend from one to three years in mission work.

The Mormon Church also has real weaknesses, and the Annes and Toms will find this out sooner or later.

There is the difficulty of reconciling Mormon mythology and documented history. Many intelligent Mormons stumble at this point. For example, it is difficult for the objective Mormon historian to accept both the church's glorified account of the life of Joseph Smith and the factual accounts given in court records and newspaper stories written when he lived.

The whole church is burdened with a weak theology. It is non-biblical and non-Christian. Doctrines have been changed from time to time because of a belief that it is still possible for revelation to be given through the president of the church. . . .

There is also an over-dependence upon organization, which leaves the church vulnerable when men fail. It seems that the organization is to be served, rather than to serve.

Though mass participation in the life of the Mormon Church is a strength, it can be a real weakness as well. So many people involved on all levels makes the organization unwieldy and difficult to move effectively. Lack of theological training on the part of those in leadership roles tends to limit their effectiveness.

The poorly trained missionary may have great enthusiasm, but it will never serve as a substitute for thorough training. He may seem quite well-versed to Anne and Tom, but will expose his ignorance quite readily when questioned concerning biblical-Christian doctrine.[23]

Jack Hurst, a newspaper writer, analyzed the work of two Mormon missionaries and the Mormon missionary program in the following words:

Elder Higley and Elder Mason had all the doors on one block shut in their faces. . . . Assigned to the Philadelphia suburbs, both are nearing the end of an austere, two-year period of service to one of Christianity's fastest-growing religions.

Mormon authorities say 24-month missionary stints are served by one-third or more of Mormon youths. At present some 18,000 of these young missionaries are in domestic or foreign fields. . . . Their success ratio among all persons contacted is probably small . . . but the mobilization is so general that even modest success produces substantial gains. . . .

Mormonism's appeal to prospective converts is wide-ranging and varied. . . .

It merges Roman Catholic-style centralization, a fundamentalist-like abhorrence of smoking, drinking and sexual promiscuity, and a modernistic permissiveness toward dancing and other forms of social contact between males and females.

The latter aspect seems to be a reason for its rapid growth — from 1 million members in 1947 to an estimated 3.3 million today. . . .

Higley and Mason present their story earnestly and gently. . . . To strangers, however, it is a hard story to get to tell. To more than two dozen attempts to tell it door-to-door on this particular day, they were not asked inside once.[24]

Robert Waldrop, a Mormon missionary to Australia (during 1972 and 1973) who later left the Mormon Church, has analyzed

23. Berton R. Hushagen, *Mormonism* (Minneapolis: The Augsburg Publishing House, tract no. 61, n.d.), pp. 9-10.
24. *Salt Lake Tribune*, September 19, 1974, p. 10A.

his own missionary experiences in a way that gives real insight into the program:

Now, what kind of people were baptized? It is very hard to draw generalizations. I know that I found among most people a very great ignorance as to basic Christian teachings. Most people acted like they had always kind of assumed that God had a body all along, and I had very few objections to the First Vision.

I think that I can draw a few generalizations, though.

1. Most of these people had little or no Biblical knowledge. Very few were active in a Church. I can think of a few exceptions, like a Pentecostal missionary family, and a family which I baptized that were attending the Jehovah's Witnesses, but for the most part they were not knowledgeable on the Bible.

2. At this period of the ASM [Australia South Mission] history, I would say that most of our converts came from the lower middle class or the poverty level. This hasn't always been the case, though. . . . I would say that the great majority of these people were middle or lower class. Working people. . . .

3. We baptized a lot more women than men, more singles than families. Oftentimes the wife would join, but not the husband. There were lots of young ladies baptized.

4. There were high rates of falling away. I think this is true of the LDS Church worldwide. Despite their recent fantastic growth, and their generally good rate of activity, a lot of these converts "just aren't sticking." . . .

5. We attracted a lot of lonely people, people with nowhere else to go. The Church offered them companionship.

I guess our converts were mostly simple people, without a strong religious base. . . . Also, a lot of them have a bad view of the various Protestant or Catholic Churches.

Also, in a foreign country you cannot discount our American accents, and neat appearance. . . . Many Australians have pleasant feelings towards America from the war, when many of them had "Yank" soldiers visiting in their homes. . . .

Also, many people, especially in the upper middle and professional classes were impressed by the fine buildings and the Church program. . . .

In January, I was transferred back to Melbourne for two reasons, one was to be one of the zone leaders of the Melbourne Zone, and two was to help with the "International Family Night" program we were putting together.

When you get 220 elders and sisters together you're bound to have some musical talent. Under Pres. Hewlett, some elders in Central Vic put together a musical show complete with a presentation about the Church and took it around to the various wards and branches. This was an enormously successful missionary tool. Members could bring their friends along for a good show and get them exposed to the LDS Church. . . . At some of our performances we had members of the Australian Parliament, the Minister of the Treasury for the state of Victoria, etc. The more "upper class" and intellectual people were greatly impressed by these programs. Imagine the psychological effect of the idea of "all those nice clean men, coming all the way from America to share their faith. Maybe there's something to it after all."

However, the main day to day activity of a missionary was TRACTING. The most scary thing on earth (at first) is to walk up to a door, knock timidly, and then give a door approach. . . .

"Hello, my name is Elder————, and this is my companion, Elder————. Your name would be?" (answer)

"We're missionaries from the Church of Jesus Christ of Latter-day Saints, and we have a very important message for you and your family about how . . . God has called a prophet, just like Moses or Isaiah in the Bible. May we come in and talk about it?" (answer). If they say no, then sell them a BOM [Book of Mormon].

"Well, if you wouldn't like for us to come back, we can leave with you a copy of an ancient history of the American Indians (open a BOM to the pictures of ancient ruins). The Smithsonian Institution has actually used this book to find ancient ruins in Central America. Would you like a copy?" (after the book is IN THEIR HANDS you say, "The way we usually leave this book is for the printing cost of 45¢ (in Australian money, in American it's 50¢). Thank you very much, I'd like to tell you that I KNOW that this book is the word of God, that Joseph Smith was a prophet, and that if you read and pray about the Book of Mormon, God himself will tell you that it is true."

That was a typical door approach. Usually you would show them "Moroni's promise" in the BOM. Above all, you would try to get a return appointment. . . .

"Every member a missionary" just hasn't caught on completely. Where it does, though, the LDS church experiences its greatest growth. . . . Nearly everyone that I actually got to teach more than two lessons was baptized. . . . The big objections

were social pressure (What will my friends think?) and the word
of Wisdom—sometimes tithing and Sabbath day observance. . . .[25]

Conclusion

We are witnessing the astounding results of a missionary
motivation and strategy that extend from the time of the founding of the Church of Latter-day Saints to the present. Since the
time of Joseph Smith the Mormon leaders have sent missionaries
throughout the world to gain converts to their church. Recently, Spencer W. Kimball, President of the Mormon Church,
made the following appeal:

> My brethren, I wonder if we are doing all we can. Are we
> complacent in our approach to teaching all the world? We have
> been proselyting now 144 years. Are we prepared to lengthen
> our stride? To enlarge our vision? . . .
>
> When I ask for more missionaries, I am not asking for more
> testimony-barren or unworthy missionaries. I am asking that we
> start earlier and train our missionaries better in every branch and
> every ward in the world. . . .
>
> I am asking for missionaries who have been carefully indoc-
> trinated and trained through the family and the organization of
> the Church, and who come to the mission with a great desire. I
> am asking for better interviews, more searching interviews, more
> sympathetic and understanding interviews, but especially that we
> train prospective missionaries much better, much earlier, much
> longer, so that each anticipates his mission with great joy. . . .
>
> The question is frequently asked: "Should every young man
> fill a mission?" And the answer has been given by the Lord. It is
> "Yes." Every young man should fill a mission.[26]

It is evident that Mormon believers have given heed to such
exhortations. Even more recently, President Kimball was able
to write, "By divine commandment we are a proselyting church.
More than 23,000 missionaries are abroad in the world today,
unselfishly giving of their time, means and talents to spread
this message of the Restoration."[27]

25. Personal letter from Robert Waldrop to Sandra Tanner, October 12,
1974.
26. *The Ensign*, October 1974, pp. 5, 7, 8.
27. *Deseret News*, April 3, 1976, p. 4.

PART SIX

South America

Donald C. Palmer

Donald C. Palmer has had wide experience as a missionary in Latin America and has used his extensive research in Latin American church affairs to good advantage. He was a missionary to Colombia with the Gospel Missionary Union from 1959 to 1971. During that time he was Coordinator of Evangelism and also served on the Field Council of the Gospel Missionary Union in Colombia. Mr. Palmer has been Area Secretary for Latin America and President of Field Affairs from 1971 to the present. He holds the M.A. degree from Trinity Evangelical Divinity School and is the author of a number of articles on evangelism, discipleship and theological education by extension course. Research for the present article resulted in his 1972 master's thesis, "The Growth of the Pentecostal Churches in Colombia," which was published by Moody Press in 1974 under the title, Explosion of People Evangelism.

11 | JESUS ONLY:

The United Pentecostal Church

Donald C. Palmer

The "Jesus Only" Pentecostals make up the largest Protestant church in Colombia today. Their growth in the past fifteen years has been greater than that of any other Protestant group in the country, and with a claimed membership of 55,000 at the halfway point of the decade of the 1970s[1] they account for over a third of the total Protestant membership in Colombia.[2]

It is known that Pentecostals are doing very well in Latin America as a whole—in fact, Pentecostalism is the fastest growing Protestant movement south of the border. By 1969 the Pentecostal churches accounted for almost two-thirds of the total Protestant membership in Latin America.[3] But it is in Colombia that the Jesus Only Pentecostals have had their most exceptional growth.

1. Rev. Domingo Zuniga, United Pentecostal Church leader, in a personal interview with Harry Jeffery of the Gospel Missionary Union, October 15, 1974.
2. Based on United Pentecostal membership estimate for 1974, and CEDEC (Evangelical Confederation of Colombia) census figures for total Protestant membership in 1972.
3. William R. Read, Victor M. Monterroso, Harmon A. Johnson, *Latin American Church Growth* (Grand Rapids: Eerdmans, 1969), p. 58.

Development in Colombia

The first missionaries to bring the message of the Pentecostal experience and the unitary nature of the Godhead to Colombia arrived in 1936. They were the Verner Larsens from Canada, sponsored by the Pentecostal Assembly of Jesus Christ. This is how Larsen describes his arrival and the subsequent growth of the United Pentecostal Church in Colombia:

> Thirty-three years ago I stepped on Colombia soil for the first time on the Caribbean Coast. At that time there was not even one Colombian baptized in the glorious *Name of Jesus Christ,* nor sealed with the Holy Spirit in Pentecostal power. Today there are tens of thousands that are people of the Name. . . . Praise His Name! . . .
>
> Colombian brethren of the Name of Jesus have carried the message to Venezuela, to Ecuador, to Peru, to Bolivia, to Panama, and have crossed the great Atlantic arriving even to the Old World. . . . Thanks be to God for all that has been done in obedience to the heavenly vision, but brethren, there is much yet to do and the time is short.[4]

In 1938, two years after their arrival in Colombia, the Larsens established the first small unitarian Pentecostal church in the city of Bucaramanga, and in the early forties, the second church in Barranquilla on the northern coast. Growth and outreach in the early years, however, were very limited.

About this time the Stanford Johnstons, already elderly and with very limited Spanish, came to Cali, the major city in the western part of Colombia. "At that time in the department of the Valle del Cauca there were no Pentecostals of any denomination, a few Presbyterians, the relatively well-established mission of the Gospel Missionary Union, and the beginnings of the Southern Baptist mission."[5]

The Johnstons were unable to start any permanent work, and because of sickness were soon forced to leave Cali. But Johnston claimed that he had received from God a special revelation that a great Pentecostal revival would take place in that whole

---

4. "From Brother and Sister Larsen," *El Heraldo de la Verdad,* March-April 1970, pp. 1-2.
5. Cornelia Flora, "History of the United States Pentecostal Church in Colombia," a mimeographed study in preparation for her dissertation (Cornell University) n.d., p. 3.

western area of Colombia, and that other United Pentecostal missionaries *must* therefore be sent to take their place.

In 1945 the Pentecostal Assemblies of Jesus Christ (Canada) and the United Pentecostal Church (the United States) merged to form the United Pentecostal Church. In 1949 this newly formed mission sent three new missionaries to take over the work in Cali. One of these was William Drost. He introduced a method of producing church growth that became the model for missionary work for the United Pentecostal Church in all of Colombia. Speaking of Drost's first day in Cali, Cornelia Flora writes:

> He immediately left his bag in the humble dwellings where meetings were held and where Johnston lived, and went out into the streets. Much to everyone's consternation, he did not return until 9:00 in the evening. He had gone out to talk to the nearby miners, and their response assured him that this was the place God wanted him to work.[6]

The Drosts first began meetings in their own home in the working-class barrio where they lived, and then at numerous other points in the surrounding region. Within one year several churches had been planted and over 500 converts were baptized. Sally Morley, who came to join the Drosts in Cali in 1951, described the beginnings of the work there:

> The Drosts had begun a church in their own home in Cali when I came, and the work had spread to the mountains. Drost was very evangelistic and got out a lot; his converts did the same thing. Some that had come from other areas to live in Cali, went back to their home areas, evangelized, then invited Drost and others to visit. Groups that formed in this way were later organized as churches, with lay leaders becoming the pastors of these churches.[7]

By 1959, just ten years after the Drosts arrived in Cali, there were twenty-five organized United Pentecostal churches in this area of Colombia. No other denomination had achieved this kind of growth during that period.

---

6. Ibid., pp. 3-4.
7. Personal interview with Sally Morley, United Pentecostal missionary, May, 1971.

The Drost method. Drost himself was what might be termed a lay missionary since he had received no formal theological education and no special preparation in missions. His strongest qualification was his intense desire to win others to the Jesus Only faith; and on winning new converts, he encouraged them to spread the message wherever they went. New converts were baptized "in the Name," led into the Pentecostal experience of "baptism in the Spirit" and speaking in tongues, and immediately sent out to win others to the faith, with the promise that the Holy Spirit would give them special power to witness and that he would accompany their witness with supernatural signs.

Not only were new converts encouraged to go immediately and spread the faith, but those who felt the desire to preach and teach were allowed to do so. They simply preached what they had believed and experienced, and invited others to do the same. Some were so successful in their preaching that they were recognized as leaders and became pastors of churches without having had any formal theological training.

In the beginning, some of the other United Pentecostal missionaries were in disagreement with Drost's way of working, and felt it wasn't wise to let new converts teach and preach without any special training for the ministry. But Drost didn't feel this way. After all, he was just a lay missionary himself and he was having success, so why couldn't the Colombian converts do what he was doing? Besides, the Pentecostal message was a simple one, consisting of a few major beliefs and the promise of the Spirit's outpouring accompanied by charismatic experiences. Moreover, this message was aimed at people of the lower classes. What better way to reach them than for new converts to take this simple but dynamic message to those of their own class?

As other United Pentecostal missionaries saw how successful Drost's methods were in producing church growth and multiplication, they also came to adopt them; these methods became the pattern for their work in all of Colombia.

So the *first major key* in the growth of the United Pentecostal Church in Colombia was the introduction of the Drost method. This can be defined simply as "immediate and spontaneous evangelization by new converts, and the development of pastors through voluntary preaching and through proven leadership abilities and results in the ministry."

Nationalization of the United Pentecostal Church. A second major development within the United Pentecostal Church in Colombia was its nationalization in 1967. In their annual convention of that year, the national delegates voted to become an autonomous Colombian church. Previous to this, missionaries had many of the administrative responsibilities. But after the church became autonomous, Colombian leaders took over all the official positions. The only responsibility the missionaries had was to give counsel when it was requested by the Colombian church leadership. Officials of the United Pentecostal Mission Board came from the United States to transfer church properties to the official Colombian board in the name of the national church.

Though there had been some hard feelings between national church leaders and missionaries during this process of nationalization, things seemed to go along fairly smoothly at first. Later, however, hostile reaction grew more pronounced until the missionaries associated with the mission board in the United States decided to sever relations with the Colombian church and to begin new churches on their own. These churches also carry the name *United Pentecostal Church,* but are affiliated with the North American foreign mission board. The great majority of the Jesus Only churches in Colombia today, however, belong to the autonomous Colombian church.

Nationalization certainly hasn't hurt the growth of the United Pentecostal Church in Colombia; if anything, it has accelerated it. At the time of nationalization in 1967 there were slightly over 200 churches and approximately 19,000 members. By 1974, the number of churches and members had practically tripled!

Major Beliefs

Who are the Jesus Only Pentecostals, and what do they believe? Like all Pentecostals, they believe that the Holy Spirit imparts to the church and to believers today the same charismatic gifts and supernatural manifestations as he did on the day of Pentecost and on subsequent occasions as recorded in the Book of Acts.

Jesus Only people share with other Pentecostals belief in the main charismatic experiences: (1) the baptism of the Holy Spirit—an experience after conversion in which the Holy Spirit comes upon the seeking believer; (2) speaking in tongues—both the initial sign of having received the baptism of the Spirit, and a continuing gift to believers; (3) divine healing—provided for all believers in the atonement of Jesus Christ; and (4) prophecy—a special gift of illumination concerning future events or matters regarding the church.

Distinctives of Jesus Only Pentecostalism. But while the United Pentecostal Church shares the above beliefs with other Pentecostals, it also differs in several of its doctrines.

(1) *Water baptism must be administered only in the name of Jesus.* This belief was first expressed during an international Pentecostal camp meeting in California in 1913. There, a Pentecostal leader named John G. Scheppe was so impressed by the healings and other miracles taking place "in the name of Jesus" that he was convinced God was giving him a new revelation concerning "the Name."

> To be sure, the "revelation" impressed many, and they hastened to examine the Bible for what teaching it contained regarding the "name of Jesus." Their research produced a revolution within Pentecostalism, for they fastened upon two texts—Acts 2:38 and John 3:5—and asserted that *true* baptism *must* be only "in the name of Jesus" rather than "in the name of the Father, and of the Son, and of the Holy Ghost." The result? Many of the early Pentecostal leaders were rebaptized. This created numerous divisions among Pentecostals as some supported this view and others denounced it as rank heresy.[8]

(2) *There is but one person in the Godhead—Jesus Christ.* The Father and the Holy Spirit are considered *manifestations* of Christ. This idea was an offshoot of the new "revelation" of the "name of Jesus" in 1913.

> The next development in this controversy . . . was a denial of the Trinity. Men like Frank Ewert and Glenn A. Cook, spokesmen for the new teaching, denied the trinity of persons in the Godhead, maintaining that while God is a three-fold Being, Father,

---

8. John T. Nichol, *Pentecostalism* (New York: Harper & Row, 1966), p. 90.

Son, and Holy Ghost, there is but one Person and that one is Jesus.[9]

The theme-text for the United Pentecostal monthly publication in Colombia *(El Heraldo de la Verdad)* is: "Hear, O Israel, the Lord our God is one Lord" (Deut. 6:4). Emphasis is also given to John 10:30 where Christ says, "I and my Father are one." It is because of this belief that United Pentecostals are known as the Jesus Only people.

(3) *Three-phase salvation.* United Pentecostals believe and proclaim that there are three steps, or experiences, that are necessary for a person to be completely saved: (1) repentance and faith in Christ; (2) baptism by immersion in "the name of Jesus"; and (3) the baptism of the Holy Spirit.

> Our doctrine on the baptism of the Holy Spirit is different from other Pentecostals. We believe that regeneration has several different steps. It begins when a person believes the message and repents. This is followed with baptism by water in Jesus' name. The baptism of the Holy Spirit is the culmination in this process.[10]

Goals and Growth

The primary objectives of the United Pentecostal Church in Colombia are: (1) to win people to the Jesus Only faith and experience; (2) to plant and build up churches throughout Colombia that are true to the fundamental doctrines of the Unitarian Pentecostal faith; (3) to bring these churches together for fellowship and outreach in a well-organized national association; and (4) to send Colombian Pentecostal missionaries to new areas of Colombia and to other countries to establish the United Pentecostal Church there.

How successful have they been? Prior to 1949 there were only two United Pentecostal churches in all of Colombia, and a few hundred members. By 1960 this had grown to 43 organized churches and 3,000 members.[11] Then in the ten-year period from 1960 to 1970 the United Pentecostal Church grew to a denomination of approximately 400 churches and 30,000 members,[12] and

---

9. Ibid., pp. 90-91.
10. Interview with Sally Morley, May, 1971.
11. *Censo de la Obra Evangelica en Colombia: 1966*, Part I, p. 4.
12. Donald C. Palmer, *Explosion of People Evangelism* (Chicago: Moody Press, 1974), pp. 31-32.

by the end of 1974 to 550 churches and a claimed membership of 55,000.[13] So in a fourteen-year period, the Jesus Only people have multiplied the number of their churches thirteen times, and their membership over eighteen times! Even if their present claimed membership is somewhat inflated,[14] their growth is still phenomenal as compared to that of the mainline Protestant churches and the "faith" missions.

As for its *outreach* and *missionary* efforts in new regions of Colombia, the United Pentecostal Church has churches in more areas of the country than has any other denomination. Its churches can be found even in isolated jungle regions such as the Guajira, Caqueta, and Putumayo.

The United Pentecostal Church may be the only Protestant church in Colombia that has sent *and supports* (and supports *well* by Colombian standards) Colombian missionaries to other countries. According to the latest reckoning Domingo Zuniga (in an interview with Harry Jeffery of the Gospel Missionary Union) claimed they have eight missionaries serving in Ecuador, Bolivia, Spain, and Canada (Montreal). Believers from Colombia were also responsible for starting the first Spanish-speaking Jesus Only church in New York.

They have also achieved their objective of a *strong national church organization*. It is directed by the "Junta" or "Board." (By 1970 the Junta was made up of fourteen leaders, six of whom, along with the President, were given the oversight of the churches and church activities throughout the country.) Next in authority are the *supervisors*, who are in charge of major regions. Under the supervisors are the *presbyters*, who have the oversight of zones within the larger regions. All of these are men of experience who have proven themselves in their ministries, and who command a great deal of respect from their followers.

The national organization also has *money* to finance missions, administration costs, building loans to churches, and literature and radio projects. This is due to the liberality of the Jesus Only people, and to a strong and well-defined program

13. Domingo Zuniga, interview with Harry Jeffery, October 15, 1974.
14. Domingo Zuniga claims that this figure is conservative. It is based on multiplying their 550 organized churches by 100. Many of their churches in the cities have 300 to 1,000 members.

in the churches. A tenth of all tithes and offerings given in the more than 500 local churches goes into the central United Fund. The responsibility for seeing that this is faithfully sent in is spelled out clearly to every pastor and every leader of a church society. In fact, one of the requirements for anyone aspiring to be a local church worker or pastor is that he promise to see that this is done.

The results are impressive. The tithe to the United Fund in 1967 was almost 400,000 pesos, or about $27,000. This means that in that year the Jesus Only people gave over a quarter of a million dollars to their churches. Today, with almost three times as many members, this total giving has gone well past the half million dollar mark, and the United Fund has increased proportionately. No other Protestant denomination in Colombia has comparable national funds to work with.

Finally, the United Pentecostal Church has placed a priority on establishing churches first in the major cities as strategic centers, rather than starting in the small rural towns and then trying to move into the cities. The United Pentecostal Church began its work in larger cities—Bucaramanga and Barranquilla to the north, and Cali to the southwest. Later it began churches in other cities—Bogota, Medellin, Pereira, and Armenia. These have become centers of outreach which send workers to evangelize and plant new churches in the neighboring towns and villages.

Leadership System

The United Pentecostal Church develops its pastors and other church leaders almost exclusively through an apprenticeship system. Even today, with 550 established churches, the United Pentecostal Church has no Bible institute or formal theological training for its pastors and leaders. And it has no program of theological education by extension courses. Yet it has successful pastors who have proved they can plant strong and growing churches, and can lead their people in an effective forward program. In interviewing some of the more prominent United Pentecostal pastors, I was impressed with the fact that *these men are leaders.* Interviews with church members made it obvious that they think very highly of their pastors, and that the pastors hold a great deal of influence and control over them.

Levels in the ministry. There are three levels of promotion in the ministry of the United Pentecostal Church.

(1) *Local license.* A man who has been a soul winner and an active lay leader in his own local church for at least one year may be put in charge of a new congregation and granted a local license. As a local worker, he will serve under the close supervision of the area leaders.

(2) *National license.* After a local worker has proved himself in the ministry for three years and has been successful in leading his church to growth and outreach, he qualifies for a national license, which is conferred by the Junta. This license gives him the right to preach or pastor a church anywhere in Colombia, as well as to administer baptism and the Lord's Supper.

(3) *Ordination certificate.* When a man has served for at least three more years as a pastor with national credentials, he may request ordination by the Junta. Ordination, however, is reserved for those who have given ample proof of leadership, maturity, and success in their ministry. Only ordained pastors qualify to serve as presbyters, supervisors, or members of the Junta. Very often ordained pastors are responsible for overseeing a number of churches and ministries in their areas.

So it takes at least seven years of proven ministry to gain ordination—one year as a lay leader in a local church, three years as a local worker over a new church, and three more years as a pastor with a national license. The essential emphasis in this process of training United Pentecostal pastors and leaders is practical experience and success in the ministry.

Advantages of the apprenticeship system. There are very positive advantages for growth in the United Pentecostal apprenticeship system of selecting and preparing church leaders. Several preaching sites are started by each organized church, and concerned lay leaders are given the responsibility of directing these outreach efforts. Every local church is able to multiply its outreach and plant many new churches because it is in itself a recruitment and training agency for new workers to fill these posts.

Then, the natural process of the apprenticeship system screens out those who do not have the leadership, vision, or gifts to go on as successful pastors. They remain as active lay leaders in local churches or at preaching sites. Only those who can build up congregations go on to become full-time pastors. This system tends to eliminate professionalism in the ministry since success in the ministry itself—leading churches to growth and outreach—is the practical requirement for advancement. Leaders simply rise to the level of their own vision, activity, and competence in the ministry.

There are some weaknesses and dangers in this apprenticeship system of training pastors and leaders. The main one, of course, is the lack of theological training and grounding in the Scriptures. Apart from the basic Jesus Only doctrines, each pastor is virtually on his own when it comes to interpreting the Bible. With little theological study or background, this results in: (1) an emphasis on charismatic experience and emotion rather than on the Bible; (2) strange interpretations of Scripture that can lead to splinter groups with some very questionable beliefs; and (3) an anti-intellectual attitude that often results in putting a premium on ignorance, and in this case, ignorance of the Bible itself.

The Appeals of Pentecostalism

The United Pentecostal Church definitely has an attraction for many Colombians, especially for those among the lower classes. This is due in part to the tremendous appeal of the message of divine healing and of miracles, and in part to the very emotionally charged meetings. These meetings hold the people in rapt attention, impressing and convincing many that what they see and hear is from God.

Happiness is healing. Consider the United Pentecostal appeal of divine healing. The average Colombian of the lower classes can't afford to go to a doctor or to buy expensive medicines, and consequently sickness can become an almost hopeless burden. Superstitions and ignorance about sickness are common, and, whenever ill, many have all their life gone to herb specialists and *curanderos*. As Roman Catholics they have been taught to look to the saints, or to miracle-working images of Christ and Mary for healing. Then they hear a message by a very convincing Pentecostal preacher that God will heal them miraculously if they will only believe and submit to him for physical deliverance. A typical United Pentecostal printed invitation illustrates this appeal:

Attention! The United Pentecostal Church of Colombia . . . invites you . . . to hear the Word of God with preachers and trios anointed with the Holy Spirit. Bring your sick and Jesus Christ will heal them, for He said, "I will go and heal them" (Matt. 8:7).[15]

Pentecostal leaders are convinced that healing is a divinely approved and most effective means for attracting and winning converts. One pastor told me that "the object of healing for the unsaved is as a bait. It attracts their attention to the power of Christ, who can also save."[16] Another said, "Healing has helped a great deal to attract and win new people to the church. In all of our services there is an invitation to receive healing; many come forward for the prayer for healing."[17]

"Moving" meetings. United Pentecostals really seem to enjoy their meetings. The emotionally charged atmosphere of their church services offers a feeling of joy, of fiesta, and of the sensational (miracles, tongues, healings) that thrills, excites, and lifts these humble believers from the dreariness and drudgery of daily life. Such meetings are especially satisfying to the Latin temperament which responds more to a meeting that can be "felt" and "experienced" than to a meeting which is reserved and formal, and where the approach is highly academic.

Then there is freedom in their meetings—liberty to pray aloud, to pray all at once, to stand and shout, and to interject an "amen," "hallelujah," "praise the Lord," as they wish. Jesus Only people call this "liberty in the Spirit," and this liberty is often mentioned by both pastors and members as a major factor in the appeal of their meetings. It gives a feeling of direct participation in what is going on to all who are present.

In personal interviews in 1969 and 1970 with many members of the United Pentecostal Church, I often asked the question: "Why do you like your church better than others?" These are a few representative answers:

---

15. Flyer inviting people to an evangelistic campaign in the city of Armenia, quoted in Palmer, *Explosion of People Evangelism,* p. 118.

16. Personal interview with Manuel Ospina, United Pentecostal pastor in Cali, January, 1969, quoted in Palmer, *Explosion of People Evangelism,* p. 117.

17. Interview with Abelardo Galvis, pastor of the second church in Pereira, September 4, 1969.

I like my church because of the liberty to pray without impediments, and because of the atmosphere there is—the presence of the Spirit.

There is continual revival—joy, prayer, evangelism, souls being saved. The brethren really work for the Lord.

Because one feels the joy of the Holy Spirit and the presence of the Lord. In other churches one doesn't feel the same joy nor warmth of the Holy Spirit.

We have liberty to preach and to testify, and there are more of God's power-working miracles in our church.

There is more life, power, enthusiasm, activity. . . . Some churches say that we are fanatic. . . . We don't speak against other churches, because we believe we have more than they have. We seek them, not to speak against what they have, but to offer them more.

Above all, I like my church better because of the manifestations of the Holy Spirit in power.

Finally, there is the cultural appeal of United Pentecostal meetings. Their music makes greater use of Colombian rhythms and beats than does the music of other churches. Their services feature not only pianos and accordions, but also guitars, maracas, and tambourines. In a Jesus Only church one can hear the kinds of music and instruments that are played in popular folk songs on the radio and in the coffee bars and cantinas. Only the words have been changed in order to convey messages of God's love and wonder-working power. These features of United Pentecostal meetings stem in part from the attitude of Drost who let the Colombians do things in their own way and as they thought best. And "their own way" naturally was Colombian. "The church that developed has been very indigenous and Colombian from the beginning, at least in the Valle. The Colombian believers were allowed to do things in their own way. If they wanted to paint a church red and pink—fine."[18]

One Pentecostal missionary couple gave this simple answer as to why church services in other denominations do not seem to appeal as much to many of the Colombians: "They are too North American."

18. Interview with Sally Morley, May, 1971, quoted in Palmer, *Explosion of People Evangelism*, p. 113.

Methods of Outreach

Besides the sociological and psychological factors present in the Jesus Only message and meetings, effective methods of outreach also contribute greatly to United Pentecostal growth.

Spontaneous personal evangelism. In one sense, spontaneous personal evangelism cannot be called a method, but it appears to be the principal means of outreach and winning others in the Jesus Only church. Every follower of "the Name" is expected to be a witness of his faith. As one United Pentecostal pastor said,

> The greatest factor in our growth is that every member of the Colombian church is an evangelist. Every believer that you see is ready to carry the gospel to anyone. . . . How is this achieved? As pastors we continually emphasize that every believer—with the power of the Holy Spirit—can and should witness to others.[19]

Another pastor added:

> Our greatest emphasis in evangelism is that *every believer be a faithful witness.* . . . There are many members that can't direct or help a great deal in the church services, but in personal evangelism—yes. Many members talk to others they know about their faith and invite them to come to our meetings—and they do this spontaneously. These are living contacts with the lost.[20]

Many non-Pentecostal pastors have expressed the wish that their church members had the same enthusiasm and high level of commitment to witness and win others as the Jesus Only people have. A pastor of the Gospel Missionary Union reported that he is impressed by "the visitation and witness carried on continually by so many, and with so much fervor," and also by "their emphasis on the Holy Spirit in the believer to overcome and witness with liberty and power."[24] A Bible Societies agent added, "These people . . . witness everywhere—on the buses, in the schools, in their neighborhoods—wherever they go."[22]

In interviewing a cross-section of United Pentecostal members, I found that the majority had been won through the witness of friends, relatives, or fellow workers who had already been

19. Interview with Domingo Zuniga, August 12, 1969.
20. Interview with Manuel Ospina, January, 1969.
22. Interview with Aldemar Pardo, May, 1971.
21. Interview with Franz Aguirre, January 20, 1971.

converted to the Jesus Only faith. I asked them which method they believed to be best for reaching and winning new people: evangelistic campaigns, home meetings, visitation, or spontaneous personal evangelism. Seventeen of twenty-three chose personal evangelism. Most of them also said that they witness every opportunity they get—in their neighborhood, where they work, wherever they can.

Why do they witness? The answer seems to be a combination of inward compulsion, the constant encouragement to do so by the pastors, and the conviction that they have found *the answer* to life's problems. One United Pentecostal member said, "We witness because we feel it in our being. We believe that we are in the true church and that we have found true salvation. And the pastor is always encouraging us to pray and to speak to others so that we will have souls for God."[23] Another member expressed much the same thing: "We witness because it is a natural thing for us to do—it is within one. And what a person has found and that is real, one wants to share. But as well as this, the church stirs us to personal evangelism by saying, 'Let's get out and witness, and preach.' "[24]

Personal witness is part of the ethos of the United Pentecostal Church, an accepted standard for the believer. The prevailing feeling is that if a member does not witness regularly, he must not be much of a Christian, and he must not be living in "the power of the Spirit."

But while spontaneous personal evangelism by its members may be the major factor in its growth, the United Pentecostal Church also makes use of more structured or organized methods of evangelism and church planting. To these we now turn.

Visitation teams. Pastors and members of the United Pentecostal Church rated visitation teams the second most influential factor contributing to growth. Visitation teams are organized for four purposes: (1) to promote initial door-to-door visitation and personal evangelism in order to find out which people are open and interested; (2) to call on interested people—those who have attended services or who have in some other way shown they might be receptive; (3) to follow up new converts;

23. Interview with Carmen Rosa Ortiz de Escobar, November 25, 1970.
24. Interview with Edilma Zapata de Valencia, November 17, 1970.

and (4) to begin new churches in neighboring towns and villages.

The second church of Pereira, for example, has three visitation teams—one of men, another of women, and the third of young people. Each group has approximately fifteen members.

> The women's visitation team goes out during the week, the men on weekends, and the young people once a week, usually on Saturdays. They go from house to house giving out tracts and other literature, and leave New Testaments and Bibles where there is good interest. Then on Sundays almost the whole church goes out in the afternoon to invite new people to the evening service. Where they find people with interest they will go back just before the service and personally bring them to the meeting.[25]

Open-air meetings. Every United Pentecostal pastor interviewed indicated that his church used open-air meetings to reach new people. The favorite places for holding these meetings are congested street corners, the market places (during the week), and parks (on weekends). At a time when this kind of meeting is considered unfashionable or a little too direct for many of the other denominations, Jesus Only people are making full use of it, often having several such meetings in a week.

Manuel Bernal, the choir director in the Bucaramanga church said, "We have six open-air meetings every Sunday—I help in these with music and preaching."[26] The pastor of the second church in the city of Palmira gave this method as a main factor in their growth: "We hold open-air meetings here in this barrio and in those around us. Music and the promise of salvation and healing play a large part in these meetings."[27]

During my years in Colombia, I remember seeing groups of United Pentecostal members coming on weekdays to the market place in the city of Armenia, and on Sundays to the large park on the outskirts of Pereira. They would arrive with their guitars and other instruments, a loud-speaking system (usually), and handfuls of tracts and flyers. Some sang, others gave testimonies,

---

25. Interview with Abelardo Galvis, September 4, 1969.
26. Interview with Manuel Bernal, November 25, 1969.
27. Interview with Jose Tason, November 12, 1970.

and another more gifted one preached the message. Then they all mixed with the listeners to give out literature and personally press the issue with those who would listen. As a young Southern Baptist pastor put it: "These people just have no laziness about them. The pastor says, 'Let's go and do this,' and they do it."[28]

The Jesus Only people also make use of the *serenata* (serenade)—a well-established and much-loved custom of Spanish-speaking people—to win new converts. In the evening, groups of Pentecostal musicians move from the house of one interested family to another and sing about God's love and his pardon for sinful men. One member gives this testimony: "How did I become a Pentecostal? A group from the church in my barrio was giving a *serenata*. I listened especially to one hymn that was so beautiful. The words kept working in my heart till I went to the church and I was converted there."[29]

Networks of preaching sites. United Pentecostals stress the reproduction principle in planting and multiplying new churches. Every organized church is responsible to: (1) evangelize the people in the surrounding area; (2) start preaching sites in neighboring barrios, towns and villages where there is no United Pentecostal work, with the purpose that these become established churches; and (3) train lay leaders who can direct these preaching sites and then pastor them as they grow and become organized churches.

An example of this is the first church of Pereira, which was started by lay leaders from the churches in Cali and Palmira. They came for a week at a time to visit and witness until they had built up a group of about fifty converts who met in one of the homes. At that point these converts received their first pastor, a layman who himself had come up through the ranks. From that small beginning the church has grown until today it has over 500 members. The church has founded six more new churches—three in the greater Pereira area, and three in other towns in the region! New churches were started in the same way the mother church in Pereira was started. Now all

28. Interview with Belarmino Dusan, March 7, 1970, quoted in Palmer, *Explosion of People Evangelism*, p. 131.
29. Part of the testimony of one member of a group from the second church in Pereira interviewed February 7, 1970.

six are established churches with their own pastors and their own outreach in their respective areas.

One of the daughter churches of the Pereira mother church is the second church of Pereira in a barrio called Cuba. It began in 1966 as a preaching site of the central church and met in the home of a member who lived in this outlying area of the city. By 1967 the group had grown to over fifty believers, so a place was rented for meetings. This church has continued to grow; by the end of 1974 there were over 400 members with their own large church building. Even more important is the fact that the second church has opened over twenty preaching sites in the area! This outreach led the Presbyterian pastor in Pereira to say:

> They have works everywhere. . . . Don't ask where they *do* work and hold meetings; ask where they *don't* work. . . . They have groups that hold meetings all around the city in the barrios, and in the surrounding villages. Often when I am returning from a service in an outlying area, I come across a group of Pentecostals either going or coming from a meeting someplace.[30]

Large united conventions. There is at least one major united convention held by the United Pentecostal Church in Colombia each year. These conventions are held in big cities which have a large, important church. In January of 1970, for example, the convention was held in the Colosseum (a civic building) in the city of Medellin—a city with a population of over 1,000,000. More than 6000 people attended the convention as busloads of Jesus Only believers came from churches throughout Colombia.

A convention like this makes a great impression on a city, but even more, it builds the morale of the United Pentecostal leaders and members. It is a tremendous shot in the arm for believers and gives them a sense of their own importance in a country where there is such a small percentage of Protestants. And it gives them identification with a church that is really "on the move." Everyone likes to belong to something that is growing and moving ahead. In a convention like this a Jesus Only believer can say to himself, "God must be with us. Look at how many of us there are, and at how God is blessing us!" Encouraged and thrilled by the very size and

---

30. Interview with Gabriel Velez, November 5, 1970.

magnitude of it all, they return to their own churches and communities to witness and serve with renewed enthusiasm and faith, convinced they are part of a church that has the truth and the power of God.

The Herald of Truth. Leaders of the United Pentecostal Church utilize attractive literature to support their programs of outreach. Most important is the publication *El Heraldo de la Verdad (The Herald of Truth)*. This eighteen-page bimonthly publication features *news* of the United Pentecostal churches— articles on special conferences, baptisms, and church leaders; *doctrine,* with a heavy emphasis on United Pentecostal distinctives; *testimonies* of believers, especially of salvation and healing; and *special features* from its youth and women's societies and on the missionary work carried on in other countries by nationals sent by the Colombian church. There can be no doubt that this publication is a valuable tool in rallying the faithful and propagating the doctrines of the United Pentecostal Church.

Relation to the Larger Society

The United Pentecostal Church is interested in evangelism, in church planting and growth, and in missions. Since radio and literature contribute more directly to accomplishing these objectives, they are used a great deal. But United Pentecostals are not interested in any institutions or efforts which are primarily humanitarian or social, such as orphanages, clinics, and co-operatives. A few local churches sponsor primary schools, but in proportion to their total membership, the United Pentecostal Church has fewer schools than any other established Protestant denomination in Colombia.

In my research I discovered that, more than the believers of any other Protestant group, the Jesus Only people and churches tend to refrain from getting involved in community affairs and social problems. While all of the non-Pentecostal pastors and leaders in my sample encouraged at least some involvement of believers and the church in community, cultural, and political affairs, almost all of the Jesus Only Pentecostals felt they should not get involved in these matters. Comparative statistics on the social involvement of one non-Pentecostal and two Pentcostal groups are given in the following chart.[31]

---

31. Palmer, *Explosion of People Evangelism*, p. 147.

Activity	Non-Pentecostals	Trinitarian Pentecostals	Jesus Only Pentecostals
Athletic team	83%	34%	0%
Accion Comunal*	78%	50%	20%
Politics	64%	6%	0%
Labor union	46%	18%	0%
Cultural club	81%	70%	7%

Accion Comunal are voluntary action groups organized in the barrios of cities and in towns and villages for the purpose of improving the community through co-operative citizen participation and effort. Projects include such things as building or improving a bridge, road, school, dispensary, or some other facility needed by the community.

In response to the related question, "In your opinion, do you feel that the evangelical church should concern itself more with the social problems of the country and declare itself with respect to these problems?" twelve of the fourteen non-Pentecostal pastors interviewed answered yes. All of the Jesus Only pastors interviewed said no, feeling that believers "shouldn't get mixed up in these things."

As for voting in local and national elections, 82 per cent of the non-Pentecostal pastors interviewed said that they do vote and encourage their members to do so as part of their civic responsibility. Of the Jesus Only pastors, only one said he voted, and none encouraged his members to do so.

A criticism leveled by many against the United Pentecostal Church is that by refusing to be directly involved in community and political affairs or in the solving of the many social problems, they are in effect supporting the injustices and sufferings that exist in their society. In their stand of extreme separation from society and its problems the United Pentecostal Church, the largest Protestant body in Colombia, removes itself from a position in which it might more directly influence society's structure for good and for justice.

But we need to see another side of the matter as well. The great majority of Jesus Only members have come from the lower and marginal classes of society. As such, most of them have never had any voice in what is happening in their country or community.

In order to understand this separation from the world . . . it is necessary to go beyond theological motivations. . . . We have affirmed that this religious movement expresses a protest against "a world without heart. . . ." Do not forget that for Pentecostals, . . . the "world" is, above all and in an experiential way, the world of misery, of sickness, and of death; the origin of its rejection is found in the panic fear of a world in which the new Christian, poor among the poor and marginal among the marginal, has only received deceptions and sufferings.[32]

Now in the Pentecostal Church the Jesus Only people have found something they may never have had before—the love and concern of a community of people, identity with a larger group that has the same beliefs and aspirations, and the promise of a miracle-working God for this life, and eternal paradise and joy in the next. This is infinitely more than they ever had before.

It should be remembered that, while the United Pentecostal Church is not directly involved in community programs or affairs as such, the mere fact that so many people have conquered drunkenness, family infidelity, and a host of other sins that have adverse social consequences, and now live a life of sobriety, honesty, and hard work, means that society as a whole has benefited a great deal.

Summary and Conclusion

There is a tendency for those who are familiar with the United Pentecostal Church in Colombia to deprecate their growth with statements like, "The Jesus Only people are all unstable—their growth won't last." But it is lasting, and is increasing.

The criticisms of many missionaries and national church leaders vis-a-vis the United Pentecostals reveal some of the reasons for their growth. At the same time they serve as an indictment of their own groups. First and foremost is the charge that "United Pentecostal believers are the worst there are at proselytizing —they win their converts from those who are already members of other Protestant churches." While this isn't entirely true, they do, by their own admission, win many from other Protestant groups. Some United Pentecostal pastors interviewed admitted (with a certain degree of pride!) that as many as a third of their members came from other churches. But would most of

32. Christian Lalive d'Epinay, El Refugio de las Masas (Santiago, Chile: Editorial del Pacifico, 1968), p. 158.

these have left other churches if they had been satisfied? *Why* did they leave?

Second, there is an implied criticism in the oft-heard statement: "The Jesus Only churches grow because their meetings appeal to the more emotional temperament of Colombians." While most members of other churches don't appreciate the emotional excesses of the Jesus Only people, it is apparent that *many are attracted to their meetings because of their liveliness.* This is quite a contrast to many who are guilty of wrapping the wonderful content of the gospel message in a package which is unattractive and unappealing to most Latins (i.e., meetings which are formal, rigid, unemotional, stereotyped).

Third, there is widespread criticism of the Pentecostal promise of divine healing, a promise which has much appeal to many Colombians (and to many throughout Latin America). But it should be remembered that while the promise of divine healing is an important factor in the exceptional growth of the United Pentecostal Church, there is more to the story. What about the attitudes, methods, and enthusiastic involvement in outreach that characterize these people?

But even these strategic factors do not tell the whole story. In the development of the Jesus Only church in Colombia two very important events took place that were not planned, but have greatly affected the growth and characteristics of this church. The first was the coming of the Drosts to Colombia in 1949 and their introduction of a revolutionary new way of working that became the pattern for Jesus Only churches throughout the country. Without them, the United Pentecostal Church would likely have followed a more traditional pattern under the direction of the other missionaries, and it is doubtful whether it would have achieved the kind of growth it has had.

The other event was the nationalization of the church by the Colombian pastors and church leaders in 1967, resulting in a church which is completely indigenous, free to "Colombianize," and responsible for evangelism, church planting, and missionary outreach. Seeing themselves as responsible for evangelism, the believers of the United Pentecostal Church have a healthy self-image—a church which gives generously and reaches out aggressively.

Actually, it is surprising to see how few foreign missionaries have served, and are serving today on a co-operative basis with the United Pentecostal Church. Numerous smaller denominations have many missionaries—as many as fifty or sixty. The United Pentecostal Church, meanwhile, has only a few.

As for the future prospects of the Jesus Only church, there are some dangers: (1) the possibility of more offshoot churches that divide over strange new (or revived old) doctrines or practices; (2) the possibility of a major split, or splits, over personality clashes or political infighting in the existing church; and (3) the tendency toward *caudillismo*—irresponsible bossism—in a culture where this has been a pattern, and in a church where pastors and leaders have so much authority.

On the positive side, my own observation is that the United Pentecostal Church is gaining top leaders who have maturity and experience, and who are becoming more tolerant and open to new ideas and change—men like Zuniga, Bernal, Ospina, and Cardozo. The church may lose its fanaticism (as concerns standards, the use of medicine, involvement in community affairs, etc.) under these men in the coming years. Basic doctrines are likely to remain the same for the foreseeable future.

The United Pentecostal Church will likely continue to grow. It may grow at an exceptional, but less accelerated, rate than it has in the past fifteen years. Or it may take off with even greater growth, filling all of Colombia with Jesus Only believers and churches.

Harmon A. Johnson

Harmon A. Johnson is a missionary to Brazil with Overseas Crusades, an interdenominational faith mission. His missionary service began in 1961. He is co-author of Latin American Church Growth *(Eerdmans, 1969), and author of* The Growing Church in Haiti *(West Indies Mission, 1970), and* Missoes *(Ele, 1974), a programmed text on missions written in Portuguese. Harmon Johnson studied at North Central Bible College, and at the University of Chicago. He holds the M.A. degree from Fuller Theological Seminary. At the present time he is coordinator for research for Pese (Pesquisa Evangelical), an evangelical research center in Sao Paulo, Brazil. He is on the board of Aette, the Evangelical Association for Theological Training by Extension in Brazil. He is married and the father of two daughters and two sons.*

12 | UMBANDA:

A Modern Brazilian Religion

Harmon A. Johnson

Umbanda is Brazil's fastest growing religion. Although its roots are ancient it must be identified as a modern religion. Drawing on Christianity, the great Oriental philosophies, African religions, and Iberian folklore, it is characteristically Brazilian.

The term *Umbanda* refers properly to a particular cult which has developed in and around the city of Sao Paulo, Brazil. In popular usage, however, it is used to refer to the belief system of the practitioners, and more generally as a generic term for similar forms of religion in every region of the country.

Religious Options in Brazil

Brazil is passing through a phase of rapid social change which affects every aspect of life. Because religion is much more an integral part of life in Brazil than is true in most of the Western world, this era of change has had profound effects on Brazilian religious patterns. The three principal options open to Brazilians today are evangelical faith, committed Catholicism, and the various forms of spiritism, of which Umbanda is one. Nominal Catholicism, which characterized Brazilians until the last few decades, is giving way to new religious loyalties.

• 247

The growth pattern of the evangelical churches can be understood with considerable clarity, thanks to the annual religious census conducted by the Instituto Brasileiro de Geografia e Estatistica, the government bureau in charge of statistics. Every local church and cult center are required to complete a census form indicating that year's changes in membership totals. The census is by no means complete but it is sufficiently accurate to show patterns of growth. The evangelical growth rate is approximately twice that of the population as a whole.

The growth of committed Catholicism is much harder to measure. The development of Bible study groups sponsored by local Catholic clergy, the *Cursillo* movement (a lay retreat program), and the revitalization of some dioceses are some clear indications that committed Catholicism is growing in Brazil.[1] Since this growth is among those who have always appeared in the census as Catholics, it is impossible to quantify it.

Most difficult of all to measure is the growth of spiritism. Only a fraction of the various spiritist movements are formally organized and an even smaller proportion of the spiritist centers are registered with the government and appear in the official religious census. A further complication is that the majority of persons who attend spiritist sessions may not consider themselves to be spiritists although they have beliefs which must be classed as spiritist, they look to spiritism for help in their problems, and effectively practice spiritism by their use of spiritist rites, customs, and artifacts.

Thus, it is necessary to estimate the extent of spiritist growth (including that of Umbanda) by such imprecise approximations as the increase of spiritist influence in Brazilian national life, the obvious proliferation of spiritist centers, the increased percentage of Brazilians who identify themselves as spiritists, and the changing attitudes of the Brazilian spiritists themselves.

> Where the Spiritists once sounded stridently anticlerical and rather unsure of themselves, they have now taken on some of the smugness and parochialism their Christian adversaries once showed. Confident that they will absorb all Christian churches, they exude good will and facile toleration. Souls—millions of them

---

1. Fausto Guimares Cupertino, "O Catolicismo Brasileiro em Crise," *O Estado de Sao Paulo*, January 11, 1973, p. 16.

—may be at stake in this parapsychological battle of the Spirits, and both sides sense its sweep.[2]

For several years, the foremost Roman Catholic apologist vis-à-vis spiritism was Boaventura Kloppenburg. Since Vatican II, his voice has been muted, but his book *O Espiritismo no Brasil* (1964)[3] continues to be the definitive statement of Roman Catholic views on Brazilian spiritism. He has pointed out that three factors make it difficult to determine the number of spiritists in Brazil.

First, the word "spiritist" itself does not have a univocally determined meaning; there is much disagreement as to definition among the Brazilian spiritistic groups themselves. Secondly, "Catholic" is the magic word in Brazil; even when Brazilians are not practicing Catholics, they continue to pledge allegiance to Catholicism. Thirdly, the official religious data of the 1960 census is still unknown and thus we can only base ourselves on estimates.[4]

The 1960 and 1970 general censuses and the religious census published annually by the Brazilian government do not serve to clarify the picture since only officially registered groups and self-identified spiritists are included. Each year, the religious groups included in the census of the previous year are sent a new form to complete and return. There is no systematic way of discovering new groups or of including groups which have escaped the attention of the census bureau.

Joining a Protestant congregation is by no means the only alternative open to those in search of a social identity. Competitive religious groups such as the various spiritualistic sects, Umbanda (a fusion of African cult forms and spiritualistic beliefs), and a number of local African cult centers variously called Candomble, Macumba, or Xango, have attracted the masses in Brazil. Conversion to Protestantism ranks as only one alternative among

2. Donald Warren, Jr., "Spiritism in Brazil," *Journal of Inter-American Studies* X (1969), 403.

3. Boaventura Kloppenburg, *O Espiritismo no Brazil* (Petropolis, Rio de Janeiro: Editors Vozes, 1964).

4. Boaventura Kloppenburg, "The Prevalence of Spiritism in Brazil," in *The Religious Dimension in the New Latin America*, ed. John J. Considine (Notre Dame, IN: Fides, 1966), p. 77.

several and there is, of course, a considerable amount of shifting from group to group.[5]

The Background of Umbanda

Approximately fifty-five years ago a spiritist group under the leadership of Zelio de Morais moved from the city of Rio de Janeiro to the interior town of Sao Goncalo in order to be free from police persecution and establish a cult center. The inspiration for this move came from a spirit known as *Caboclo das Sete Encruzilhadas* (Indian Spirit of the Seven Crossroads). In Sao Goncalo they established a center known as the Circle of the Indian Spirit of the Seven Crossroads in honor of their guiding spirit. Later, the group purchased a house to which they gave the name *Tenda Nossa Senhora da Piedade* (The Hut of Our Lady of Piety). This was the first of the centers of what later came to be known as Umbanda. "Here was the essence of religious and racial syncretism: Negro and white worshippers together, practising a more evolved form of African ritual, under the influence of Europe's Kardecism, under the leadership of an Indian spirit guide, and under the name of Our Lady of Piety."[6]

Umbanda as a movement arose as an effort, whether conscious or not, to unify the diverse elements of Brazilian religious values. It is significant that the rapid growth of Protestantism in the last few decades has resulted in an effort to include Protestant elements in Umbanda practices. Since Umbanda is overtly syncretistic, it includes elements from as far back as we can go in the history of man as well as many modern innovations and adaptations. However, the result of this effort has been the emergence of a religion that is new and different and greater than the sum of its parts. The historical development of Umbanda as a religion can best be seen through an analysis of its Brazilian nature.

Umbanda is a deliberate synthesis of various aspects of traditional Brazilian religious beliefs and practices. At least part of its appeal can be attributed to the fact that it expresses the religious convictions of a majority of Brazilians.

5. Emilio Willems, *Followers of the New Faith* (Nashville: Vanderbilt University Press, 1967), p. 123.
6. Pedro McGregor, *Jesus of the Spirits* (New York: Stein and Day, 1966), pp. 169-70.

In a special project conducted in 1971 by MARPLAN, a Brazilian research organization, 312 adults of all social classes and of both sexes were interviewed.[7] Sixty-eight per cent of those interviewed felt that attendance at Umbanda cult centers was very high. Forty-three per cent believed that the supernatural phenomena in the spiritist centers are genuine. The sample was made up of 72 per cent Catholics, 10 per cent spiritists, 8 per cent Protestants, 1 per cent from other religions, and 9 per cent who professed no religion. Over half (52 per cent) believed that all religions are true, 56 per cent believed that religiosity is decreasing among men, while 41 per cent believed that only one religion is true, and 31 per cent believed that religiosity among men is increasing.

As regards the reason for the appeal of Umbanda, 35 per cent attributed it to the healings, psychological peace, charity and spiritual comfort to be found in the cult sessions. Twenty-six per cent thought that the reason for Umbanda's appeal is the anguish of modern man as he faces life's problems, the desire to get ahead in life, and the yearning for material improvement. We shall look at these factors again when we come to consider the factors involved in the growth of Umbanda. At this point, the significant thing is that the general acceptance of Umbanda is remarkably high and that Umbanda is seen by many as a valid religious option.

Kloppenburg has aptly summarized a number of the strange syncretistic elements found in Umbanda:

> Supernatural communications, apocalyptic prophecies, redemption messages, statues that come alive, celestial figures that appear among the trees, diabolic nocturnal persecutions, images that bleed and cry, new cults that promise salvation to the world, messages and secrets, stigmas and healings, millenarian prophecies, secret and esoteric instructions, haunted houses, spoken voices, transcendental photographs—there is a whole world, disordered, fascinating, and surprising.[8]

In order to understand this kind of religious attitude, we must understand the type of Christianity which developed in Brazil. Roger Bastide has described various types of Catholicism

---

7. MARPLAN, "Umbanda tem no Rio Alta Frequencia," *Jornal do Brazil,* September 9, 1971, p. 20.
8. Kloppenburg, *O Espiritismo no Brazil,* p. 64.

in Brazil.[9] He contrasts the austere Catholicism of the religious orders (principal among them the Jesuits), the familial Catholicism of the Portuguese colonists, and the Catholicism which developed among the African slaves.

The Iberian Catholicism brought to the New World was already predisposed to accept the basic premises of spiritism. German Arcineagas describes how Bartolomé de las Casas dealt with spirit powers:

> Fray Bartolome lists as the first line of defense: the cross, holy water, and naming the Holy Trinity. But he adds that there are also "things found in the gamut of items created by nature which are said to have the virtue of driving away demons and undoing the magic tricks and spells cast by sorcerers, magicians, and enchanters."[10]

No doubt others, more ignorant and less well prepared, brought with them even stronger ideas. The cult of saints, as practiced in Brazil, shows the effect of this legacy. Charles Wagley's description of *Ita* is typical of much of Brazil.

> The content of their religion includes many local variations of archaic Iberian beliefs which, while not in direct conflict with contemporary orthodox ideology, often overshadow many of its main precepts. God and Christ are worshiped, but more important in local religion are the Virgin and the saints . . . St. Anthony, St. Benedict, St. John, St. Apolonia, and the Virgin are identified by the people with their local images. Each saint is considered a local divinity. . . . To the people of Ita, the saints are protectors, benevolent powers to whom they may go for help and protection.[11]

Portuguese settlers put their simple faith in a rather nebulous God and in very specific and knowable human saints.[12] This extreme credulity and pragmatic approach to religion created an atmosphere ripe for spiritism.

9. Roger Bastide, "Religion and the Church in Brazil," in *Brazil: Portrait of Half a Continent,* ed. Lynn T. Smith and Alexander Marchant (New York: The Dryden Press, 1951), pp. 335-38, 346-48.
10. German Arcineagas, *Latin America: A Cultural History* (New York: Alfred A. Knopf, 1967), p. 534.
11. Charles Wagley, *Amazon Town: A Study of Man in the Tropics* (New York: Alfred A. Knopf, 1964), pp. 220-21.
12. Parke Renshaw, "A New Religion for Brazilians," *Practical Anthropology* 13 (1966), 126-32.

According to Freyre, the church which affected the cultural development of Brazil most directly was the plantation chapel.[13] The resident priest became the servant of the plantation owner.

This familial Catholicism possessed neither inflexibility of dogma nor puritanism of conduct. It was all indulgence, softened by the heat of the tropics and by the sensuality of the Negro women [sic]. It let itself be contaminated by the superstitions of the Indians and the religions of the Africans, belief in forest spirits, water mothers, love potions.[14]

The educative efforts of the orders did succeed in creating a different type of Catholicism which was more orthodox and more Roman. While it could coexist with familial Catholicism it never succeeded in replacing it.

Catholicism among the slaves was overtly syncretistic. The plantation owners encouraged the slaves to maintain their own life-style. Many Roman Catholic priests of the time felt that as long as people were faithful to the church it did not matter what else they were mixing with their Catholicism.

To the Catholicism of the religious orders, the Portuguese colonists, and the African slaves Bastide adds two other types of Catholicism: present-day rural and urban Catholicism. Due to the scarcity of priests, rural Catholicism follows the patterns of familial Catholicism. In rural Brazil, persons known as *benzedores* (blessers) and *rezadores* (prayers) are common. They mix into their Catholic ritual many non-Catholic practices.

In contrast, urban Catholicism is tied closely to the diocesan system. The direct influence of the hierarchy keeps this type of Catholicism much freer from admixture. The result of this, however, is that the lower class urban dwellers of a rural mind-set have had to look outside the church for the explanations of the mysterious which they were accustomed to find in rural Catholicism. One of the reasons for the proliferation of spiritist sects in the cities of Brazil may be this dissatisfaction with the type of Catholicism found in the cities. Kloppenburg comments on the religious illiteracy of these people:

---

13. Gilberto Freyre, *The Masters and the Slaves* (Casa-grande and Senzala): *A Study in the Background of Brazilian Civilization,* trans. from the Portuguese by Samuel Putnam, second Eng. lang. ed., rev. ed. (New York: Alfred A. Knopf, 1971) p. 192.
14. Bastide, "Religion and the Church in Brazil," p. 336.

Our people lack an elementary religious education. Certain religious practices, good in themselves and Christian, are manifested more by folkloric impulses than for religious motives. There is no Christian conscience formed. Our people do not have available sufficient criteria to be able to discern truth from error, superstition from religion, or pagan practices from Christian worship. They want to be Christians but they do not know what Christianity is. For this reason they are easy victims of wrong propaganda that comes with a Christian façade.[15]

Although Kloppenburg obviously is writing from the point of view of a churchman who is disappointed at the inadequate religious understanding of his countrymen, his evaluation of Brazilian Catholicism is objective. Emilio Willems concurs with his judgment: "Folk Catholicism itself, even without African or Indian ingredients, seems to have an unlimited capacity for the absorption of religious innovations at variance with the teachings of the Church."[16]

The second and largest element of the Brazilian religious scene is the strong prevalence of beliefs and practices surviving from African religious systems brought by the slaves and to a much lesser extent from Amerindian religions. In the area around Sao Luis, Maranhao, Dahomean religion has been kept alive, complete with the Dahomean pantheon.[17] The related Yoruba system dominates in Candomble, best known of the African religions in Brazil.

The Yoruba designation for their gods, Orixa, has come to be the accepted term in Brazil for the various African deities of whatever pantheon.

These Orixas are now personifications of natural forces, natural phenomena, and the basic activities of man. They are represented by fetishes in which the divinity can rest. Every Orixa has a shrine which may be a hut, a room in a temple, a tree, or a spring which is its assento (resting place) and in which the fetish is kept. The spirit enters the fetish by means of a special magical act and can be called to leave it through another ritual.

---

15. Kloppenburg, *O Espiritismo no Brazil,* pp. 33-34.
16. Willems, *Followers of the New Faith,* p. 258.
17. Manoel Nunes Pereira, "A Casa das Minas: Contribuicao ao Estudo das Sobrevinencias Daomeinnas no Brazil," *Publicacoes da Sociedade Brasileira de Antropologia e Etnologia* I (1947).

But the gods are also free to roam at will. These fetishes are not idols; they are not prayed to nor worshipped in any way.[18]

The head of the pantheon is Oluran, supreme and unapproachable. The African slaves would find a close parallel in the attitude of their masters to the Christian God who was also unapproachable except through the mediation of the saints. In modern variations of African religions, the supreme god is maintained and identified as the Christian God. In the many changes which the pantheon has undergone, perhaps the most significant has been the general syncretism with Catholicism and the specific identification of African gods with particular Catholic saints.

> The elements ancestral to the present-day organization of worship have been retained in immediately recognizable form. . . . This phenomenon . . . is marked by the following characteristics: the Negroes profess nominal Catholicism while at the same time they belong to "fetish cults" which are under the direction of priests whose functions are essentially African and whose training follows more or less well recognized channels of instruction and initiation; the ceremonialism and idealogy of these "fetish cults" exhibit Catholic elements more or less prominently; and everywhere specific identifications are made between African gods and Catholic saints.[19]

This particular phenomenon had significant implications for Umbanda which developed later. It helped to make Umbanda acceptable to nominal Catholics who interpreted it as a Christian religion because of the references to the saints and the use of artifacts and practices commonly associated with Catholicism.

Except in Belem and other centers in the Amazon basin, most of the Amerindian elements of Brazilian religion are not survivals but are recent accretions which are part of the current idealization of Brazil's Amerindian heritage. Some of these are obvious, such as the war bonnets of the North American Plains Indians which appear in some Brazilian cults.

---

18. Kalervo Oberg, "Afro-Brazilian Religious Cults," *Sociologia* XXI (1959), 135.
19. Melville J. Herskovits, "African Gods and Catholic Saints in New World Religious Relief," in *Reader in Comparative Religion: An Anthropological Approach*, ed. William A. Lessa and Evan Z. Vogt (New York: Harper and Row, 1965), p. 542.

The other major component of Brazilian religious expression is what is known in Brazil as "high spiritism," a term used to distinguish it from "low spiritism" which would include those cult groups of essentially African or Amerindian origin. While most high spiritists would object, Umbanda is considered to mediate between the two spiritisms. High spiritism is rationalistic and essentially European in origin, although the influence of Eastern mystical religions (via Europe) is conspicuous.

High spiritism, known in Brazil as Kardecism after Allan Kardec, the codifier of modern spiritism, has developed into a highly evolved system of cult centers and a world view emphasizing charity, the reality of spirit activity, and the inevitability of progress. The rational emphasis, the reinterpretation of Christianity, and the stress on charity and the Golden Rule have won the sympathy of most Brazilians and the adherence of many. "Many good Brazilians of various classes, disillusioned or neglected by the Roman Catholic Church, are attracted by the moralistic preachments on love and brotherhood, the charity projects, the scientistic ring of the cosmology, and the assurance of the reality of the spiritual world and of immortality."[20]

While the Afro-Brazilian cults emphasize ritual acts of worship of the deities, high spiritism emphasizes communication with the spirits. The heart of Kardecism is the seance. The healings, divinations, counseling, and communications from the dead are all understood to be an essential part of the practice of charity. Kloppenburg has developed a working definition of spiritism:

In a general manner, "Spiritism" is understood as a pretentiously evoked, perceptible communication with spirits from the beyond, whether to receive news from them, to consult them (necromancy), or to place them at the service of man (magic); either to do good (white magic) or to perform some evil (black magic). To be a spiritist, therefore, it suffices to accept this minimum doctrine: that spirits exist; that these spirits are ardently interested in communicating with us in order to instruct or help us; that we men can evoke perceptible communication with these spirits.[21]

20. Renshaw, "A New Religion for Brazilians," p. 131.
21. Kloppenburg, "The Prevalence of Spiritism in Brazil," pp. 77-78.

The appeal of Kardecism was always to the rational and intellectual. Magic as such was impossible because everything was explained in terms of spirit activity. Personal problems were dealt with by enlisting the aid of the spirits and by educating the lower classes of spirits which were held to be responsible for most of the ills which humanity suffered. "Since Kardecism had made the acceptance of spirits as such respectable, however, the time was ripe for a religious movement embracing the generality of his principles but adding the mysticism, the ceremonial, the music and color that he lacked. Thus Umbanda...."[22]

Umbanda Belief and Practice

In Umbanda there are seven lines of spirits corresponding roughly to the orders or classes of spirits of Kardecism. Each line is made up of many spirits which form ranks within the line. Each line is identified with one of the Yoruba Orixas, although not all Umbandists agree as to what the seven lines are or with what Orixa they should be identified. A typical list includes the following:

(1) Oxala—Jesus Christ
(2) Yemanja—the Virgin Mary
(3) Ogun—St. George
(4) Oxossi—St. Sebastian
(5) Xango—St. James
(6) Oxun—St. Catherine
(7) Omulu—St. Lazarus

The spirits of a line and rank share characteristics, but each spirit is distinct in personality with its own unique nature and function.

Umbanda as a religion is made up of a multitude of sects which display a remarkable lack of unity.

If Spiritism is belief in search of an institution, Umbanda is religious aspiration in search of a form. Really, what are seen in Sao Paulo are changing variations of religious organizations, without doctrinal or ritualistic unity. Each terreiro has its system and each director thinks he monopolizes the most perfected truth.

---

22. McGregor, *Jesus of the Spirits*, p. 166.

This picture is varied, not only by the multiplicity of the forms it includes, but by its internal dynamism, which brings instability of concepts and a disposition toward the syncretism of all factors.[23]

Kardecism has been unified by the codification of Kardec, and Candomble and other "purer" Afro-Brazilian cults have maintained a relative stability by their appeal to tradition, but Umbanda, which sets out to be syncretistic, has lacked a unifying force. How, then, should we define Umbanda? "Umbanda stands for those Negro-derived practices now performed to a greater or lesser degree under the influence of Kardecism, its purpose being to help man overcome the difficulties of this life."[24]

The key to this definition is the expression "to a greater or lesser degree under the influence of Kardecism." Umbandists hold that Umbanda is just a different way of practicing spiritism. Within the movement there is disagreement as to just how much of Kardecism there ought to be. Leaders have tried from the beginning to discourage those aspects of the African religious practices which seem most primitive and most offensive to the public and to the authorities.

The *terreiros* (cult centers) of Umbanda are located in specially constructed buildings, in rented halls, in private residences, or in shacks or outbuildings. In accordance with the practice of the African cults there is always a little altar outside the building which is dedicated to Exu, the "Mercury" of the Yoruba pantheon, identified by many as Satan of Christian theology. This altar is always kept locked to prevent the god from wandering away to practice evil. In accordance with the pattern of Xango, the syncretistic African cult of northeast Brazil, the main altar in the *terreiro* includes many images of the various Orixas in the form of Catholic saints; these images stand side by side with figures representing the *pretos velhos,* the old black men whose spirits communicate with the worshipers during cult sessions, and the *caboclos,* the Indian spirit guides. The only thing to indicate the African origin of Umbanda is the figure of Exu.

---

23. Candido Procopio Ferreira de Camargo, *Kardecismo e Umbanda* (Sao Paulo: Liveraria Pioneira Editora, 1961), p. 33.
24. McGregor, *Jesus of the Spirits,* p. 183.

The cult sessions are known as *giras* (literally, turnings). Under the direction of the head of the center known as the father- or mother-of-saint, the session begins with a special "fumigation" of the *cavalos* ("horses"—the mediums who will be possessed by the spirits), the *cambonos* (their helpers), and the drums. A second fumigation includes everyone in attendance in order to remove any evil influences. In the more African forms of Umbanda, Exu is dispatched and sacrifices similar to those used in Candomble are offered. Then, to the rhythmic beating of the drums, the drinking of *cachaca* (cheap Brazilian brandy) and incantations, the *cavalos* are possessed by the spirits. Each is possessed by a different spirit and makes characteristic gestures and sounds which indicate the particular spirit in possession. Finally, the music is stopped and the *cambonos* lead the *cavalos* to a place where they may sit. Lines of inquirers form to ask aid of the various spirits. Under the possession of the spirit, each *cavalo* helps those who have brought their problems. The session ends with a special song which sends away the spirits.

The trend in Umbanda is toward a closer approximation with Kardecism. Many *terreiros* no longer use alcoholic beverages and some have eliminated the use of drums.

Umbanda is concerned primarily with those spiritual problems which reflect Brazilian beliefs about the nature of supernatural power. The opening and closing of the body, the opening and closing of the "way," *amarrar* (to tie), *desmanchar* (the undoing of a spell), and the evil eye are common concepts. By means of special ceremonial acts the body may be "closed." "The closing of the body has the purpose of protecting the individual against visible and invisible evil, freeing the body from knife and bullet wounds."[25] The person whose body has been closed is immune to all evil attempts against him. Opening the body would have the opposite effect. A closed "way" is inability to achieve one's goals because spiritual forces obstruct him. A way is opened by means of the correct ritual. *Amarrar* is the process by which a person is *bound* to perform a particular

---

25. Tancredo Silva Pinto and Byron Torres de Freitas, *Guia e Ritual para Organizacao de Terreiros de Umbanda* (Rio de Janeiro: Editora Eco, 1968), p. 90.

act or feel a particular way, a ritual much used by lovers. *Desmanchar* is the process by which magic can be undone.

The Growth of Umbanda

Among the various types of spiritism, Umbanda is the most pervasive. Even Kardecism, which has looked down on Umbanda and all other Afro-Brazilian cults as inferior, is conforming to Umbandist practices. Some Kardec centers now use candles and images, set restrictions on food and sex on the day of a session, and use white vestments—all of which are Umbandist in origin.[26] Because of its syncretistic nature it is quite possible that eventually Umbanda will swallow up all of the other forms of spiritism.

"Spiritism is growing in a cultural milieu characterized by religious pluralism, the formalization of religion, and the condition known as *anomie*."[27] However, as will be shown later, *anomie* is not the final chapter in the process, but is only a phase in the "resynthesis of the mazeway."[28] Religious pluralism has always characterized Brazil, but the condition was accentuated and reinforced by the religious freedom which developed with the evolution of Brazilian political institutions. The growth of evangelical Christianity and of committed Catholicism has served to educate Brazilians as to what is and what is not Christian.

Both Charles Wagley[29] and Eduardo Galvao[30] foresaw the development of a more orthodox Catholicism in the Amazon region: "Socio-religious change in the Amazon region, then, is not one of simple and gradual secularization, accompanying a growing influence of urban patterns. Rather, formal religious practice gains in importance as the penetration of new forces from the outside continues."[31] But what actually happened there as elsewhere is that the move toward formal religion which they

---

26. Ferreira de Camargo, *Kardecismo e Umbanda*, p. 23.
27. Harmon A. Johnson, "Authority over the Spirits: Brazilian Spiritism and Evangelical Church Growth," M.A. thesis, Fuller Theological Seminary, 1969, p. 57.
28. Anthony F. C. Wallace, "Revitalization Movements," *American Anthropologist* 58 (1956), 264-81.
29. Wagley, *Amazon Town*, p. 263.
30. Eduardo Galvao, "The Religion of an Amazon Community," Ph.D. dissertation, Faculty of Political Science, Columbia University, 1952, pp. 4-6.
31. Ibid., p. 5.

anticipated has been the formalization of spiritism and not of Catholicism. Formerly, Brazilians felt free to practice other religions while maintaining their nominal Catholicism. They felt no disloyalty in this nor were they aware of any paradox in their attitude. Now they must choose. While Umbandists and other spiritists accept anyone without requiring exclusive allegiance, the Roman Catholic Church and the various evangelical churches have called for an either/or choice.

The result has been that many Brazilians have had to evaluate their religious allegiances. Many have chosen to identify themselves as practicing spiritists. This has tended to hasten the process of conversion of others. As already described, Umbanda presents a world view which is essentially animistic and is a serious attempt to deal with all of reality. In Umbanda, Brazilians are finding a satisfactory explanation of the irrational and mysterious in life (at least from their point of view).

Typically, the pattern of conversion to Umbanda, as to other types of spiritism, takes place in four stages.[32]

(1) The conversion process begins with a personal problem which is brought to the Umbanda medium. The problem may be physical illness, emotional distress due to alienation, sorrow over a death, disappointment in love, economic deprivation, or frustration with life. The sharing of the problem itself may grant a certain emotional release. The significance of this stage is that the person is looking to Umbanda for the solution to life's problems. For many Brazilians, their contact with Umbanda never goes beyond this. However, a significant step which prepares the way for subsequent stages has been taken. This is particularly true if the person has been disappointed in seeking help from other religions. Umbanda speaks to that which is most profoundly religious in humanity in that it includes all of human experience in the province of religion.

(2) The second phase of conversion to Umbanda is a stage of experimentation in which the person tests the results obtained in the first stage. Seeing the medium in a state of possession tends to reinforce the conviction that the spirit world is real. The person involved sees others being helped by Umbanda. Only those who have been helped to their own satisfaction

---

32. Ferreira de Camargo, *Kardecismo e Umbanda*, pp. 77-81.

usually reach this stage. By immersion in the world of Umbanda, the person experiences the reality of the religion. In this stage, the person may, for the first time, experience possession by a spirit.

(3) The next stage is crucial. Until this point there has been no commitment as such. Now, convinced of the validity of experiences with spiritist phenomena and satisfied with the result of the stage of experimentation, the person commits himself. It is significant that this commitment does not necessarily require an overt act. It is rather an attitudinal change. From this point on, the person counts himself as an Umbandist, at least in some sense, and will defend Umbandist beliefs and practices.

(4) The last stage or phase of conversion is internalization. All prior experience, all prior learning, all prior orientation are fitted into the new Umbandist orientation resulting in a new world view. Much which had been implicit in prior beliefs becomes explicit. Not that the new world view is completely consistent—that would be too much to ask of anything—but values are rearranged to the satisfaction of the new convert. At this point, he takes an overt stand as an Umbandist if such a stand has not been taken before.

Because conversion to Umbanda takes place in stages, there are three kinds of Umbandists. Pedro McGregor has differentiated between "seekers" who visit cult centers to find solutions to personal problems and "followers" who regularly attend a particular center and participate in cult activities there.[33] A third category must be added. There are also those who participate in decision-making for the cult center. Although leadership in Umbanda is primarily based on personal charisma with spirit possession as a prerequisite, almost all centers have an "in group" responsible for the well-being of the center on a more or less democratic basis.

There is little overt proselytism by Umbandists. Naturally enough, those who have had unusual experiences through Umbanda or who have become excited about the Umbandist world view will share this with friends, relatives, and neighbors. When confronted by anyone in difficulty they will praise Umbanda and suggest that Umbanda may solve the problem. Umbandists,

---

33. McGregor, *Jesus of the Spirits*, p. 203.

as a rule, do not feel any compulsion to win others to commitment to Umbanda. There is in Brazil an astonishing toleration of religious diversity.

> The way in which many people drift back and forth between
> various forms of religion, perhaps without ever developing a
> lasting allegiance to any faith in particular, especially the nai-
> vete with which many Brazilians profess to be Catholic while
> participating in Umbanda or Spiritist cults, suggests not that all
> existing faiths are perceived as equally true, but that all are
> regarded as potentially true. Thus the pattern of religious
> experimentation, traceable to folk Catholicism, sets the stage,
> so to speak, for the proliferation of new sects.[34]

An Umbandist's approach to a non-Umbandist might then be:
What have you tried in order to solve your problem? Perhaps
if your own religion doesn't help you with this problem you
ought to try something else. How about trying Umbanda?

Growth Factors

The growth of Umbanda is overwhelmingly, although not
exclusively, an urban phenomenon. Part of the reason for this
is that rural and small-town Brazil is far more traditional than
the larger cities. In the more conservative societies there is still
considerable community pressure to hinder anyone who is
tempted to change religious affiliation.

The phenomenon of urban religious growth is far more
complex, however, than the absence of conservative social pressures. "Newly emergent social groups are, at least in the context of a society in which the religious view of the world
dominates, likely to need and to evolve new patterns of religious
belief to accommodate themselves in their new situation."[35] As
Gino Germani has explained, the city itself can serve as a
mechanism to integrate individuals and groups into modern national society.[36] In response to Germani, Glen Beyer points out
that migration to the city often creates crisis states for the
migrants and that many of the city's institutions fail to provide

---

34. Willems, *Followers of the New Faith*, p. 258.
35. Brian Wilson, *Religion in Secular Society* (Baltimore: Penguin Books,
1966), p. 230.
36. Gino Germani, "The Concept of Social Integration," in *The Urban
Explosion in Latin America*, ed. Glen H. Beyer (Ithaca, NY: Cornell
University Press, 1967), p. 175.

a sense of belonging for them.[37] Access to groups and associations which could foster transition to urban life is often limited for the migrant. Umbanda provides a place to belong, a supportive social context, as well as a value system to explain reality.

Anomie (the breakdown of traditional social controls) is the state in which the masses live on their way to a new integration of values. This state is due in part to the tensions arising from the rapid social change inherent in urbanization. Ferreira de Camargo sees this as a negative destructive thing which destroys true religion.[38] However, since it is a phase in the process of integration, this stage is not all negative. On the contrary it is the stage at which the old unsatisfactory ways are abandoned to clear the way for the new synthesis of values.

Umbanda helps to integrate men into urban society. Spiritism of whatever type gives men status. Since leadership in Umbanda does not require the mastery of any corpus of material, status becomes easier to achieve than in Kardecism. For lower-class persons—despised by others in their own land—Umbanda provides a way to get ahead socially. It grants a sense of belonging and of social support from one's peers.

> Faced with the uncertainties of life under the new technological system and the impersonal relationship of employer and employee, the modern Brazilian tends to feel that all of life is irrational and mysterious. In this kind of atmosphere those systems which attempt to provide an explanation of the irrational and mysterious have a certain appeal.[39]

I have already referred to the re-emphasis on religion which accompanies urbanization. In this connection, Alex Inkeles wrote: "When a man goes to the city . . . he reintegrates himself, if you like, with the formal things around him, one of which is his religion."[40] What results under the pressure of *anomie* accompanied by the frightening freedom of urban life is that the

---

37. Glen H. Beyer, ed., *The Urban Explosion in Latin America*, pp. 197-208.

38. Ferreira de Camargo, *Kardecismo e Umbanda*, p. 66.

39. Johnson, "Authority over the Spirits," p. 61.

40. Alex Inkeles, "The Modernization of Man," in *Urbanism in World Perspective: A Reader*, ed. Sylvia Fleis Fava (New York: Thomas Y. Crowell Company, 1968), p. 365.

religious values of Brazil (which are essentially those of Umbanda) are reworked and reformulated. Often this formalization
of religion takes the form of adherence to Umbanda. As M. G.
Barnett has put it, "Unsettlement for any cause creates a fluid
condition in which the old values are no longer operative. With
the old sanctions gone or of doubtful validity, the way is open
for the creation and the acceptance of new interpretations."[41]
For some Brazilians this is the route into Umbanda. All that is
needed is a new interpretation of an old value system. For
others, the route is different, but the end result is the same.
There are other innovative adaptations to extreme deprivations.
"Compromises, syncretisms, imitations, and sublimations are alternative reactions to the loss of essentials."[42] In the same way
that the cult itself is an attempt to explain reality the choice of
affiliation with the cult is *a deliberate, organized, conscious
effort to construct (or adopt) a more satisfying culture (or life
style, or symbol system)."[43]

My own experience in Brazil bears out Ferreira de Camargo's
assertion that *anomie* is a major factor in the growth of Umbanda. However, Seth and Ruth Leacock have come to quite
another conclusion in their study of the Batuque, the Afro-
Brazilian cult of Belem.

> Judging from our data, however, rural-urban migration does not
> appear to be a major factor in inducing individuals to join the
> Batuque. Admittedly, Belem is not as impersonalized or urban-
> ized as are the southern Brazilian cities, and an individual mov-
> ing to the city from the rural interior would not have as difficult
> an adjustment problem as the rural migrant to Sao Paulo or Rio
> de Janeiro. However, economic hardship and health problems
> are as great in Belem as in any of the southern cities. Medium-
> istic religions (spiritualism and Pentecostalism as well as the
> Batuque) are rapidly growing in Belem as in the south. Such
> religious movements may represent responses to the stresses of
> rapid social change but our data suggest that the possession

---

41. M. G. Barnett, *Innovation: The Basis of the Cultural Change* (New
York: McGraw-Hill, 1953), p. 89.
42. Ibid.
43. Vivian Garrison, "Sectarianism and Psychosocial Adjustment: A Controlled Comparison of Puerto Rican Pentecostals and Catholics," in *Religious Movements in Contemporary America*, ed. Irving I. Zaretsky and
Mark P. Leone (Princeton, NJ: Princeton University Press, 1974), p. 329.

religions attract the native-born, lower-class urban population more than recent rural migrants.[44]

Although this may place in question the significance of migration for the growth of Umbanda (Ferreira de Camargo's data are at least as well documented and based on a larger sample, however), this argument by the Leacocks does not necessarily invalidate the thesis of *anomie* as a factor in the growth of Umbanda.

It is true that native urbanites enjoy decided advantages over migrants.[45] However, these advantages are primarily economic. The most perplexed and frustrated of all urban dwellers in Brazil today are those who are native urbanites, whose status in the city was unchallenged and whose role was understandable until rapid urbanization changed the ground rules, as it were. Suddenly, they are in competition for things which they had taken for granted—and in competition with migrants who appear to them as interlopers. Migrants come to the city expecting things to be different, but rapid urbanization catches many (if not most) native urbanites by surprise. In such a situation it is understandable that *anomie* should result. And with *anomie* the trend toward the growth of Umbanda.

Another factor in the growth of Umbanda is that it has provided many with small group participation and its attendant sense of belonging and social homogeneity.[46] This is related to the way in which Umbanda fits into Anthony Wallace's classification of religions.[47] He writes of four types of religious culture: shamanic, communal, Olympian, and monotheistic. The shamanic includes those religions in which ritual is performed by part-time practitioners or even occasional practitioners. Communal religions include as well pantheons of deities and a more specialized practice. Olympian religions center on a pantheon of several high gods and a full-time priesthood. In Wallace's classification, monotheism includes all of the so-called world

---

44. Seth and Ruth Leacock, *Spirits of the Deep* (Garden City, NY: Doubleday Natural History Press, 1973), pp. 113-14.
45. Seymour Martin Lipset and Reinhard Bendix, "The Patterns of Opportunity in Large Cities," in *Urbanism and World Perspective: A Reader*, p. 324.
46. Cupertino, "O Catolicismo Brasileiro em Crise," p. 17.
47. Wallace, "Revitalization Movements," p. 88.

religions. With a brief nod to monotheism, Umbanda succeeds in incorporating all of the significant aspects of the other three types of religion.

> Perhaps the most highly eclectic and complex form of syncretism is the Umbanda religion of Brazil. . . . It does not have its principal appeal and support among the disinherited members of the lower class. In Sao Paulo its appeal appears to be to the upwardly mobile members of the lower and lower middle class. . . . Umbanda, then, perhaps alone among the various syncretic religions with African components, has made the transition to a religion of the social whole. Indeed, one is tempted to see it as a new religion facilitating as well as symbolizing the development of a new society. . . . Umbanda appears to be able to provide its members with help in the processes of decision making and in dealing with the inventory of new statuses and roles provided by the rapid social and economic changes inherent in the development of new social forms in contemporary urban Brazil.[48]

In many very pertinent ways, the growth of Umbanda follows the patterns which have been described for the growth of sects in other parts of the Western world. It is not strange that this is so, since adherence to Umbanda involves a deliberate choice of commitment to a religion which is a faithful representation of traditional Brazilian religious values but at the same time is not a traditional religion. This heightens the sense of belonging and of small group participation.

> One of the functions of sects has obviously been the heightened sense of commitment and distinctiveness which sectarianism implies. . . . This particular characteristic may often be associated with the intensity of sect life, of the drawing together of a community which is often small, and which demands a strong communal allegiance among its members. The sect provides a context of social involvement which quite apart from the specific advantages which the ideology offers to the faithful, demands responsibilities of a much more compelling kind than are found in most voluntary organizations, interest-groups, service agencies or welfare associations.[49]

48. Erika Bourguignon, "Introduction" in *Afro-American Anthropology: Contemporary Perspectives,* ed. Norman E. Whitten and John F. Szwed (New York: The Free Press, 1970), pp. 37-38.
49. Wilson, *Religion in Secular Society,* p. 210.

The other major factor in the growth of Umbanda is that it has provided the meaningful role for the layman which was lacking in traditional Brazilian religion. It was Ivan Vallier, among others, who pointed out that the two most significant new forces in twentieth-century Latin America are the leftist political groups and the churches labeled Pentecostal.[50] Both of these movements have emphasized their laity, have granted status and responsibility with authority to all who belong to the group. To these two movements must be added spiritism and, particularly, Umbanda.

Perhaps more important than the giving of a meaningful role to everyone in the movement, however, is the potential the movement provides to rise to a position of prestige and status. Every member of Umbanda knows that not everyone can or will rise to the top, but at the same time it is common knowledge that every leader rose from the ranks and that the way is open for others to follow the same path to the top. Since leadership is not formally validated the empirical ability to lead is its own validation.

While the number of those attracted to Umbanda because of the leadership possibilities is small in proportion to the total number of adherents, it is a very significant part of the whole because it continues to provide the movement with a never-ending supply of gifted leaders.

Conclusion

Of all the religious options in Brazil, the most attractive *as a new option* at the present time is Umbanda. It is the most Brazilian of the various popular religions of Brazil, including as it does every significant element of Brazilian religious belief. The Christian elements in Umbanda do not predominate. In fact they are limited to the use of Christian artifacts without the corresponding theological content which the various forms of Christianity have assigned to these artifacts. In ethos, Umbanda fits with the religions of the Orient in that it is existential, eclectic, and nonrevelatory.

---

50. Ivan Vallier, "Religious Elites: Differentiations and Developments in Roman Catholicism," in *Elites in Latin America*, ed. Seymour Martin Lipset and Aldo Solari (New York: Oxford University Press, 1967), p. 195.

Umbanda deliberately assumes a mediating position between the spiritism of Kardecism with its heavy traces of French positivism and the more traditional animism of Candomble and other Afro-Brazilian cults. In effect, Umbanda offers Brazilians all that Kardecism's philosophical system can provide, together with the richness of the imagery of the Afro-Brazilian cults in all their depth of meaning.

The growth of Umbanda is particularly significant because it does not result from systematic campaigns of proselytism to win converts from other religions. It is a religion built on the convictions of its adherents and dependent entirely on their commitment and the excitement they generate because of their commitment.

In the midst of the kind of social change through which Brazil is passing, Umbanda with its urban orientation provides modern Brazilians with a satisfactory religious option which does not degenerate into secularity. In a context which provides relatively few opportunities for enhancement of prestige or advancement in status, Umbanda provides both. As long as these conditions obtain, Umbanda will probably continue to be the leading religious option in Brazil.

PART SEVEN

Southeast Asia

Victor L. Oliver

Victor L. Oliver has studied in nine different institutions of higher learning in England, Canada and the United States. He holds degrees from Nyack College (B.S.) and Syracuse University (M.A. and Ph.D.). His field is anthropology and he has done research in Asian religious movements with a concentration on Southeast Asia. He has written articles for a number of journals. His book Caodai Spiritism: A Study of Religion in Vietnamese Society *has been published by E. J. Brill, Leiden, Netherlands. He has been a research fellow at Southern Illinois University and has taught at Nyack College and Canadian Bible College. He has served as a minister, missionary (Vietnam) and as associate professor and vice-president of Canadian Bible College. Presently he is managing editor of Tyndale House Publishers.*

13 CAODAISM:

A Vietnamese Socio-Religious Movement

Victor L. Oliver

This is an essay on Caodaism, a fast-growing indigenous Vietnamese religion that originated in South Vietnam and has shown its greatest development in that part of the nation. Caodaism is not only concerned with ritual and other practices generally considered to be of a religious nature. The movement is also interested in social, administrative, political, and economic activities. Caodaism is, therefore, both a social movement and a religion.

After establishing the original Caodai holy see in 1926 at Tay Ninh (approximately sixty miles northwest of Saigon) the Caodai founders sought to propagate the new religion. They attracted adherents from all classes of the Vietnamese. Many of the early followers were employees of the French colonial administration in Cochinchina, the southern third of present-day Vietnam. By 1956 the number of Caodai converts had increased until they amounted to approximately one-eighth of the South Vietnamese population.[1] By the end of 1971, Caodaism had

---

1. G. Miellon, *Les Messages Spirites,* ed. Tran Quang Vinh (Tay Ninh: n.p., 1962), p. 14.

acquired a following of approximately 2,000,000 persons. This estimate includes adults and children, although the latter are not considered disciples until they formally join the religion at eighteen.

From 1926 to 1956, when the major elements of the Caodai armed forces were incorporated into the South Vietnamese army, Caodaism played a significant role in the religious, political, and military developments of South Vietnam. Until the Buddist-sponsored revolution of the 1960s the Coadai was one of the two major politico-religious forces in South Vietnam.

The strength of the Caodai influence in political affairs may be seen in the composition of the National Congress (1953), formed to discuss the terms of a Vietnamese independence treaty with the French. The Caodai were given seventeen seats at the congress, the largest delegation of any of the politico-religious groups operating in South Vietnam.[2] At this same congress the Caodai leader of the Tay Ninh "mother" organization, Pham Cong Tac, was chosen to read the political objectives of the congress to the press.[3]

The late Bernard Fall, a noted Vietnamologist, stated:

> For a short time after French power collapsed in March 1945 the Cao-Dai came close to gaining preponderance over all other groups (including the Viet Minh) operating in the South. However, in the absence of the *Ho Phap* [the above-mentioned Pham Cong Tac], still imprisoned in Madagascar, the subordinate Cao Dai leaders quarreled and failed to exploit the situation.[4]

These factors indicate the extensive influence of Caodaism upon South Vietnamese society.

Since 1926 when the movement was organized, Caodaism has suffered and, in some ways, benefited from a continuing tendency towards sectarianism, the development of sects which have broken away from the "mother church." In field studies the author identified over fifty such groups. Only a few (approximately four) of these sects have succeeded in significantly influencing, challenging, or threatening the Tay Ninh mother

2. Bernard Fall, "The Political-Religious Sects of Vietnam," *Pacific Affairs* 28 (September, 1955), 241-42.
3. Ibid., p. 242.
4. Ibid., pp. 239-40.

church (identified as Tay Ninh because this is the name of the town near which the original holy see was located).

The Establishment of Caodaism

The role of Ngo Minh Chieu and other early adherents. Ngo Minh Chieu (also known as Ngo Van Chieu) was the first disciple of Coadism. He was born February 28, 1878, in Cholon, South Vietnam. He passed his civil service examinations in 1917 and soon became Tan An district chief. In 1920 he was sent to Ha Tien where he remained only eight months. He requested a transfer to Phu Quoc, an island off the coast of Cambodia. Ngo Minh Chieu had served as district chief on Phu Quoc for four years when he received orders to return to Saigon. He worked first in the Second Bureau, now the Commerce Department, and finally, until his retirement in 1931, as county chief in the Central Ministerial Building.

From his childhood Chieu was interested in religion. He read widely in the Asian classics and studied Western spiritism through the works of Kardec, Leon Dennis and Durville.

His experiences with spiritism began in 1902. At Tan An, Ngo Minh Chieu first became acquainted with the spirit Cao Dai. In contrast to others in the group, Chieu seemed to have an extreme sensitivity in religious affairs. In February, 1920, when Cao Dai first appeared, Chieu believed the spirit's presence to be of great importance because of the tone of authoritative communication given in the seance.[5]

When transferred to Phu Quoc, Ngo Minh Chieu gathered together a group of interested spiritists and began seances at the Quang Am Tu pagoda, using young people for mediums. During his residence on Phu Quoc he received further revelations from the spirit identifying himself as Cao Dai. Obeying Cao Dai's directive, Chieu became a total vegetarian on February 8, 1921. Later, in a vision, Cao Dai gave him a revelation of the divine eye which became the symbol of the religion.

In July, 1924, Ngo Minh Chieu returned to Saigon where he met others who were interested in the spiritist movement. Among these were Vuong Quang Ky, who worked in the same Saigon office as Chieu and had attended other types of seances

---

5. Toan Anh, *Tin-Nguong Viet-Nam* (Saigon: Kim-Lai, 1967), p. 431.

at Thu Dau Mot, and Nguyen Huu Dac, who worked in the same administrative building as the other two men. When they began to hold seances at various homes, others joined their group. Chieu shared with these men the doctrines and rituals he had been taught by Cao Dai during his years of discipleship on Phu Quoc. He also taught the new adherents a simple ritual of chanting prayers and the presentation of offerings to Cao Dai. Each disciple was to observe the ritual four times daily— 6:00 A.M., 12:00 noon, 6:00 P.M., and 12:00 midnight. All the rituals were performed in front of the altar, above which was the all-seeing divine eye of Cao Dai.

According to the Caodai historian, Tran Thai Chanh, numerous people came to worship at the seances, but there was no official attempt to receive new converts into the group through the performance of a special rite.[6] This supports the premise of the Chieu Minh (one of the Caodai sects) who claim that Ngo Minh Chieu was primarily an ascetic, and was averse to making an appeal to the masses. Hue Luong, another Caodai commentator, agrees that because of Chieu's ascetic life he could not allow himself to become involved with many people, thus defiling himself.[7]

Among the group of early adherents was Le Van Trung (1875-1934), a former elected official of the Colonial Council of Cochinchina and a member of the Conseil Supérieur de l'Indochine. Mrs. Cao Quynh Cu, a Caodai disciple, notes that on January 11, 1926, Le Van Trung came to her house to see her husband. Cu was a leading member of the *Pho loan,* the first group of Caodai mediums. Le Van Trung wanted to become officially a disciple of Cao Dai.[8] Two of the first three Caodai mediums, Cao Quynh Cu and Pham Cong Tac, made a return visit to Trung's home on January 18, 1926 (under the direction of Cao Dai). On that occasion they held a seance, and Cao Dai revealed himself to Trung as the one who had previously sent Ly Thai Bach, a spirit messenger, to teach

6. Tran Thai Chanh, *Lich-Su Cao-Dai Dai-Dao Tam-Ky Pho-do: Phan Pho-Vi* (Saigon: Hoa-Chanh, 1967), p. 86.

7. Hue Luong, *Dai-Dao Tam-Ky Pho Do; Cao Dai Giao So-Giai* (Saigon: Thanh Huong, 1963), p. 19.

8. Huong Hieu, "Dao Su Xay-Ban," Tay Ninh, 1968, p. 37 (mimeographed).

and minister to Trung. Again Trung was urged to follow a religious life. From that time on, Le Van Trung began to take a leading role in the administration of the Caodai movement.

The role of the Pho loan. The term *Pho loan* indicates a medium whose office is to be the recipient of divine law. Formerly, it was used to designate those who "received" the emperor. This term was borrowed by Tran Thai Chanh in his *Lich-Su Cao-Dai Dai-Dao Tam-Ky Pho-Do: Phan Vo-Vi* (1967) to refer to the first group of Caodai mediums.

In June 1925, three Vietnamese white-collar workers in the French colonial government began meeting together to investigate *table-tournante* (table-turning). These men were Cao Quynh Cu (1887-1929), a clerk in the Saigon railway office; Cao Hoai Sang, Cu's nephew, who worked in the customs department; and Pham Cong Tac (1893-1958), also a clerk in the customs office.

Mrs. Cao Quynh Cu (her religious name is Huong Hieu) acted as their secretary. Her reports indicate that the first time they sat around the four-legged table with their hands resting on its surface, the table began to shake. In answer to the men's questions the table legs would knock on the floor—the specific number of successive raps indicating a corresponding letter of the Vietnamese alphabet.

The men developed their ability to communicate with spirits. Reports indicate that the different spirit-visitors gave messages in various languages: English, French, Chinese, and Vietnamese. Among the spirits identifying themselves were relatives, friends, heroes, patriots, and even strangers. Reports of the success in contacting the spirit world reached others.

Unlike Ngo Minh Chieu, an ardent student of religion, the *Pho loan* were not well-versed in the traditional Vietnamese religions. Jean Ross, quoted in Gabriel Gobron, incorrectly claims that they were all Buddhists.[9] Actually, Pham Cong Tac was a Roman Catholic, and the other two men were primarily followers of the traditional family cult.

In July, a spirit called "AAA" (the first three letters of the Vietnamese alphabet—distinguished by diacritical marks) identi-

---

9. Gabriel Gobron, *History and Philosophy of Caodaism* (Paris: Dervy, 1950), p. 23.

fied himself to the *Pho loan* and proceeded to assert himself as a spirit of primary importance in the nonmaterial world. Convinced of the reality of the spirit world and of the possibility of communication with departed spirits, the three *Pho loan* informed AAA that they wanted to involve themselves more fully with spirit communication. This initiated a crisis of dedication for the *Pho loan*. AAA demanded a public display of their commitment to him. On December 16, 1925, the three men, holding nine joss sticks, knelt outside on the sidewalk, praying that AAA would give them sufficient grace to reform their ways.

AAA dramatically revealed his real identity to the group on Christmas Eve, 1925, after several months of communicating with the *Pho loan*. During this time he had given instructions concerning religious affairs, answered questions, and acted as an interpreter for seance messages the *Pho loan* did not understand. On this Christmas Eve he claimed to be Ngoc Hoang Thuong De viet Cao Dai Giao Dao Nam Phuong, meaning "Jade Emperor alias Cao Dai, Religious Master of the Southern Quarter." Immediately after this, the revelation continued:

> Be joyful tonight on this the anniversary of my appearance to teach the religion in the West. Your allegiance to me brings much happiness to me. This house will be filled with my grace. You will see more miracles which will lead you to further honor me. . . . For some time I have used the symbol AAA to lead you into the religious life. Soon you must help me establish the religion. Have you seen my humility? Imitate me so that you may genuinely claim to be religious men.[10]

On January 1, 1926, Cao Dai emphasized his identity more strongly by claiming to be another revelation of Jesus, "the one who shed His blood because of His love for the world."[11]

Already by the end of 1925 the *Pho loan* had grown to include several others who were mediums. By this time they often met in two groups, one using the *xay ban* (table-tapping) and the other the *ngoc co (corbeille à bec)*, a writing instrument used in the seances.

---

10. Tran Thai Chanh, *Lich-Su Cao-Dai Dai-Dao Tam-Ky Pho-do: Phan Pho-Vi*, p. 90.
11. Ibid., p. 91.

Then contact occurred between members of the *Pho loan* and the followers of Ngo Minh Chieu. Vuong Quang Ky, one of Chieu's first converts, began to meet regularly with the *Pho loan* as the result of a seance session they had held in which Ky's father appeared with a message for him. In January 1926, the *Pho loan* mediums were directed by Cao Dai to seek Ngo Minh Chieu and receive instructions from him. They were told that he was to be their leader.[12] Chieu taught them how to construct the Caodai altar after the pattern given him on Phu Quoc. He gave them copies of prayers to replace the ones borrowed from the Minh Thien, another religious group, which the *Pho loan* had been using.[13]

Division: The two "schools" of Caodai thought. On January 27, 1926, the *Pho loan* held the first seance under the direction of Ngo Minh Chieu at his home on Bonard Street. For the next three months they practiced spirit communication and the worship of Cao Dai. This apparently harmonious relationship did not last long, however. Conflict occurred among the leaders of the movement. The result of this conflict was that Ngo Minh Chieu separated from the *Pho loan*. With a few followers he dedicated himself to the pursuit of personal holiness through a life of quiet asceticism. Ngo Minh Chieu chose the life of an ascetic, seeking to cultivate within himself those necessary religious characteristics that would guarantee his escape from rebirth, and entrance into a heavenly union with Cao Dai.

Within the Caodai movement, and among students of Vietnamese religions, there has been misunderstanding about this split in Caodaism. (The reasons for this division are discussed in the author's book on Caodaism published by E. J. Brill). The division resulted in the formation of two radically different schools of Caodai thought.

The distinction between these two schools of thought is based upon differing goals, values, and methods within Caodaism. "Esoteric" Caodaism is called *vo vi* (inaction) and emphasizes self-cultivation of the inner life by progressive eradi-

12. Nguyen Trung Hau, *Dai-Dao Can-Nguyen* (Saigon: Hoa-Chanh, 1957), p. 9.
13. Tran Thai Chanh, "Lich-Su Cao-Dai Dai-Dao Tam Ky: Phan Pho-Do," Saigon, 1970, p. 40 (typewritten).

cation of the inferior self and the resultant development of the divine element within the self. "Exoteric" Caodaism is called *pho do* (to ferry across, to help others) and emphasizes the propagation of the Caodai message to win converts and change the world.

Ngo Minh Chieu's "esoteric" sect became known as the Chieu Minh Tam Thanh. It began a way of life which was unique among Caodaists and which to this present day is followed by only about two hundred adults. They believe that each member must be "called" to a special life of asceticism. This calling must be confirmed at special seances. Their way of life becomes progressively more difficult as they apply secret techniques necessary to develop spiritual maturity. Little wonder, then, that in 1970 there were only six small chapters of this sect in South Vietnam.

The *Pho loan* mediums, on the other hand, provided the major leadership for the "exoteric" Tay Ninh mother organization. That group established their holy see in Tay Ninh province near Long Thanh. They have committed themselves to spread the message of the "Third Amnesty of God" as widely as possible from that center.

Some Basic Aspects of Caodai Teachings

The spirit world. The term *Cao Dai* literally means "high tower or palace." When using "Caodaism," I refer to the religion itself; "Caodai" means the disciples of the religion; "Cao Dai" is the term used by Caodai adherents to refer to God. This last term was part of the terminology used by spirit AAA when he identified himself on Christmas Eve, 1925, to the *Pho loan* as Ngoc Hoang Thuong De viet Cao Dai Giao Dao Nam Phuong. The most commonly used title for the deity Cao Dai in official Caodai terminology is *Cao Dai Tien Ong Dai Bo Tat Ma Ha Tat* (High palace, Immortal, His Honor the Eldest Bodhisattva, the Venerable Saint). The Caodai believe that God has no name. The use of the word *God* is a divisive element among humanity. This explains why they prefer such terms as *the most high* and *the absolute*, and also why they use the term *Cao Dai*.[14]

14. Gobron, *History and Philosophy of Caodism*, p. 172.

There is divergent opinion among the Caodai concerning the essential nature and attributes of the Creator. This is caused in part by their acceptance of the ancient Chinese supposition of the *Yin* and *Yang* duality as the two essential elements in the formation and harmonious balance of the universe. There are two important deities, Dieu Tri Kim Mau or Duc Phat Mau (the Mother Goddess) and Cao Dai (God), though, originally, there was only one cosmic principle in the universe. From this principle came these two deities, one male and the other female. There is debate among Caodaists as to which of these was the primary source of creation. Most believe it was the male principle, Cao Dai. They believe Cao Dai to be the heart of the universe, the common Father of all human beings. Since he is a spirit, men (who are spirits wrapped in the frame of material bodies) can communicate with him.

On the other hand, some recognize the Mother Goddess as the Mother of the Universe. At the Tay Ninh holy see there is a special temple dedicated to her. Daily worship ceremonies are conducted there, mostly by female dignitaries. The Tay Ninh Caodaists recommend that all of their local congregations build a separate smaller building in which the faithful may worship the Holy Mother, Duc Phat Mau. Some of the more philosophical Caodaists (members of the Co Quan Pho Thong Giao Ly, for example) are explicit in their belief that since Duc Phat Mau is the Mother of the Universe, she is responsible for giving birth to all life. This difference of opinion concerning the roles and status of the two principal deities is not a cause for division and acrimony among Caodaists. The primary concern of all Caodaists is to worship both Cao Dai and Duc Phat Mau.

As Father of the Universe, Cao Dai, since the beginning of time, has communicated with human beings, revealing his will to men. Indeed, according to Caodai religious beliefs, history is divided into three major revelatory periods *(Tam Ky)*. In the first two of these periods there were selected individuals (people like Buddha and Moses) who received Cao Dai's instructions. These human agents served suffering humanity by founding and developing religions (Nhan Dao, Than Dao, Phat Dao, Thanh Dao, and Tien Dao). In their pristine form the revelations given by these human messengers were "truth," but because of the human frailty of the messengers and their disciples, the messages were corrupted. The Caodai also believe that these messages were culture-bound, that is, they were applicable only to the people of the area in which the founders lived; moreover, they were primarily intended for specific ages. In all, the effect of the revelations given during these two periods gave but a partial picture of Cao Dai's will. Therefore, Cao Dai decided to give a third and final amnesty and revelation to the world through his new religion, Caodaism.

Caodaism presumably avoids the failures of past religious leaders because spirit agents are used to communicate divine truth. The original teachings of the other great religions are combined to form an entire statement of truth. The Caodai were chosen to be the primary agents in the world-wide propagation of the message which has been basically given in their sacred texts—the *Religious Constitution,* the *New Law,* and the *Compilation of Divine Messages.*

Most Caodaists believe that there are various categories of spirits: *phat* (buddhas), *tien* (holy spirits), *thanh* (saints), and *than* (lower-ranking spirits). Each of these categories may be divided into three grades: *thien, nhan,* and *dia.* This twelvefold categorization is posited as the heavenly equivalent of an earthly hierarchy in Caodaism, beginning with the acting pope and descending to the lowest lay disciple. Humans are part of the spirit hierarchy, and they pass through a "humanity" stage before entering the nonmaterial sphere. Not only are humans a part of the spirit hierarchy, but so are animals, and even plants. All spirits evolve out of a material world and progressively attain higher rank based on the law of karma: future states depend on present deeds.

Disembodied spirits fulfill a number of roles. They are benefactors of mankind, messengers of salvation, and instructors of doctrine. The Caodai have contacted numerous such spirits through seance communication. These include deceased leaders of the Caodai church, patriots, heroes, philosophers, poets, political leaders, military warriors, religious personalities, and ordinary individuals.

During field research I noted the names or titles of over seventy different spirits that have appeared in Caodai seances. Non-Asian spirits included Descartes, Joan of Arc, Victor Hugo,

Pasteur, Shakespeare and Lenin. Asians include Ly Thai Bach, Sun Yat Sen, Quan Am (Kwan Yin), Mencius, and Quan Thanh De Quan.

In the official seances held at Tay Ninh spirit communication generally was limited to contacts with "key" spirits. For example, because of his frequent seance appearances to the Caodai mediums living at the Phnom Penh center in Cambodia, Victor Hugo was named the chief spirit of foreign missions endeavor! The Ho Phap, Pham Cong Tac, deceased since 1957, gives directions concerning the law, its development and interpretation. Among the Chieu Minh disciples, Ngo Minh Chieu is believed to be the reincarnation of Jesus Christ. Therefore, Chieu is the most important spirit communicant in their seances.

The practice of religion. The underlying goal of a Caodai disciple is to escape the continuing cycle of reincarnation by virtue of the deeds he performs in this life. To achieve a heavenly union with Cao Dai it is essential that man performs successfully his duty on earth. What is his duty? First, his duty is to devote himself to the practice of good and the avoidance of all kinds of evil. He must observe the five interdictions against killing, lying, luxurious living, sensuality, and stealing. This is a commitment to human brotherhood. Second, his duty is to show kindness to animals and to avoid any unnecessary destruction of plant life, recognizing that they are part of the reincarnation cycle. Third, he must serve society. Caodaists must represent God's image to the world. "God is you and you are God."[15] Moreover, "God's love of life is immense and in the earthly life a disciple ought to manifest this virtue by concentrating all his actions and thoughts to one purpose of supporting and conserving all living creatures. In other words, a disciple has to serve all living beings."[16]

Caodaists view themselves as the salt of the earth. The underlying philosophy of the "exoteric" school is that all Caodai disciples are to participate in the affairs of life, political, military, educational, medical, and so forth, and through these activities demonstrate love and understanding to all. They attempt to avoid discrimination in all its forms. Representatives

15. Nguyen Long Thanh, p. 12.
16. Ibid.

of other religions are heartily welcome as members of a universal brotherhood. When pressed, leaders admit that Caodaism eclipses other religions because it is all-encompassing, and they insist that the final path of salvation was established by Cao Dai. On the other hand, they deliberately avoid any suggestion that other religions are not adequate to lead men to salvation.

Involved in being of service to mankind is the practice of vegetarianism. Through vegetarianism the Caodai believe they are observing their responsibility not to harm or destroy the opportunity of fellow travelers in the spiritual hierarchy to progress in their spiritual evolution. They also believe that vegetarianism is a means of self-purification.

Caodai worship and ritual. Another major concern of Caodaists is participation in ritual acts of devotion and worship to Cao Dai. Caodai rituals have maintained the same basic pattern that was given in the seances during the 1920s. The regular schedule of rites involves the four daily ceremonies mentioned previously. These four services must be observed in all Caodai temples. For Caodai adherents a daily minimum of one act of obeisance before the Caodai altar is required. Whether a Tay Ninh member worships in his house or at the temple, white robes and a black hat (for men) must be worn. On ceremonial occasions, all dignitaries and members of the various hierarchies wear special ceremonial dress and hats. These temple rites involve prayers to Cao Dai and other spirits, and (depending on the day) selected offerings of incense, tea, alcohol, fruit, and flowers. These offerings symbolize the main concern of the worshipers, the offering of the total self to Cao Dai. They offer tea in the morning and evening, wine at noon and midnight. Tea is poured in one altar cup, holy water in another. On major ceremonial days, and the fourteenth and thirtieth of each lunar month, fruits and flowers are offered as well as the tea and alcohol.

Since the establishment of the first temple at Long Thanh, daily ceremonials as well as special bimonthly and anniversary celebrations have been observed with orchestral and choral accompaniment.

Most Caodai rituals are performed in front of altars which may differ in form and accoutrements depending on the sect or group. The one common characteristic of all Caodai altars is the presence of the divine eye above the altar. Yet this symbol appears in a variety of forms in the various temples. The eye became the official symbol of the religion after Ngo Minh Chieu saw it in a vision on Phu Quoc island in the Bay of Cambodia.

The altars of the Tay Ninh churches have five tiers, each tier indicating the rank of the representative statuary. On the first and highest tier are statues of Buddha, Confucius and Lao Tze. The second tier has Quan Am, Ly Thai Bach and Quan Thanh De Quan, who are recognized as the three "Lords of the earth." Jesus Christ is on the third tier, ranked below the others because "he appeared in a later era." Khuong Thai Quan, the head of the ancestral spirits, is on the fourth tier. On the fifth tier are the altar accoutrements.

On the altar, the lamp symbolizing the eternal light of the universe *(thai cuc)* is always lit. Two candles and five joss sticks are lit at the beginning of ceremonies. The candles represent the male and female *(am* and *duong)* principles; the five incense sticks represent the different levels of spiritual development available to humans: purity, meditation, wisdom, superior knowledge, and liberation. The *Yin* and *Yang* duality occurs in other aspects of Caodaism. For example, Caodai architecture emphasizes it. The temples are built so that male and female disciples enter on opposite sides. Generally, there are smaller altars on either side of the main altar; these smaller altars are dedicated to masculine and feminine deities. The left side represents the female principle, the right side the male. When worshiping in the temples, women are on the left and men on the right.

Other regularly scheduled rites involve the normal *rites de passage*—naming children, entrance into the church, and so forth. Crisis rites are observed for accidents, sickness, death, and entry into the priesthood. Both the regularly scheduled and crisis rites have specific prayers prepared for the use of the choristers and participants. These prayers are listed in the official prayer book with directions for those involved in the rituals.

For some Caodai groups the seance has become a crisis ritual, used only when matters of extreme importance demand spirit counsel. Other groups like the Chieu Minh and the Pho

Thong Giao Ly regularly participate in seances. They believe the seance is essential to maintain an intimate relationship with the spirits, and an open channel for additional teachings from Cao Dai.

The ritual calendars of the Caodai sects and organizations differ considerably because each group recognizes different saints, founders and previous leaders of their respective movements. Scattered throughout the calendar year are major holy days, for example, Buddha's birthday, the memorial for the Caodai pope, and Christmas Day. On these occasions, major ceremonial observances are held. This type of service normally is scheduled for midnight, but security problems during wartime necessitated a rescheduling to noon. At Tay Ninh, officials line up in rank outside the great temple and enter in procession. The ceremony lasts approximately two hours. Included with the regular prayers and prostrations are the offerings of fruit, flowers, tea, and alcohol, and the reading and burning of the written prayers to Cao Dai. On these occasions the Tay Ninh temple (which can accommodate approximately 1300) is filled.

Caodai Organization

Caodaism has no closed priesthood. From the beginning the movement was open to male and female clergy. A layman can serve as a priest if he is willing to observe the regulations of the religious laws, *Phap Chanh Truyen* and *Tan-Luat,* and to meet the other basic requirements. Normally this requires a period of service as an elected lay official followed by an application for entrance into the student priest category. This is the beginning of a life as a Caodai functionary which theoretically can lead to an opportunity for election to the papacy.

In 1926 Cao Dai indicated that the religion was to have three branches—the Bat Quai Dai, Hiep Thien Dai and Cuu Trung Dai. The Bat Quai Dai (the Eight-sided Palace of God's Presence) is the seat of God's throne and altar, and the center of spiritual power and authority. It is symbolized in the temple by the altar with the all-seeing divine eye above it. The Bat Quai Dai, unlike the other two branches which are composed of men and women, is a "spiritual" community having no human members, but is the locus for humans to commune with and worship Cao Dai.

The Hiep Thien Dai (the Heavenly-union Palace) is composed of spiritual legislators. It is symbolized by the Ho Phap's altar at the end of the temple opposite God's altar. The Ho Phap is the senior official of the Hiep Thien Dai and the head medium of this branch of the religion. The members of the Hiep Thien Dai are the protectors of the sacred laws. Their role is to be either mediums through whom the administrative branch (Cuu Trung Dai) communes with Cao Dai via seances, or legislators who protect the law by seeing that all the priests in the administrative branch correctly fulfill their tasks.

There is a threefold division of the legislative branch: the College of Mediums, the junior officers, and the technical academicians. The College of Mediums has three units concerned with religious, legislative, and secular affairs especially. Each unit is directed by one of the three founders of the Tay Ninh religious organization. The Ho Phap (Superior) is the overall leader of the entire legislative branch. The twelve members of the College of Mediums are called the "twelve zodiacs." These men are the officially recognized mediums. The second division is comprised of junior officers, cadres of the second rank. The third division is a group of skilled academicians who may be asked for advice by the legislative leadership. When the official inauguration of Caodaism took place in November 1926 the offices of the Hiep Thien Dai were filled through the twelve-member College of Mediums.

The Cuu Trung Dai (the Nine-sphere Palace) is the administrative and executive branch of Caodaism. In the temple the Cuu Trung Dai is symbolized by the central section of the building, the place where the worshipers kneel and offer themselves to Cao Dai between the Bat Quai Dai, Cao Dai's altar, and the Hiep Thien Dai, the rear altar. This branch of Caodaism composes the majority of the priesthood. The hierarchy of the Cuu Trung Dai is ranked in nine levels with limited positions at the first six levels. It is the branch of Caodaism concerned with administration. It trains adherents, administers various programs, and directs the movement to the attainment of its stated goals, such as the development of the Caodai structure nationwide, the maintenance of a highly organized, effectively administered movement from the local village level to the central offices at Tay Ninh, the regular observance of Caodai rituals in local temples, the collection of fees, and so forth. It controls the total church program, whereas the Hiep Thien Dai enforces adherence to the sacred laws during the enactment of that program.

The Growth of Caodaism

The results of propagation. After Ngo Minh Chieu's departure from the *Pho loan,* Le Van Trung, with specific direction from seance messages, began to assert administrative leadership over the fledgling movement. Under his direction, the new group sought to expand their religion by holding seances in the suburban and rural areas. The Caodai historian, Tran Thai Chanh, claims that this plan was initiated by instructions given during a seance.[17] At each location, two mediums belonging to the *Pho loan* conducted a worship and seance session. M. Dujeil notes that in these meetings "on n'a pas manqué de recouvrir aux pratiques secondaires: miracles, eaux de guérison, imposition des mains, prédiction par medium ou par la corbeille à bec."[18]

Cao Dai had given instructions that the original meeting place at Doan Van Ban's house in Cau Kho was to be expanded to five additional locations—Cholon, Tan Kim, Loc Giang, Tan Dinh, and Thu Duc. A special place, the home of Tran Van Ta, was selected for services held exclusively to heal the sick. These meetings were directed by leaders of the fledgling movement. In some cases, the seances were led by officers of the College of Mediums. Writing in a Vietnamese newspaper, Nguyen Trung Hau indicates that meetings were held at many other locations to spread the religion to new adherents.[19]

Fifteen of twenty-one "oratories" for which Le Van Trung requested government permission in May 1926 were in Saigon, the provinces of Gia Dinh and Cholon (adjoining Saigon), Tay Ninh and Bien Hoa.[20] The other six "oratories" were in the

17. Tran Thai Chanh, "Lich-Su Cao-Dai Dai-Dao Tam Ky: Phan Pho-Do," p. 74.
18. Nguyen Tran Huan, "Histoire d'une Secte Religieuse au Vietnam: Le Caodaisme," *Review de Synthèse* 3 (11-12, 1958), 276.
19. Nguyen Trung Hau, *Tien Viet,* no. 1659:1.
20. R. B. Smith, "An Introduction to Caodaism 1. Origins and Early History," *BSOAS* 33 (2) (London: University of London, 1970), p. 342.

central provinces of the Mekong delta at My tho and Ben Tre (two each), Sa Dec and Vinh Long.[21]

Statistical data on the growth of Caodaism during these earliest years are unreliable and confusing. Nguyen Van Tam states that there were almost 30,000 converts in six months. By October, 1926, the membership had increased to 50,000.[22] Dennis Duncanson, who is critical of the Caodai, insinuated that Le Van Trung, as a labor contractor of some fame, was able to muster the 50,000 people he claimed were present at the official inauguration. Duncanson implies that these members must be considered questionable "followers."[23]

In 1928 Le Van Trung claimed over 1,000,000 followers. In the same year, the newspaper *l'Opinion* published a membership figure of 700,000. This figure was rejected by Maurice Monribot in *La Presse Indochinoise;* he wrote that there were only about 200,000 Caodai members.[24]

Nguyen Tran Huan writes that by 1931 the Caodai had about 500,000 followers.[25] Other writers have contradicted this estimate, believing it to be too low. For example, Ellen J. Hammer believes that the Caodai had over 1,000,000 followers by 1930.[26] G. Abadie writes that by 1932 Caodaism's followers in Cochinchina numbered "more than one million out of three and a half million inhabitants."[27]

The divergence of opinion on the actual numerical strength of the Caodai from 1925 to 1932 seems to indicate reluctance, on the part of some, to admit the success of Caodaism. On the other hand, extravagant claims by others suggest a defensive posture in the face of criticism. These inflated estimates were an attempt to exaggerate the movement's success and to improve the image of religion for the public. I believe a conservative

---

21. Ibid.

22. Nguyen Van Tam, "Caodaisme et Hoa Hao," *Extract de l'Education* 14 (Jan.-Feb., 1949), 4-5. (This journal is published in Saigon by Nguyen Van Cua.)

23. Dennis Duncanson, *Government and Revolution in Vietnam* (London: Oxford University Press, 1968), pp. 125-26.

24. Smith, "Introduction to Caodaism," p. 341.

25. Nguyen Tran Huan, "Historie," p. 273.

26. Ellen J. Hammer, *The Struggle for Indochina* (Stanford, CA: Stanford University Press, 1954), p. 79.

27. Gobron, *History and Philosophy of Caodaism*, p. 103. •

estimate of Caodai membership (adult and children) in 1930 would be 500,000. In any case, even in terms of the most modest estimates, the rapid growth in the early years is significant. Though the rate of growth subsequently slowed down, the movement grew to approximately 2,000,000 adherents by 1971, as we have seen.

The involvement of Cambodians and Vietnamese living in Cambodia is important to any analysis of the early growth of Caodaism. In 1927 the Caodai officially opened a "foreign mission center" in Phnom Penh on Lalan de Callan Street. At first, this center was directed by Pham Cong Tac. The first officials were chosen by seance directive on July 27, 1927. Caodai officials claimed that 10,000 Vietnamese living in Cambodia were converted to the religion during the first year. Also, many Cambodians living near the South Vietnamese border joined Caodaism. The Caodai erected a huge statue of Siddhartha at the entrance to their newly purchased property at Long Thanh, Tay Ninh. Reports state that thousands of Cambodians came to see the statue because rumors developed that it was a representation of one of their old Cambodian monarchs who reputedly would return to restore a golden age in Cambodia. The Cambodians worshiped Buddha and sought further blessings through Caodaism. Thousands came to Long Thanh to worship and work on the new site of the holy see. Local police reported as many as 5000 Cambodians at one time sitting around the statue of Siddhartha.[28] Laws were passed by the French administrations to stop these mass defections by Cambodian Buddhists. King Monivong of Cambodia signed a decree (April 1, 1930) forbidding conversions to Caodaism and restraining Caodaists from propagating in Cambodia. Caodaism was not accepted as one of the officially recognized religions.[29] In spite of official French and Cambodian harassment, however, the Caodai reported over 30,000 converts in Cambodia by 1937 and more than 70,000 by 1951 (64,953 Vietnamese and 8,213 Cambodians).[30]

28. Le Huong, "Hoat-Dona cua cac Chuc-Sac Cao-Dai Viet-Kieu tai Cao-Mien," *Su Dia* 16 (1969), 95 (published in Saigon by Khai-Tri); Le Van Trung, *Le Caodaisme ou Bouddhisme Rénové* (Saigon: n.p., 1931), p. 41.
29. Le Huong, "Hoat-Dona," pp. 95-96.
30. Ibid., pp. 98-99.

The Caodai have not been very successful in their foreign missions activity apart from the early mission in Cambodia. They attempted to establish a mission in south China but had no success and so disbanded the mission. A few French nationals were won to the faith—the most notable being Gabriel Gobron, who has written on the Caodai movement. In spite of the massive United States presence in South Vietnam over a long period of time, hardly any Americans became converts. The Caodai do claim a few adherents in Africa.

Reasons for the Success of Caodaism

In discussing the reasons for the growth of Caodaism it is important to make several preliminary comments. First, it is extremely difficult to measure qualitatively or quantitatively the relative importance of the variables noted as likely causes of growth. Second, because of limitations of space, it is possible to make only a comparatively brief comment on each variable. Third, it should be noted that some of the factors mentioned here were more applicable in the initial growth of the movement than they have been in its later development. With these cautions in mind, we will consider the factors which seem to account for Caodaism's rapid growth.

(1) As a new religious movement, Caodaism is culturally relevant to the society in which it originated and developed. Its rituals, doctrines, dress, music, instruments, food, symbols, and literature are readily understood by Vietnamese. This relevancy is in sharp contrast to the "unrelatedness" of many other religious groups which often have displayed an insensitivity to indigenous cultural factors. Caodai rituals, for example, are not difficult to perform and are typically Asian and Vietnamese in their character and activity. Many of the ritual components— the offerings, the kowtowing, the use of incense sticks, the dragon ceremonials, to name a few—have much in common with either Vietnamese ancestral or Buddhist rituals.

(2) Although Caodaism was not officially inaugurated until 1926, its roots are found in other Asian religious movements and Western philosophical thought. The religion is syncretistic in its organizational structure, philosophy, theology and ritual practices:

Much of Cao Daist doctrine is drawn from Buddhism of the Mahayana tradition, and mixed with it are concepts of Taoist and Confucianist origin. The Buddhist ideal of "the good man" provides the basis for Cao Daist ethics, and the whole complex of little-tradition Vietnamese taboos and sanctions is incorporated into their ideal behavioral scheme.[31]

This synthesis of elements adapted from other religions into a functioning religious movement manifests itself in such common Caodai practices as priestly celibacy, vegetarianism, seance inquiry and spirit communication, reverence for ancestors and prayers for the dead, fervent proselytism, and sessions of meditative self-cultivation. Credence is given to the teachings of the great religious and cultural leaders of the past, both foreign and (especially) Vietnamese.

(3) Caodaism has attempted to meet the emotional needs of a people who have known more than their share of hardship, oppression and war. Promised benefits have included more than the usual healing and other provisions for physical well-being. As one who has witnessed the various ceremonies of Caodaism, it seems apparent to me that one of the major effects of these ceremonies is the reinforcement of a feeling of belonging. Every believer who participates in one of the rituals has his specific garments to wear and a particular area in the temple in which to worship; he is recognized by others as a fellow believer. Again, there can be little doubt that in the days of French colonialism the secretive nature of the society and its rituals promoted the idea among the South Vietnamese populace that here was an indigenous organization potentially capable of mounting a threat to French authority. As a matter of fact, some evaluators have considered Caodaism to be a secret society.

(4) Though basically a religious movement, Caodaism has concerned itself with various areas of secular life and thought. Caodai military, administrative, governmental and social branches have been prominent in influencing their counterparts in the larger Vietnamese society. At times Caodaism has exerted a powerful influence over the government of South Vietnam.

31. Gerald C. Hickey, *Village in Vietnam* (New Haven, CT: Yale University Press, 1964), p. 291.

Though generally most concerned with caring for the needs of fellow believers, Caodaism has undertaken to provide relief for all refugees in times of crisis. Schools, clinics and a hospital are maintained in or near the Tay Ninh central offices. This activity has unquestionably resulted in greatly increased numbers of contacts for Caodai propagandists and has added weight to their message.

(5) Strong leadership has been another significant factor in the success of the movement. The rapid expansion of Caodai temples, the creation and development of the Caodai militia, and the ability to relate to governmental authorities cannot be explained without reference to the quality of Caodai leadership. While studying the development of Caodai sectarianism (over fifty sects in approximately forty years!) I found that the leadership of key men strongly influenced the character and success of the sects which they directed. For example, under Pham Cong Tac, the Tay Ninh organization became militaristic, authoritarian and chauvinistic in the eyes of Caodaists who were not members of that particular group. After Tac's death, Cao Hoai Sang, the new leader of the Tay Ninh, insisted on a course of rapprochement and a rejection of militarism in any form. Even he, however, was prepared to apply political pressure when it counted and thus achieve advantages for Caodaists in Vietnam.

(6) The organization of Caodaism—in particular the Tay Ninh—has been an important factor in the growth of the movement. From the beginning there has been a functional system of control spreading through the entire organization. Lines of command are clear. Opportunity is offered for men and women from every level of society to advance to higher levels of office and authority. Advancement cannot occur, however, without ratification from a higher authority within the hierarchy. This mechanism has enabled strong leaders to control the major sects, and usually has enabled these sects to present a unified front during times of confrontation. On the other hand, this system also has caused the development of a number of sects and groups which have left Tay Ninh to establish their own Caodai movements.

(7) The early establishment of the holy see at Long Thanh, along with its various enterprises, has also been a positive factor

in the growth of Caodaism. An established central headquarters with its flurry of activity and impressive buildings and rituals has seemed to be most important to the average Vietnamese.

(8) Enthusiasm and an effective method for propagating the faith cannot be overlooked in evaluating the growth of the movement. In fact, Caodaism presents one of the clearest illustrations of the importance of an active program of propagation. Ngo Minh Chieu's "esoteric" approach to religion was not calculated to produce new disciples. From the very beginning, the case of the "exoteric" Tay Ninh was different. Le Van Trung divided his leaders into three groups and sent them into the various provinces of South Vietnam to proclaim the Caodai message and win converts. Down through the years there have been strong co-ordinated attempts to proselytize at home (particularly in the dense population areas of the Mekong delta) and abroad. For the most part those attempts have been rewarded handsomely.

(9) Since Caodaism was inaugurated in 1926 women have had an effective role in the development of the religion. The special women's branch has had the same basic hierarchical structure as the men's administrative branch, thus giving all female adherents the potential for advancement, influence and participation in the movement. Women have been quick to take advantage of this opportunity, and the success of Caodaism is in significant measure due to the enthusiasm with which they have spread the faith.

(10) Finally, mention is made of the Caodai seances, the significance of which requires extensive comment. According to Pham Cong Tac, seance communication served a fourfold purpose: to establish the religion in the early stages of development, to provide the laws and sacred revelation, to aid in propagation of the Caodai message, and to teach the mysteries of Caodaism.[32]

Every Caodai seance involved at least five individuals. First, the *Phap Dan* or *Phap Su,* the spiritual leader of the meeting, had to see that all the necessary arrangements for the seance had been made. Were the altar accoutrements correctly in place? Were there a sufficient number of officials to hold the

---

32. Tran Thai Chanh, "Lich-Su Cao-Dai Dai-Dao Tam Ky: Phan Pho-Do," pp. 163-64.

seance? Was there any evidence of the presence of evil spirits? To avoid attack from the spirits, the *Phap Dan* cleansed the temple in each direction. He used a fresh flower to sprinkle holy water and write the traditional sacred symbols that ward off the spirits. Also, ritually, he cleansed the hands of the mediums who wrote the messages, and he cleansed their entire bodies symbolically by sprinkling the water over their heads.

Ritual prayers were chanted before the altar where offerings were made to Cao Dai. The seance began with specific prayers requesting that spirit communication would be fruitful. The two mediums sat facing one another with their hands holding the *corbeille à bec* under the lattice work, the writing end of the instrument hovering above the table. When the mediums received a revelation the head of the *corbeille* was lowered to the table and the message written.

The *Doc Gia*, the official interpreter, stood to the side of the mediums and read the message aloud so the *Dien Ky*, or the secretary, could hear and transcribe it into a book. During the communication, the *Phap Dan* knelt behind the mediums, in front of the altar.

These seances attracted many curiosity-seekers. To stand outside and view the proceedings or to enter and kneel soberly was not unusual for the Vietnamese. Many of these seances took place in local Buddhist pagodas and the Vietnamese populace in general was familiar with various types of seance communication, spirit-inquiry, and astrological observations.

The types of communications given through the seances differed in content, quantity and quality. Reports of these early seances indicate that on occasion miraculous healings of supernatural character allegedly occurred, convincing many to convert to Caodaism. I talked with a well-known, retired university professor who stated that as a young man, unknown to anyone, he had attended a seance. Suddenly, during the seance, his name was called and the spirit indicated he was to live a religious life by following Cao Dai. This convinced him that the spirit communication was genuine and he should become a Caodaist.

The seance was the most common means of attracting converts. People at the meetings would hear their names called in a seance message and be invited to come into the building if they were outside. Often they would be given a spirit message *(bai thi)* in verse, sometimes a four-line poem. The poem would be applicable to the individual, and he would then request permission to join the religion.[33]

Those who wanted to enter Caodaism would kneel before the altar. The mediums, acting as intermediaries, asked permission of the spirit for the reception of the individual. If the answer was yes *(thau)*, instructions about the religion were given and the convert would swear allegiance to Cao Dai.

The seance was a powerful force in winning new converts to Caodaism. In *Le Caodaisme ou Bouddhisme Rénové,* the author states that it was the grace of spiritism, the love of God manifested in the seance, and the decisive influence of the messages in the seance which brought mass conversions.[34] Huan writes that the seances attracted the attention and excited the curiosity of the people. They desired a fellowship with God because they were under the yoke of oppression.[35]

Conclusion

Historically, Caodaism has played an active and significant role in Vietnamese religious, societal, and political spheres. It is doubtful whether the Caodai will have again an opportunity to affect the ways of the Vietnamese as effectively as they did from 1926 to 1956. Nevertheless, as a unique, indigenous, Vietnamese socio-religious movement Caodaism is representative of an exciting era in Vietnamese history—an era and a movement to be studied and not forgotten.

From the perspective of evaluating the growth pattern of Caodaism the religion was very successful in the first ten years and continued to expand until the Second World War began. In 1946 Caodaists initiated another period of growth which lasted until 1956 when their continuing military involvement became the cause of their downfall. Since that time they have had trouble in maintaining their membership, one major reason being the divisions (sectarianism) that have occurred in the movement.

---

33. Tran Thai Chanh, *Lich-Su Cao-Dai Dai-Dao Tam Ky Pho-do: Phan Pho-Vi,* p. 98.

34. *Le Caodaisme ou Bouddhisme Rénové* (Saigon: Dao-Ton, 1949), p. 11.

35. Nguyen Tran Huan, "Histoire," p. 270.

CONCLUSION

What Causes Religious Movements to Grow?

David J. Hesselgrave

The case studies we have examined make their contributions to our understanding of the growth of religious movements independently of comparative analysis. In fact, it is difficult (if not impossible) in making such an analysis to do justice to the authors, the movements and all the growth factors involved. Nevertheless, it does not seem proper to conclude our study without an attempt in this direction. It must be understood that the conclusions expressed in this chapter reflect the editor's understanding and are not to be assigned to the contributing scholars.

Preliminary Considerations

In this study we have entertained one primary question: how do certain religious movements attain rapid growth in their respective cultures?

There are four important aspects to this question. First, we are concerned with *growth* as explained in our introductory chapter. Growth can be measured in quantitative and qualitative terms. These are closely related for, as we shall see, "quality characteristics" of the members of a movement affect quantitative growth. But it is primarily an interest in numerical growth that has occasioned this study.

Second, we are concerned with the *relationship between culture and the growth of religion*. On the one hand, we want to know which growth factors are evident in all or most of the case studies. On the other hand, we want to ascertain the extent to which growth factors mirror cultural differences. The word *culture* is one of those omnibus words in the English vocabulary which have a wide variety of meanings. To social scientists, however, it has basically one meaning. That meaning was given to the word when, in the nineteenth century, anthropologists sought a covering term for what we might call "human custom." *Culture* means "the totality of learned, socially transmitted behavior or 'custom'" and *a culture* is used to refer to "a localized and more or less different and unique system of behavior, e.g., Eskimo culture, or Cherokee Indian culture."[1]

Third, in order to proceed with our inquiry in an orderly fashion we must determine the *categories of religious systems* in which innovations that relate to growth can be introduced. From his anthropological perspective, Felix Keesing says that every religious system shows a universal framework consisting of belief or dogma, group organization, ritual or rites, religious objects or paraphernalia, linguistic behavior, and affective or emotional elements.[2] This framework is not without problems. For example, one is at somewhat of a loss to know where to subsume such an important facet of religion as the propagation and dissemination of religious teachings. Therefore, certain modifications will be made as we proceed, but Keesing has provided us with a basic framework in which to analyze many of the factors contributing to growth.

Fourth, we are inquiring into *growth factors*—the causes, reasons or conditions for the rapid increase of adherents to these movements. The concept of causality is by no means a simple one. The establishment of causal relationships is even more complex. An exhaustive discussion of such questions would

---

1. Felix Keesing, *Cultural Anthropology: The Science of Custom* (New York: Holt, Rinehart and Winston, 1958), p. 16.
2. Ibid., p. 335.

take us far beyond the bounds of this study. It would be presumptuous, however, to talk about causes of growth without clarifying what we mean and what we are about.

It is important to distinguish the various *types of causation*. Numerous discussions of the growth of religious movements and churches fail in this regard. Indiscriminate identification of causes, however, obscures even as it clarifies. Reflection on four basic types of causes will serve to indicate the importance of their differentiation:

(1) A *necessary cause* is one that *must* occur if (in this case) religious growth is to occur.

(2) A *sufficient cause* is one that is *always* followed by growth.

(3) A *contributory cause* is one that makes it *likely* that growth will occur. (It is only one of multiple factors which *may* produce growth.)

(4) A *contingent cause* is a factor that makes it possible for another factor to function as a contributory cause.

To distinguish among the types of causes in this way is to open Pandora's box—especially when one is concerned with the growth of religious movements.

Religious growth must be viewed from both theological and scientific viewpoints. When I examine the Scriptures (or a book like C. S. Lewis' *Screwtape Letters*), I am reminded that there is a very real sense in which the only *sufficient cause* for the growth of the church of Jesus Christ is the sovereign and gracious action of the Triune God. Our Lord said *he would build his church* and the gates of hell would not prevail against it (Matt. 16:18). When our Lord admonished his disciples to bear much fruit he also reminded them that apart from him they could not do anything (John 15:5). When the greatest "church growth specialist" of them all wrote concerning his role in the growth of the church at Corinth he said, "I planted, Apollos watered, *but God was causing the growth*" (I Cor. 3:6, NASB, italics mine). In fact, from a theological point of view, insofar as the movements in this study are in accord with God's truth and purposes, their growth is primarily due to the sovereign activity of God. Insofar as they are in accord with

Satan's lies and purposes, their growth is primarily due to Satan's activity as permitted by God.[3]

Again within the limitations of that which God has revealed to us we may also say that the only *necessary cause* for church growth is that men of God go forth to faithfully preach the gospel in accordance with his command (Rom. 10:13-15). That first phrase is important. A sovereign, all-wise and loving God may have ways to effect his purpose of gathering the elect into his church apart from the instrumentality of obedient human servants. But that truth should be the occasion for a greater faith, not the excuse for a lesser obedience. For his own (sometimes mysterious) reasons and in the vast majority of cases, God has ordained that the necessary condition for the salvation of men and the building of the church be the activity of faithful heralds and obedient co-laborers.

Turning now to the scientific point of view, the scientist qua scientist may insist that there is no demonstrable *sufficient cause* (i.e., one that will *always* be followed by growth) for the growth of a Christian or any religious movement. He may, however, conclude on the basis of the data he has that there is a *necessary cause* (i.e., one that *must* occur if growth is to occur) for such growth: namely, the emergence of able leadership.

It will be immediately apparent that the "theologian of mission" and the "scientist of mission" may very well disagree, or they may agree for different reasons. We may expect that disagreements will be less pronounced when it comes to *contributory causes* and *contingent causes*. Even in these cases, however, a cause which may be overlooked by the scientist (e.g., prayer) or one which may be only a contributory cause from his perspective (e.g., a unique message) may prove to be a necessary cause when re-examined and interpreted in the light of Scripture. The missiologist (who is both a scientist *and* a theologian), therefore, must keep in mind that there are two aspects of his task—the theological (exegetical) and scientific aspects. The former takes precedence. Scientific investigation is important, but it cannot be the last word.

---

3. Cf. Edmund Perry, *The Gospel in Dispute: The Relation of Christian Faith to Other Missionary Religions* (Garden City, NY: Doubleday & Company, Inc., 1958), pp. 88-96.

Obviously, the approach of this book is scientific. In fact, it is a particular type of scientific approach. In this book we are "proceeding backwards" from the effect to the (probable) cause(s). One could, of course, move in the opposite direction. One could proceed a priori to conjecture, for example, that certain strategies of propagation will result in great growth. Then one might put these strategies into operation to see if great growth does, in fact, occur. This kind of a priori procedure is particularly well suited to the physical science laboratory, but it has some real liabilities in relation to religious propagation. In any event, it is not what we are about here. We are engaging in a posteriori reasoning which takes the following form: G (growth) has occurred in religions A, B, and C (the religions dealt with in the case studies); something has caused it; that something was probably X, Y, and Z (causes). In and of itself, this kind of reasoning can never place the alleged causes of growth beyond doubt. It is always characterized by a certain degree of tentativeness. But when, in case after case, great growth is attended (preceded) by certain factors (J. S. Mill's so-called method of agreement) the researcher is on rather solid ground in assuming a cause-effect relationship.

The causes of growth that come to light in this volume are based on a very limited number of case studies. Our conclusions are, therefore, tentative and the causes are best categorized as contributory or contingent (apart from further scientific and theological investigation). These are important points for our reflection. Theorists and practitioners of mission need to think in terms of the tentativeness of many of their conclusions and also of the widest possible variety of potential causes of the growth of the church. There is a tendency to think simplistically. The common idea that a single event (the cause) produces another (the effect) is very often unwarranted. Usually a given effect is the result of a multiplicity of causes. Failure to understand this simple fact has occasioned the erroneous notion—rife in Christian missions—that there must be *some one key* which unlocks the door to great religious growth. Strategists and practitioners alike have made one false start after another—carefully devising a plan of evangelism and church growth, only to abandon it after a few months or years in favor of another plan that has new promise. The resultant loss of time and effort to Christian missions is incalculable. It would seem far better to recognize that growth is the result of a confluence of factors, and to devise an overall plan which takes as many of them as possible into account. Minor adjustments and innovations will, of course, always be in order. But the disruption that results from repeated backtracking and starting along new paths can be averted only by thinking in terms of *multiple causes.*

For Everything a Time

No set of circumstances in and of itself occasions religious growth. It is important to note, however, that most of the movements in our case studies have thrived in relatively free societies. It is very doubtful that they would have had the same measure of success in circumstances of continued and concerted repression. To be sure, a religious movement may survive a *measure* of persecution—in fact, it may even thrive on it. Some persecution may serve to unite believers and strengthen their resolve. Kimbanguism, Mormonism, Caodai, Ahmadiya and the Soka Gakkai would be cases in point. But none of these religions have grown in an environment of severe and sustained oppression or under governmental regimes staunchly opposed to religion per se. In a world where the march of anti-religion totalitarianism continues unabated,[4] strategists of the Christian world mission should ask themselves whether more attention should be given to survival strategies. Is there nothing that can be done to help prepare the church in the free world to survive—and even grow—under anti-religion or anti-religious propagation regimes that may oppress it in the future? Caodai now finds itself under the authority of a government that may prove to be adamantly opposed to religious propagation and expression. Iglesia ni Cristo and Kimbanguism must accommodate themselves to governments that are in a position to place severe restrictions on religious freedom! For that matter, a great segment of the Christian church finds itself under (or potentially under) governments whose policies are inimical to

---

4. It is reported that of the 105 nations in the Third World, 48 have totalitarian governments, 15 are free, and the rest are in between. See David Abshire, "Is the U.N. Committing Suicide?" *Readers Digest,* (March, 1976), pp. 173-83.

church growth, and outside efforts to assist persecuted religious minorities to sustain themselves and grow have often been criticized as doing more harm than good. *In a period of political disruption and instability a much higher priority should be placed on dialogue that is concerned with the development of strategies on how to cope when religious freedoms are swept away or severely curtailed. If this is not done, the churches will be left to ad hoc decisions as to ways and means of survival and growth.*

At the same time, our studies would seem to indicate that religious growth is in part contingent upon threatening, unsettling, and less than ideal conditions within the particular movement or within the society in which the movement exists. Tong-il growth no doubt has been made possible in part by unsettled social and political conditions and the communist threat that have been part and parcel of South Korean national life since the Korean war. The colonial and postcolonial situation in which African Zionism and Kimbanguism have flourished has been an important aspect of their growth. New Apostolic Church leaders repeatedly pointed to the apostasy that has pervaded Christendom. The Jehovah's Witnesses equate Christendom with Babylon. Umbanda makes its greatest impact in the mushrooming urban centers of Brazil where uprooted peoples grasp for new values and relationships. In short, when citizens grope in the twilight of uncertainty or when the members of a movement feel a creeping coldness in their institutions, it becomes pre-eminently possible for Moseslike leaders to persuade them to gather their possessions, march through the wilderness, and take hold of the promised land. When people enjoy the settledness of their respective Zions, it is most natural for them to feel at ease, and the call of the prophet becomes unpersuasive if not inaudible.

Circumstances are "givens." They cannot be ordered. But they can be discovered and exploited. Fortunately, they can be exploited for good—and, unfortunately, they can also be exploited for ill. From the standpoint of growth strategy, then, perhaps the best way to think of circumstantial causal factors is in terms of timing. Ahmadiya leadership recognized the significance of Islamic instability on the subcontinent of India and was able to capitalize on it. Umbanda leaders recognized the possibilities occasioned by rapid urban growth in Brazil and took advantage of the situation. As Eric Hoffer has indicated, the time must be right to effect a new and successful movement.[5] But circumstances of and by themselves do not occasion the growth of any movement, secular or religious. More is required. Rapid growth is contingent upon the ability of perceptive people to identify—or even predict—the *right time* for growth. Only by virtue of such perceptiveness will plans be made, resources marshaled and the moment seized. Without it the moment (for that is what it usually is when viewed from the perspective of history) will be lost, and the verdict will be "too little and too late." We have been looking at movements that have grown because the time was right and because men took advantage of it. The great unknown is how many other religious movements, perhaps with teaching more true and purposes more noble, were aborted or failed to grow during the times when and at the places where these movements flourished.

Culture and Growth

To be successful, any religious movement must be simultaneously "of the culture" and "not of the culture." Or so these studies seem to indicate. By "of the culture" I mean that to be widely accepted, *a religious movement must be meaningful in terms of indigenous world views and values, and traditional ways.* If the movement grows up within the culture it tends to communicate and exemplify these views, values and ways as a matter of course. If it is introduced from the outside, it must make appropriate accommodations to local understandings or else achieve growth at the expense of reinterpretation or syncretism.

At the same time, each successful religious movement seems to represent some significant parting with that which is commonly believed and practiced within its culture. It is this combination of similarities and differences, affirmation and negation, the simultaneous "yes" and "no" which, in proper balance, contributes to growth.

---

5. Eric Hoffer, *The True Believer: Thoughts on the Nature of Mass Movements* (New York: The New American Library of World Literature, Inc., A Mentor Book, 1958), p. 103.

Examples are not difficult to come by. Each case study exemplifies this. Kimbanguism and African Zionism represent forms of Christianity so adapted to African culture that it has become difficult for observers to determine the degree to which they are faithful to the tenets of biblical Christianity. But by-passing for the time being the question of whether or not these movements are fully Christian, there can be no doubt that they are culturally meaningful to their converts. Missionaries from other lands could hardly have been expected to introduce many of their beliefs and practices, not simply because of doctrinal objections, but also because of cultural foreignness.

Obviously, prophet movements flourish in Africa because contemporary Africa needs prophets. And prophets gain followers because they personify and reintroduce traditional cultural ways of thinking and doing things. At the same time, only myopic vision would fail to see that there is another side to "prophethood" in Africa. From the Prophet Harris movement in Liberia to Kimbanguism in Zaire, there have been the "thou-shalt-not," the pointed finger, the iconoclastic bent, and the parting of the ways with culture and society. We recall, for example, that Simon Kimbangu opposed polygamy. (And, to leave Africa, Felix Manalo opposed the eating of *dinuguan*.)

Cultural negation, then, accompanies cultural affirmation. If affirmation insures the identity of the society and the worthwhileness of its customs as over against those of other societies and cultures, the negation accomplishes something similar for the "elect" as over against the larger (indigenous) society and culture. That both the negation and the affirmation are essential becomes even more apparent if one reviews the case studies from Asia, Europe and the Americas. But more than a facile "no" or "yes" is involved. *Both* must be brought into the warp and woof of work, worship and witness. Culture is too pervasive and too ingrained to be successfully duplicated by veneer. For those involved in crosscultural Christian ministries it would be an eminently worthwhile exercise to carefully analyze those aspects of these rapidly growing movements which distinctly reflect or adapt to the native culture.

Belief or Dogma

Our case studies reveal a wide variety of beliefs and a diversity of authorities for those beliefs. Teachings range from the intricate and elaborate systems of Tong-il, Soka Gakkai, Jehovah's Witnesses and the Mormons to the comparatively simple tenets of Zionism, Kimbanguism and Umbanda. Appeal is made to the authority of new revelation given in the form of visions and dreams (Ahmadiya, Caodai, Tong-il, the Jesus Only movement), to the teachings of special leaders (Soka Gakkai, Tong-il, Iglesia ni Cristo), to the authority of sacred scriptures (Ahmadiya, Soka Gakkai, Jesus Only, New Apostolic Church), and to various combinations of these. But several characteristics merit closer examination.

A unique message. The message of each movement is *unique* as far as its members are concerned. Even when that message is obviously syncretistic (Umbanda, Caodai, Zionists, Tong-il), it is nevertheless exclusive and distinctive in the understanding of its adherents. Limited (if any) credence is given to the teachings of other religions. Indeed, other religions and their beliefs are often the targets of open attack (Iglesia ni Cristo, Ahmadiya, Soka Gakkai).

A corollary of this exclusivism is the call for conversion. Without exception, these movements preach a message which requires a new beginning. The message may seem relatively simple to the newcomer and the initial requirements for becoming a believer may not seem to be overly demanding (Zionism, Umbanda, Soka Gakkai) but continuation in the faith entails significant changes in allegiances and priorities.

Practical beliefs. The beliefs are *practical* and *related to life* as it is lived out in a world of challenge and frustration. Whether one lives with the racial tensions of South Africa, with the burgeoning economies of Brazil or Japan, or with the struggle for identity and improvement of the Philippines, life has its traps and pitfalls which eventually snare the feet of even the wary. These growing religious movements speak to the victims of contemporary living and offer forgiveness, healing, success and a new song. The message may be the uncomplicated preachments of the Zionist prophets. It may entail the complicated interpretations of a Felix Manalo or Sun Myung Moon. In most cases (including the latter two) it is *both* uncomplicated and complicated, simple and complex. *But ultimately it is down to earth.* It speaks to people where they are. It takes the newspaper headlines and interprets their "true" significance (Jehovah's Witnesses, Ahmadiya, Soka Gakkai, New Apostolic Church, Tong-il). It takes the hurdles and hurts of living and describes a way to surmount the former while prescribing a balm for the latter. The common themes are healing, forgiveness, reconciliation, peace, success, prosperity, happiness, identity and belonging in this life and in the "life to come" (however that may be interpreted). These themes are not dealt with in a purely theoretical manner. Prayers for healing and reconciliation may be offered as soon as the message is preached (Zionism). They may be promised as one faithfully fulfills the requirements (Soka Gakkai). There may be an elaborate system of caring for the needs of believers (Iglesia ni Cristo). These approaches are not mutually exclusive, of course, even in the cases mentioned. The point is that dynamic religious faith is practical, and honored deities and believing saints "join hands" to make it so.

All-encompassing teachings. The teachings of these religions are all-encompassing. They tend to spell out the implications of faith for every area of life. Individual members are not left to think through these implications. In one way or another, leaders, revelations or group experiences communicate the expectations that attend the faith (Caodai, Jehovah's Witnesses, Iglesia ni Cristo). When the life-encompassing nature of the faith is further reinforced by organizational arrangements that control the behavior of members by involving them in the activities of subgroups which specialize in art, music, athletics, and science, for example (Mormonism, Soka Gakkai, Iglesia ni Cristo), the life of the individual member becomes almost totally absorbed into the movement.

Apocalyptic faith. The beliefs of growing religious movements are *apocalytic.* They impart to the movements what might be called a "destiny complex."[6] The coming kingdom is, of course, described differently in accordance with basic religious orientations. It is sometimes tied in with a very definite and elaborate view of history (Ahmadiya, Caodai, Jehovah's Witnesses). Quite

---

6. The term is not original but I cannot determine who originated it.

often the founder of the movement occupies a primary role in
the announcement (New Apostolic Church, Iglesia ni Cristo)
or governance (Tong-il) of the "golden age" yet to come. However these aspects may vary, the teachings of these movements
point toward a life to come, thus making "sense" out of world
history by crowning it with a kingdom which rights its many
wrongs.

Group Organization

Under this rubric we will give attention to organizational
structure, special leadership, and member participation.

Organizational structure. Religious movements such as those
in our case studies are variously termed voluntary organizations,
voluntary or free associations, and sodalities. In some respects
they differ rather markedly. Zionism in South Africa and the
Umbanda in Brazil are composed of numerous "sects" within
the larger wholes and seem to grow by "division," whereas
Kimbanguism in Zaire and the United Pentecostal Church in
Colombia are tightly-knit and grow by "addition." In the case
of Caodaism in Vietnam the "mother church" retains primary
importance but numerous "sects" have been spawned. The
Iglesia ni Cristo in the Philippines has managed to retain a
high degree of unity. Some movements are much more highly
organized than others. This seems to be true where the larger
society is highly organized.

While we acknowledge these and other differences occasioned
by cultural and circumstantial variability, two organizational
characteristics common to all the movements seem to emerge.
First, the organization of growing religious movements tends
to be decidedly hierarchical. The three branches of Caodai,
the "apostle" orientation of the New Apostolic Church and
Mormonism, the "prophet" orientation of Zionism and Kimbanguism, the president and board of directors arrangement in
Soka Gakkai—all exhibit authority patterns which are at once
definite and graded. Sometimes the organization extends right
down to the local levels with an efficiency and explicitness that
is reminiscent of the military (Iglesia ni Cristo, Jehovah's Witnesses). On the other hand, the nomenclature used may seem
to be democratic and egalitarian (United Pentecostal). In either
case the organizations tend to be authoritarian. Lines of au-

thority are seldom blurred or disregarded. Checks and balances there may be, but these seem to be operative mainly at secondary and tertiary levels of leadership. Believers know where real authority lies, and it is usually at the top!

Second, below the primary levels of authority there tends to be considerable opportunity for the disciplined, gifted and knowledgeable believer to "move up" in status and authority. The Soka Gakkai is somewhat unusual in that they have a specific testing and evaluation program for advancement to explicit rankings in the organization. But in most of these movements the member who "performs" well will "move up" in responsibility, authority and respect. This is true even in a movement of the diversity of Umbanda. It is worth noting that the key to promotion in dynamic movements is merit rather than "political pull" or "arm-twisting." At least it would appear so to the outside observer.

Special leadership. From a scientific point of view one is tempted to say that if there is any necessary or sufficient cause for the success of a movement apart from the purely spiritual factors we mentioned earlier, it is that the movement have outstanding leadership. Most of the founders and top leaders of the movements in our study would probably qualify as charismatic. They also exhibit a deep sense of call and mission. It would be highly instructive to make a comparative study of such leaders as Judge Rutherford, Joseph Smith, William Drost, Felix Manalo, Ghulam Ahmad, Josei Toda, Sun Myung Moon, Simon Kimbangu, Le Van Trung and others. It would reveal notable differences, of course. But whatever else that study would reveal it would certainly bear out Eric Hoffer's contention that dynamic movements need good leaders and leaders need able lieutenants.[7]

It should be noted that with but one or two possible exceptions (Drost in Colombia and, perhaps, Moon in the United States) these studies indicate that successful leadership arises out of the culture in which the movement flourishes. An overwhelming sense of call and mission, the insistence upon divine authority, an unusual capacity for sacrifice and work, the ability to communicate—these and other characteristics of suc-

---

7. Hoffer, *The True Believer*, p. 106.

cessful leaders may indeed be universal. But they must be translated into words and actions which are meaningful and persuasive *in situ*. For that reason a religious movement has a great advantage if it has its roots in the culture. But movements from the outside can "invade" a society with singular success *if their message* and objectives are embodied in, and translated by, local leaders who think, speak and act in culturally meaningful ways.

Much has been said and written about the importance of national leaders to a successful missionary enterprise. This cannot be overemphasized. Missionaries who for any reason fail to recognize, encourage, inspire and help train native leadership do their cause a great disservice. There are risks here. The native leader will likely chart new and untried paths. The missionary will have to place his own ego on the line. But squelching native leadership potential by insisting on conformance to the missionary's (not necessarily scriptural) notions of leadership or by promoting one's own person, position, and ideas entails a far greater risk. A number of the leaders in our case studies were rejected by Christian missionaries. Were this not so these histories might be more to our liking!

Individual participation. Growing religious movements emphasize the importance and participation of individual members. Members are *people*. More, they are "chosen people" who do not simply fold their hands and await a future utopia. With but one possible exception (the Umbanda) these movements not only *stress* the importance and role of the layman, they *involve* laymen in disciplined, organized activities. To appreciate this one need only rehearse the lay orientation of the local churches of the New Apostolic Church, the "companies" of Jehovah's Witnesses, the "locals" in Iglesia ni Cristo, the *zadankai* in Soka Gakkai, and the "spiritual retreats" in such diverse organizations as Tong-il and Kimbanguism. (Even when the movement does not place great emphasis on individual members winning others to the faith, as in the case of Umbanda, there is a meaningful role for the layman.)

One is tempted to conjecture that, far from discouraging lay identification and participation, hierarchical organization tends to promote them because in such systems individuals at the lowest levels are informed of their importance, place and role with a precision that might well be lacking in movements that are more democratic and egalitarian. Time and energy that would be "wasted" in the decision-making processes of organizations of the latter type can be devoted to the carrying out of the programs and directives of the movement as determined by recognized authorities. The "employment" of large numbers of financially self-sufficient believers to accomplish movement goals, whatever the goals may be, is characteristic of these movements from the New Apostolic Church in Germany to the Witnesses and Mormons in America to Tong-il in Korea.

Worship, Ritual and Rites

As one would expect, the ritual observances of the movements in our case studies are as variegated as those of the traditions from which they come. A knowledge of the worship and rites of spiritism, Islam, Buddhism and Christianity will enable one to predict with reasonable accuracy the basic patterns of individual and collective religious observances in these movements. Of course, an intimate study of the movements themselves is essential to an understanding of the unique symbolism and significance of such observances as Tong-il mass weddings, Caodai worship ceremonies, Umbanda fumigation and "opening and closing" rites, Zionist massaging, Kimbanguist *nsinsani*, and so forth. Certain characteristics of the ritual observances of most of these groups do stand out, however.

Incorporation rites. For the most part these movements emphasize conversion and incorporation rites. In Umbanda this does not seem to be as carefully spelled out as it is in the other movements. But even there, once the "experimenter" experiences "possession by a spirit" and the "reality of religion" he reaches a new stage. Though his acceptance as a member does not require any special overt act or ritual it does demand a definite attitudinal change. One enters the Soka Gakkai by the simple procedure of procuring a *honzon*, repeating the sacred title inscribed thereon, and attending the local meeting. But this simple beginning receives such immediate and positive reinforcement from the faithful that appropriate private and public worship before the *honzon* becomes a most integral part of human experience. Conversion to Zionism is attended by a rite that is as definite and important as any of the rites of passage of traditional Africa. The New Apostolic Church has its "sealing rite" by which the person becomes a child of God. It seems safe to conclude that these growing religious movements do not leave conversion *or* incorporation to chance or the vagaries of individual initiative. In informal and formal (and, often, highly symbolical) rites they incorporate new believers into the group. *This would seem to be an exceedingly important observation for that distressingly large segment of Protestant missionary personnel by whom conversion is understood to be of life and death importance, while definite and undelayed incorporation into local churches is understood to be of but little significance.*

Believer participation. The participation of believers in some rituals and rites—particularly those which are related to worship —is greatly stressed and often mandatory. In these rituals the believer is not simply a passive observer. He is actively engaged in them. Caodaism and undoubtedly Ahmadiya (though Inniger does not stress this) have worship rituals that are exceedingly formal and make daily demands on the faithful. Jesus Only and Kimbanguist worship "rituals" are less formal and less frequent. But one need only rehearse accounts of these spiritual exercises and utilize a minimal imagination to realize their attraction to participants. One can almost picture the intensity of concentration, the pain of anguished seeking, and the sheer delight of the rapture of "finding" that must be evident on the faces of these worshipers. In these gatherings there are activity, movement, emotion, engagement. The whole of the personality is somehow involved.

Focus on needs. It is important to emphasize in this connection also that the worship and other rituals of these movements tend to focus on the needs which people feel, such as the psychological need for acceptance and the physical need for healing as well as the spiritual needs of mankind. In fact, one would not be far wrong in calling these religions "healing religions." In almost every case the healing of the body and the healing of human relationships are complementary to the "healing of the soul." However one might interpret what actually happens when, for example, Kimbanguist and Jesus Only hands are laid upon the sick or when the Soka Gakkai believer chants the *daimoku* in faith, it is apparent that a majority of these fast-growing religions place great emphasis on the well-being of the body.

Meeting Places and Material Objects

Be they ever so otherworldly and nonmaterialistic, religious movements nevertheless must concern themselves with the world and cultures in which they live. In fact, they often appear to be as enamored of material culture as are nonreligious groups. For religious people, however, there is always the necessity of determining the point at which material goods become obstacles to the achievement of stated goals, or even idols which take the place of supreme objects of devotion. Religions, of course, differ widely at this point.

What about the religious movements of our present study? The truth seems to be that they exhibit in microcosm the wide variegation of religions in macrocosm. Witness the elaborate altars and their furnishings among the Caodai and Umbanda, the robes and symbols of Kimbanguism, and the various insignia of the Tong-il propagator. Contrast these with the material simplicity which characterizes Jesus Only or Jehovah's Witnesses. Look at the grandeur of Temple Square and other Mormon buildings, Soka Gakkai's Taisekiji, and Iglesia ni Cristo cathedrals. Contrast these with the buildings of the movements in Africa and South America. What can one conclude other than that here as elsewhere variety seems to be the spice of religious life? But it does appear that most of these religious movements share in this: materially speaking they do have their "home place(s)" and "cultural possessions."

What do we mean by "home place(s)"? Simply that these movements have places or buildings which are in some way and sense made "sacred" if only by virtue of the fact that the "chosen people" meet there in the presence of the divine. More than that, a number of them have headquarters where they carry out the "secular" functions of their spiritual programs. Soka Gakkai lays claim to the "earth's center" with the "largest temple on earth" and the sacred site where Nichiren's *honzon* and relics reside and where the coming kingdom will be located. Kimbanguism and Zionism would seem to be at the opposite end of the spectrum, but this is not so. Though they may never match the magnificence of Taisekiji, they have their own N'Kamba (where Kimbangu's remains are kept) and local "Mt. Zions." Ahmadiya devotees can point to the place in Srinagar where Jesus' remains are held to be buried; they can assemble in "their" Qadian and, on occasion, journey to their Mecca.

It has often been pointed out that Christianity is universal in various senses including the fact that it has no one sacred spot on earth, no one central shrine hallowed by its founder. True as that is, it is noteworthy that even so Spirit-oriented a movement as Jesus Only has its churches—unpretentious as most of them very likely are. Some groups, it would seem, take great pride in their holy places and buildings and, in visiting and beholding them, draw great spiritual encouragement and motivation. Others look upon their places and buildings of meeting as quite unimportant except that *believers meet there*. When they do meet the place is hallowed, and when they leave they are better prepared for life's struggles. In either case, the places are there and they serve "kingdom" purposes. Believers indeed may meet in houses or halls, in forest or field. But the believers of growing movements do have those places that they call "home."

It may be noted in passing that there are important psychological and cultural factors in all of this. In terms of buildings, there can be little doubt that the magnificent Iglesia ni Cristo churches reflect, and in most cases surpass, the grandeur of the Roman cathedrals of the Philippines. In terms of material symbols, it is revealing that Kimbanguists tend to use the cross sparingly in order to avoid Christo-pagan misunderstandings, but use stars and doves without similar misgivings. Inspired personalities are no doubt far greater factors in the growth of religious movements than are mortar and art—but there is a definite and important place for both mortar and art in religion if they are religiously, psychologically and culturally meaningful.

Revelation and Linguistic Behavior

Fundamental to the dynamic of growing religions is an authoritative word or experience by which other words and experiences are measured. From a purely scientific perspective, it would seem to be true that the authoritativeness of the "word" is one of the most important qualities of these movements. To some of us the differences between the Christian Bible, the Koran, the Lotus Sutra and the Book of Mormon

make the Grand Canyon look like a drainage ditch by comparison; but as perceived by the adherents of these growing religions, these books have one thing in common: *they speak with
an absolute authority on the fundamental concerns of mankind.*

No sooner has that statement been made, however, than we
find that qualifications and even exceptions must be made.
In some cases the authority and meaning of the sourcebook
are mediated—or even superseded—by another authority (or
authorities). Thus, although Ghulam Ahmad uses the word
ilham (the lower level of inspiration) in relation to his own
writings, he makes the reader feel that those writings have the
force of *wahy* (the infallibility accorded the Koran). Sun Myung
Moon and his followers appear to be explaining an authoritative
Bible, but in actuality the explanation is so farfetched that only
by elevating the *Divine Principle* itself to the level of a final
interpretation do they achieve their ends. For the Soka Gakkai,
the Lotus Sutra is absolute truth, but only as the "beneath
the letter" meaning is elucidated by Nagarjuna and Nichiren
(and, finally, Makiguchi, Toda and Ikeda?). Iglesia ni Cristo
elevates Felix Manalo's words to final arbiter of truth. Caodaism
furnishes an intriguing approach to the problem of authoritative
revelation. There the failure of two revelational periods of
history is attributed to the humanity of the intermediaries. These
failures are overcome in the current and final period because
spirits are used to communicate truth. Nevertheless, even the
contemporary message is contained in sacred texts.

Such movements as Kimbanguism, Zionism and Jesus Only
are difficult to analyze on this score. Each points to an authoritative Scripture to be sure, but it is almost impossible to tell
where the primary authoritative component for the *average
believer* really resides—in the Scriptures themselves, in the word
of the authoritative prophet-teacher, or in the subjective experience of the believer. Umbanda leaves little room for doubt.
Here the spiritual experience is primary.

One might conjecture on the basis of these studies that any
religious movement found to be without a fully authoritative
revelatory record, interpretation or experience probably did not
begin that way, and, all things being equal, is most likely
destined for slow growth or a slow demise. That much seems
clear. How these authoritative words and experiences interrelate,

however, is not so easily ascertained. In each case there seems to be a kind of practical hierarchy. One of the revelatory records or experiences is primary, the others secondary and tertiary. As far as growth is concerned, any hierarchical ordering will do, but in our studies the emphasis is on an objective *word* (spoken or written, a sourcebook or its interpretation) and then on *subjective experiences*.

From a Christian point of view these conclusions need first a theological and then a practical evaluation. The former is beyond the scope of the present study but veritably cries out for attention in the so-called Age of Aquarius. A church without a fully authoritative Word of God *and* believers who have known the illumination and regeneration of the Holy Spirit is a contradiction in terms. Interpretation and teaching are also essential to the continuation and growth of the church. The sourcebook of Scripture, the experience of the believer, and the interpretation of teachers—all are essential, but each in its own order. The Bible is its own best interpreter and also must be allowed to judge the experience of the believer. In fact, to act on the basis of the Bible truth *is* to realize truly Christian experience. Moreover, to *fully hear* the biblical Word is, as Karl Barth reminded us, to hear that Word in the church.[8] In this way one is delivered from private interpretations and misinterpretations. *But, of course, much of this can be concluded only on the basis of theology. What can be concluded on the basis of the dynamics of growth would seem to be that the fully authoritative word—or vision—must be there.*

If in these movements there are verbal symbols or formulas which are efficacious in and of themselves in the manner of the mantras in Indian religions or the so-called powerful words in primitive religions, they are not a prominent feature except in two or three instances. More prominent seems to be the use of hymns and songs. In Kimbanguism, Zionism, Jesus Only, Tong-il, and Soka Gakkai, joyous hymns or martial songs are extremely prominent. The place of music as such in the Mormon movement is well-known, and Tong-il also seems to have employed music not only as a means of worship or rally-

---

8. Cf. Karl Barth, *Credo* (New York: Charles Scribner's Sons, 1962), pp. 179-83.

ing the faithful, but as a strategy for attracting others to the faith. Just how important hymns and songs (and music in general) are as a part of the dynamic of growth in the other religions is not clear from these studies, but overall they would seem to play an important role.

Affective and Emotional Elements

No aspect of these movements presents a greater challenge to analysis than the emotional element. Affective states are extremely difficult to measure. But explicitly or implicitly the studies indicate that identity, belonging, security, awe, ecstasy and zeal are part and parcel of religious growth. Each of these elements deserves considerable attention, and a review of the case studies will reveal that in significant measure most of the movements do evidence each of them. Here we confine ourselves to some of the most illuminating examples.

Identity, belonging, and security. Very little imagination is required to empathize with the feelings of lostness, aloneness, estrangement and insecurity that must have gripped Muslims on the Indian subcontinent, Africans under the domination of white leaders, the Japanese during an occupation, and Brazilians in a time of rapid urbanization—to cite once again but a few examples of the circumstances that cause people to cry out for identity, belonging, and security. Each of these has spiritual, psychological and social dimensions. And growing religions seem to answer to these needs in a very real way. If the Jehovah's Witnesses tend to represent a somewhat lower stratum of society than do the traditional Protestant churches of North America, they nevertheless do regard themselves as being the "elite" of Jehovah. If the multiplied thousands of Umbanda believers formerly felt themselves without a "home" in rapidly urbanizing Brazil, they have now been "integrated" and have achieved a new status. If Filipino followers of Felix Manalo once feared for their future, the church now offers them a security that has social and economic dimensions as well as spiritual. If South African blacks formerly believed that they were marching to oblivion, thousands of them have reason to feel that now—hand in hand—they are indeed "marching to Zion."

Awe and ecstasy. Awe and ecstasy, though not twins, would seem to be closely related affective states in these movements. Jesus Only believers stand with hands upraised before a holy God who nevertheless deigns to fill them with his Spirit and crown their meetings with joy unspeakable. The African movements evidence very similar if not identical emotional states. The spirits in Caodaism and Umbanda evoke strong feelings of dependency and—responding to "proper" prayers and rituals—reward believers with information and experiences that can only call forth joy and ecstasy. I have listened to supposedly unemotional Japanese who, after long periods of waiting, gathered in worship before the *honzon* at Taisekiji. I have heard them break out in spontaneous song and extol the virtues of faith upon taking leave of that temple.

Zeal. Perhaps that affective element which seems least necessary to mention—much less elaborate—is zeal. The zeal of believers in these movements takes various forms, but its presence among laity as well as leaders is unmistakable. On almost every page of our case studies one will find, in one form or another, zeal, zeal, zeal. Perhaps that is the single characteristic of leadership that counts most for the growth of these movements. Leaders can impart information and it will remain in musty books or tired minds, unused and unavailing. They can organize the movement and the members will stand in place, immobile and ineffective. They must take those ideas and make them burn. Having reviewed the troops, they must lead them forward. However it is accomplished, believers must be infused with zeal for the cause. Only then will it triumph.

It must remain as the primary indictment of a great portion of the church of Christ that its truth remains closeted and cloistered while lesser causes advance, borne on by the zeal of ordinary believers.

Propagation and Continuity

From the perspective of this study no feature of a religious movement is more important than its strategy and program for the dissemination and continuation of the faith. Ways and means must be found to extend the faith laterally so as to include a widening territory and increasing numbers of people, and lineally through time to succeeding generations. Most of the movements under study have aggressive and forward-looking programs of outreach that distinguish them from nongrowing movements. The characteristics of those programs are rather easily discerned.

A vision for the world. Of the twelve movements under study at least ten keep in view the dissemination of the faith *among the peoples of other nations.* At least nine of them have *organized efforts* to reach people of other countries and convert them to the movement's teachings and goals. This is indeed significant because the roots of some of these movements reach so deeply into their own national and cultural soil (Tong-il, Mormonism, Caodai, Ahmadiya, Iglesia ni Cristo, Kimbanguism, Soka Gakkai) that they might be expected to be myopic and confined in their outlook. Such is not the case. Even where economic and other conditions militate against actual missions to places and people very far removed geographically (e.g., Kimbanguism), the vision is still there. And some groups such as Tong-il, Soka Gakkai, Ahmadiya, the Latter-day Saints, and the Witnesses, have foreign missionary organizations and programs that are amazingly extensive and active! Of course if such activity is effective in making converts abroad, it is also helpful at home for it serves to reinforce world-encompassing goals with world-embracing programs.

Aggressive programs of propagation. Propagation programs involve large segments of the faithful. The New Apostolic Church, the Umbanda, and perhaps Zionism have campaigns of proselytism which are less systematic than those of the other groups, but the rest of these groups have somehow succeeded in mobilizing their membership and mounting highly successful efforts to win outsiders. Indeed, in at least three cases—the Latter-day Saints, the Caodai and Ahmadiya—there are vivid illustrations that these programs are highly important for growth. In each of these three movements there are two major subgroups, one of which tends to give more attention to the development and nurture of individual members and the other of which is disciplined and zealous in outreach as well. The subgroups which really concentrate on converting outsiders are the rapidly growing ones!

Far and away the most important means of propagating the faith is face-to-face communication. Groups such as the Soka

Gakkai, Mormons, Jehovah's Witnesses and Tong-il have extensive training programs to turn ordinary believers into effective missionaries. But even those who may not have such training programs (Umbanda and the New Apostolic Church) nevertheless rely on believers to spread the word and win others. These studies would indicate that there is no substitute for this—on buttons to press, switches to pull, or surrogates to send. *Either ordinary believers win others by means of person-to-person witness, or the movement is not likely to exhibit unusual growth.* It should be noted that this is not confined to "individual-to-individual" witness. Some of these movements emphasize "individual-to-group" and even "group-to-group" witness. The Soka Gakkai counts membership by families—not by individuals!

The use of mass media. It should not escape our notice that several of these movements utilize dramatic presentations, choral groups, special retreats and other innovative means of propagating their beliefs. But more important than these approaches, and next to person-to-person witness, is the effective use of the mass media. Of course, the significance of the media is lessened in countries like Zaire and South Africa. But where literacy rates are high and media use is developed, growing movements emphasize the use of the mass media—especially the printed media. They do so in two ways: (1) by drawing the attention of the secular media to their movement, and (2) by developing their own publications.

Tong-il is perhaps one of the most successful of the various movements we have studied when it comes to commanding space in the secular press. In the United States much of their press coverage has been negative, but it seems evident that in Korea Tong-il press tends to be mostly positive. The cases of such groups as the Latter-day Saints, Caodai, Ahmadiya, Iglesia ni Cristo, Jehovah's Witnesses, and Soka Gakkai are very similar in that secular press coverage is *both* positive and negative. Some of the criticism is probably justified. On the other hand the favorable mass media exposure greatly enhances the possibility of growth. And, as we have seen, not all negative commentary necessarily impedes growth. Religious movements thrive on a certain amount of "persecution."

We mentioned that for the most part these groups also have their own publications. It is impossible to review here the books, periodicals, newspapers and other printed materials published by these groups. Anyone who has seen Iglesia ni Cristo's *Pasugo* magazine, the Witnesses' *Awake!*, Soka Gakkai's *The Seikyo Graphic* or *Seikyo Shimbun* or Ahmadiya's *The Muslim Sunrise* will be aware of the high quality materials prepared by these growing movements. But it should be noted that "quality" here entails more than artistic and technological know-how. The content of these publications intimately relates the teachings of the movement to the *contemporary concerns of society*. In other words, religious teachings are not left floating in space, somehow removed from the common concerns of men whose feet are planted on *terra firma*. Furthermore, these publications are not simply funneled into society in the vague hope that sometime, somehow they will affect the movement's growth. They are utilized by believers in their person-to-person contacts and their contents become the subject matter for group discussion or public forum.

If the evangelical wing of the Christian church has succeeded in the translation and distribution of the Scriptures and the production and dissemination of quality literature—and it has—it has largely failed to attract the secular press and to utilize the materials it has produced in ways which will contribute most to rapid growth. This failure demands analysis and correction if optimum growth is to be achieved.

The establishment of schools. This is by no means one of the most prominent aspects of the "propagation and continuation" features of these movements as the authors have analyzed them, but it is perhaps worthy of mention. The schools mentioned in these studies perform at least one of three basic functions. First, they inculcate the precepts of faith in the coming generation. Kimbanguism's hastily developed "schools under the trees" are a good example of this. Second, schools train ministerial and missionary staff. The rapid development of the Kimbanguist seminary and the short-term Mormon missionary school are examples. Third, schools are used as a means of missionary outreach in target areas. Mormonism and Caodai furnish illustrations of this.

But perhaps the most important kind of education for both the propagation and continuation of the faith is not intimately related to formally organized schools at all. It is the education that takes place in the homes of believers, and in their churches, assemblies or small group meetings. These are the places where instruction that is really basic to growth occurs. Probably each of these growing movements could be used to demonstrate this principle, but perhaps the outstanding example is the Jehovah's Witnesses. Review once again their program for instructing their young and their new believers in the retention, defense and dissemination of their faith. Then look again at the various other movements such as the Latter-day Saints, the Soka Gakkai and the New Apostolic Church for reflections of this type of instructional program. Look—and weep—if you belong to a religious movement that piously claims to possess the truth and yet offers but faint reflections of these effective approaches to the training of home-bred and adopted sons and daughters in the faith!

Conclusion

Religion can be (and has been) defined in such a way as to downgrade supernaturalism. Thus numerous secular faiths such as communism and humanism can legitimately be termed religious. After all, they too can involve "ultimate concerns about the ultimate"—to use Paul Tillich's phraseology. And they rest upon assumptions of faith which have less "proof" to commend them that does true supernatural religion. These "secular religions" will survive on the earth as long as man does. Man cannot live without meaning. And meaning cannot endure without faith. Even secularism can survive only as a faith.

But what about the sacred? What of religion defined—as we have defined it in this study—so as to explicitly *include* supernaturalism? Anthony F. C. Wallace concludes that, given several hundred years, supernatural religion will die out:

To the question put in this way, the answer must be that the evolutionary future of religion is extinction. Belief in supernatural beings and in supernatural forces that affect nature without obeying nature's laws will erode and become only an interesting historical memory. To be sure, this event is not likely to occur in the next generation; the process will very likely take several hundred years, and there will probably always remain individuals, or even occasionally small cult groups, who respond to hallucination, trance, and obsession with a supernaturalist interpretation. But as a cultural trait, belief in supernatural powers is doomed to die out, all over the world, as a result of the increasing adequacy and diffusion of scientific knowledge and of the realization by secular faiths that supernatural belief is not necessary to the effective use of ritual. The question of whether such a denouement will be good or bad for humanity is irrelevant to the prediction; the process is inevitable.[9]

Wallace seems to be altogether too convinced of his conclusion. The rapid rise of Eastern religions with their bizarre supernaturalisms would seem to belie his prophecy, although it must be admitted that some of them so dilute their supernaturalism with materialism and hedonism as to raise serious questions. Biblical Christianity, of course, insists not only that supernaturalism will survive but that the final kingdom will be the kingdom of Christ. Christ himself, however, raised the question, ". . . when the Son of Man comes, will He find (the) faith on the earth?" (Luke 18:8, NASB). We may safely conclude, therefore, that supernaturalism—at least, supernaturalism in its true form—is not destined to survive without significant struggles.

Elizabeth Nottingham believes that religious movements go through *stages* of growth.[10] In the innovating, creative phase the movement is dominated by the personality of a charismatic founder. In the second phase "the successors of the founder are forced to resolve and clarify important matters pertaining to organization, belief, and ritual. . . ."[11] A "second founder" is sometimes needed to resolve these issues. During the third stage, the leaders must answer why the original objectives have not been realized. This stage is especially difficult for movements which have an apocalyptic message.

Nottingham's analysis would seem to have some validity. It is important to note that in the opinion of the authors of the studies in this book, some of these rapidly growing religions already show signs of leveling off. And it is true that movements such as the New Apostolic Church and Jehovah's Witnesses have

9. Anthony F. C. Wallace, *Religion: An Anthropological View* (New York: Random House, 1966), pp. 264-65.
10. Elizabeth Nottingham, *Religion and Society* (New York: Random House, 1954), pp. 60-61.
11. Ibid., p. 60.

had special problems growing out of unfulfilled apocalyptic predictions.

The apostolic church not only survived the challenges inherent in stages two and three, it gave impetus to a growth that has continued until, as Bishop Stephen Neill says, today for the first time the world harbors a truly universal religion—the Christian religion.[12] More than one-fourth of the population of the world claims the Christian faith, and the Christian church is represented in almost every nation on earth. Truly the "gates of Hades" have not overpowered the church (Matt. 16:18, NASB).

But growth has not come easily or steadily. Growth has come by starts and fits. Moreover, the growth of the church universal has not been duplicated in all of the numerous movements, denominations, fellowships and localized expressions of which it is comprised. Far from it. The history of Christian churches and movements has all too often been marked by birth in vision, advance with fervor, retreat to mediocrity and, finally, surrender to sterility. This history should prod true Christians to continually return to the apostolic record in order to see how they measure up. But that record should also prod us to look at rapidly growing movements such as those in this study to discover blind spots which blur our vision. By so doing we may uncover the "secrets" of rapid growth in contemporary cultures. After all, never in their wildest dreams did the apostles envisage the potential for growth inherent in the technological developments of the twentieth century, much less the pitfalls inherent in those same developments.

But more than that, perhaps a careful look at these contemporary movements will jar us into a new awareness of the necessity of returning to irreplaceable aspects of apostolic methodology and motivation of evangelism and church growth.

I would suggest that a discovery (or rediscovery) of contributing causes of growth in these movements, for example, should prod numerous Christian churches, denominations and missions to re-examine themselves vis-à-vis the following factors:

(1) The recognition of the necessity for accommodation to (not compromise with) the culture(s) in which the church is to be propagated and nurtured.

---

12. Stephen Neill, A History of Christian Missions (Grand Rapids: Eerdmans, 1965), pp. 14-16.

(2) The readiness to be "different" people, judging both society and themselves by the objective standard of the Word of God and willing to suffer the consequences of that judgment.

(3) A realization of the "right time" for special growth efforts in the various target areas of society (but with a corresponding willingness to work for growth irrespective of circumstances).

(4) A message which is authoritative, unique, practical, holistic and apocalyptic (in other words, the message of biblical Christianity).

(5) Organizations in which there are clear lines of authority with leadership based on spiritual maturity and achievement, and with a disciplined and trained "laymanship" *geared to participation in the fundamental (not peripheral) tasks of the church.*

(6) The immediate formal and informal incorporation of new believers into the fellowship of the churches, with provision for their active participation in worship and other aspects of church life, and a practical concern for their needs. Christians must find identity and a measure of security in the "believing family" if they are to be faithful, producing members.

(7) A place—whether simple or ornate—that believers think of as a spiritual "home."

(8) An emphasis on *both* the objective, fully authoritative Word of God in the Scriptures *and* subjective experiences which are enjoined by—and also judged by—that Word. A Christianity that is either "noncognitive" or "unemotional" is both unbiblical and "unsalable." An apologetic that is not both logically sound and existentially relevant is deficient.

(9) A definite, positive, ordered program for winning the people of the world to Christ which has as its basis the face-to-face witness of individuals and groups.

(10) A use of the mass media which supplements—but does not supplant—the face-to-face witness and instruction in the churches and church-related groups.

Prognosticators of church growth in the last quarter of this century fall into three categories. There are the optimists who see great movements of men, nations and even continents into the fold of the church. At the other end of the spectrum there are the pessimists who foresee fewer and fewer open doors for the preaching of the gospel and an ever-decreasing percentage of the world's population identifying themselves with the church of Christ. Finally, there are the realists who believe that the church faces momentous challenges from within and without, and that where she draws upon her deepest spiritual resources and employs her best strategic forces she will grow, and where she does not she will languish.

I rush to the side of the realists, with the prayer that the church will be the church. And that the prods to thought and action contained within this volume will contribute to its dynamic!